PHARMACOLOGY - RESEARCH, SAFETY TESTING AND REGULATION

THE PET MEDICATION INDUSTRY

OVERVIEW, COMPETITION AND DISTRIBUTION ISSUES

PHARMACOLOGY - RESEARCH, SAFETY TESTING AND REGULATION

Additional books in this series can be found on Nova's website under the Series tab.

Additional e-books in this series can be found on Nova's website under the eBooks tab.

PHARMACOLOGY - RESEARCH, SAFETY TESTING AND REGULATION

THE PET MEDICATION INDUSTRY

OVERVIEW, COMPETITION AND DISTRIBUTION ISSUES

ANITA R. ALVAREZ
EDITOR

nova publishers
New York

NOTICE TO THE READER

Library of Congress Cataloging-in-Publication Data

ISBN: 978-1-63485-316-3

Published by Nova Science Publishers, Inc. † New York

CONTENTS

PREFACE

The U.S. market for pet medications is growing, and is in a state of transition. Although many pet owners continue to purchase their pet medications directly from veterinarians, this traditional distribution model has been challenged by the entry and expansion of retail businesses (both online and brick-and-mortar) that sell pet medications, as well as changes in the business practices of pet medication manufacturers, distributors, veterinarians, and retailers. This book provides an overview of the pet medications industry then examines prescription portability (prescriptions that can be filled by someone other than a veterinarian). The book also looks at distribution practices and the topic of generics. Recommendations on potential policy choices are made and areas that could benefit from additional study are identified.

In: The Pet Medication Industry
Editor: Anita R. Alvarez

ISBN: 978-1-63485-316-3

Chapter 1

COMPETITION IN THE PET MEDICATIONS INDUSTRY: PRESCRIPTION PORTABILITY AND DISTRIBUTION PRACTICES*

Federal Trade Commission Staff

I. INTRODUCTION AND EXECUTIVE SUMMARY[1]

The U.S. market for companion animal medications ("pet medications") has grown significantly in the last decade. This growth is reflected in increased sales of both prescription and non- prescription (also referred to as "over-the-counter" or "OTC") medications.[2] Recognizing the economic importance of the pet medications industry for American consumers,[3] and in response to legislative proposals regarding prescriptions for pet medications,[4] the Federal Trade Commission's ("FTC" or "Commission") staff compiled information concerning historic and current business practices in the sale of pet medications.[5] Staff primarily focused on two related issues that directly affect consumers' access to competitively priced pet medications:

* This is an edited, reformatted and augmented version of a report issued by the Federal Trade Commission, May 2015. This report represents the views of the staff of the Federal Trade Commission. Stephanie A. Wilkinson, Office of Policy Planning is credited as the Principal Author.

- the availability of "portable" pet medication prescriptions, obtained from veterinarians and used to purchase prescription pet medications somewhere other than the prescribing veterinarian's office; and
- manufacturer distribution policies and practices for both prescription and OTC pet medications.

Drawing on the Commission's significant competition and consumer protection expertise, FTC staff sought to collect information related to the following three questions:

- To what extent, if any, is competition in the pet medications industry adversely affected by limited consumer knowledge of and access to portable prescriptions?
- To what extent, if any, is competition in the pet medications industry adversely affected by manufacturer distribution practices that restrict non-veterinary retailers' access to pet medications?
- To the extent that competition in the pet medications industry may be adversely affected by current industry practices, are there less restrictive approaches that could be used to enhance competition without compromising animal health and safety?

Although this report may not answer all of these questions definitively, it does offer insight into each of these issues and identifies areas for further research and study.

On October 2, 2012, the FTC conducted a public workshop to advance its understanding of these issues.[6] A variety of industry stakeholders participated in the workshop, including pet medication manufacturers and distributors, veterinarians, retailers, pharmacists, and consumer advocates, representing a broad range of perspectives on these issues. In addition, the FTC received and reviewed over 700 written public comments submitted in response to the workshop.[7]

This report summarizes the information reviewed by FTC staff regarding these issues, makes recommendations on potential policy choices concerning prescription portability, and identifies areas that could benefit from additional study. The report is based on the workshop transcript and public comments received in response to the workshop, discussions between staff and various industry stakeholders in preparation for the workshop, and other publicly available information compiled by staff before and after the workshop. FTC staff intends for this report to be useful to a range of stakeholders – including businesses and policymakers – who are interested in economic developments in the pet medications industry, and who may be considering new business practices, laws, or regulations that could affect competition and consumer protection in that industry. This report may also better inform pet owners in their pet medications purchasing decisions. FTC staff was particularly interested in exploring the role of competition in the market for pet medications to determine whether and to what extent additional competition might help to reduce pet ownership costs while ensuring the availability of safe and effective pet medications.

The U.S. market for pet medications is growing, and is in a state of transition. Although many pet owners continue to purchase their pet medications directly from veterinarians, this traditional distribution model has been challenged by the entry and expansion of retail businesses (both online and brick-and-mortar) that sell pet medications, as well as changes in the business practices of pet medication manufacturers, distributors, veterinarians, and retailers. These changes in distribution patterns and methods of sale have had varying effects on these market participants who tend to have different perspectives on how consumers should obtain pet medications. Some key observations regarding this industry include:

- Major manufacturers of pet medications have historically distributed their products exclusively through veterinary practices. One reason for adopting this type of distribution model may have been to promote sales by providing incentives for veterinarians to learn about, recommend, and prescribe their products. Manufacturers argue that this model is necessary to distribute their products efficiently and to ensure the safe use of their products. Others have suggested that these exclusive distribution policies restrict competition and have questioned whether the purported justifications offered by manufacturers are valid, particularly with respect to OTC medications approved for safe use without direct veterinary oversight.
- Most manufacturers use independent, authorized distributors who focus on sales to veterinarians and veterinary practices. These distributors also argue that pet medications should be distributed exclusively through veterinary practices. In addition, some manufacturers may have agreements with distributors preventing them from selling competing branded or generic animal drugs.
- Veterinarians traditionally have been the principal source of pet medications for consumers, and many appear to believe that they are

best suited to dispense these products safely to consumers. In addition, veterinary practices typically derive a significant portion of their income from the sale of pet medications, and many veterinarians have expressed concern about the financial impact to their practices of losing these sales. For these reasons, many veterinarians favor a distribution model in which they are the exclusive seller for most pet medications and oppose any changes that would make pet medications more readily available through other distribution channels. Some veterinarians stated, however, that they accept these changes as inevitable and have already adjusted their practice models to rely less on profits from pet medication sales. Furthermore, some veterinarians appear to have already responded to price competition from other retail distribution channels by lowering their prices for certain pet medications.

- Retailers[8] believe that they, too, can dispense pet medications to consumers safely. They seek to compete with veterinarians not only on price, but also on non-price factors such as convenience (for example, supplying maintenance prescription drugs for chronic conditions via home delivery or supplying OTC pet medications at regularly visited retail stores). Some retailers believe they could more effectively compete with veterinarians if portable prescriptions were more widely available to consumers and if it were easier for them to obtain supplies of pet medications. Manufacturers and veterinarians have expressed concerns, however, about the ability of retail pharmacists to dispense pet medications safely.
- Coinciding with the increased presence of non-veterinary retailers, as well as increased consumer demand for pet medications, some manufacturers have departed from the traditional distribution model and now supply both veterinarians and non- veterinary retailers. In addition to this seemingly authorized expansion of distribution, a secondary distribution system (or "gray market") for pet medications also has emerged, supplied by products that are diverted from the traditional veterinary distribution channel. This system allows non-veterinary retailers to purchase pet medications despite stated manufacturer restrictions on sales other than through veterinary practices. Some view the secondary distribution system as procompetitive, because it allows for increased competition between veterinarians and non-veterinary retailers, at least to some degree. Some retailers, however, view the current secondary distribution

system as inefficient, and contend that it leads to higher prices for pet medications than would otherwise prevail if primary distribution were not restricted to veterinarians only.

- Consumers appear to have benefitted from increased competition between veterinary practices and alternative retail channels, particularly for OTC flea and tick control products and prescription heartworm products. Pet owners now have many more choices for purchasing pet medications than they did a decade ago, and several industry stakeholders believe this has led to lower prices, greater convenience, and improved service.[9]
- However, these benefits may have been reduced by the inconsistent availability of portable prescriptions. Some retailers claim that many consumers are unaware of the option to obtain portable prescriptions from their veterinarians, which would allow them to purchase prescription pet medications from other retail outlets. Furthermore, it appears that some veterinarians may be reluctant to inform their clients that portable prescriptions are available and to provide portable prescriptions to their clients, or may otherwise try to discourage their clients from requesting portable prescriptions. Some stakeholders argue that if limitations on prescription portability and restrictive distribution practices were eliminated, the market would continue to develop in ways that are more responsive to consumer preferences. They suggest that this might, in turn, enable pet owners to further reduce their pet care costs and provide them with additional purchasing options. Other stakeholders contend, however, that such changes would not reduce prices or increase convenience, but would instead undermine pet health and the financial stability of veterinary practices.
- Compared to the human drug industry, there are relatively few animal drugs that have generic substitutes. Furthermore, the generic animal drugs that do exist have not achieved the same degree of market penetration as human generic drugs. There appear to be several factors that may have deterred the development and marketing of generic animal drugs. Some stakeholders suggest that changes in restrictive distribution practices, as well as legislative and regulatory measures that would allow for the automatic substitution of generic animal drugs, could facilitate the development and use of these products. Greater availability of generic animal drugs would likely benefit consumers.

As part of the workshop, FTC staff considered whether limitations on prescription portability and restrictive distribution practices reduce the availability of pet medications at non-veterinary retail outlets, and thereby inhibit competition for the sale of pet medications. Staff concluded that portability likely benefits consumers, and therefore generally supports policies that would increase consumer awareness of the availability of portable prescriptions and veterinarian release of prescriptions to consumers. Consumers could then choose whether to purchase pet medications from their veterinarian or an alternative retail outlet. More information is necessary, however, to determine the extent to which consumers are aware of their ability to receive portable prescriptions and the extent to which veterinarians refuse to provide portable prescriptions to their clients. Likewise, more information is needed to determine the full economic impact of greater prescription portability.

With respect to manufacturer distribution practices, FTC staff concludes that it is difficult to evaluate the effect of current practices on competition. More information about the impact of these practices is necessary to make such a determination. As with any market in flux, it is likely that participants in the pet medications industry – including manufacturers, distributors, veterinarians, and retailers – will continue to reevaluate and adjust their competitive strategies in light of consumer demand, supply conditions, and any legislative and regulatory developments.

Finally, FTC staff has identified some issues that might benefit from further study. First, at present there is a lack of empirical analyses of how prices for pet medications vary across different channels of distribution and how changes in the competitive environment have affected prices for pet medications. Second, consideration of whether safety concerns regarding retail pharmacists are justified may be useful. Third, analysis of the effect of any future changes in state legislation regarding prescription release for pet medications may shed light on the economic impact of such requirements, including the potential effect on consumer awareness of retail options and veterinary services pricing. Lastly, more information regarding the secondary distribution system for pet medications could allow for deeper analysis of the economic and product safety concerns alleged by industry stakeholders.

II. Overview of the U.S. Pet Medications Industry

This section of the report provides general factual background regarding the U.S. pet medications industry, including an explanation of important regulatory characteristics that influence how it operates. This section then frames the key issues explored by FTC staff, with an emphasis on current competitive dynamics.

A. General Facts and Trends Regarding Pet Medications

Companion animal products and services constitute a major consumer expenditure in the United States. Approximately 65 percent of U.S. households own pets, the most common being dogs and cats, which equates to 79.7 million homes.[10] In 2014, Americans spent approximately $58 billion on their pets, including food, supplies, veterinary care, prescription and OTC medications, and other pet services and products. This figure is expected to reach $60.6 billion in 2015, representing tremendous growth since 2001, when comparable expenditures totaled $28.5 billion.[11] Many industry stakeholders agree that this rapid expansion has been driven, in large part, by a shift in Americans' attitudes towards their pets. In recent years, an increasing number of Americans have come to think of their pets as members of the family. Coinciding with this shift in attitude, many pet owners are willing to spend a significant amount of money to feed and care for their pets.[12] Pet health care products and services comprise a significant portion of these expenditures,[13] and may continue to increase as pet life spans lengthen and the pet population ages.[14]

Another important factor contributing to the growth in pet medication sales has been the introduction of new therapeutic medications approved by the Food and Drug Administration ("FDA").[15] Many large pharmaceutical companies have increasingly focused on the pet medications market in the last ten years, researching and developing new pet-specific drugs that are often adapted from human drugs (for example, treatments for arthritis, anxiety, and infections).[16] Moreover, significant improvements have been made to traditional pet medications, such as flea, tick, and heartworm preventatives. As veterinarians and pet owners have become more aware of these treatment options, the products have gained widespread acceptance and, in turn, reports indicate that overall pet health care has improved.[17] The availability of a larger variety of pet medications has, however, increased the cost of pet ownership, as pet owners with the means to do so are more likely to purchase medications that will keep their pets as healthy as possible.[18]

Prescription and non-prescription pet medications comprise a significant portion of pet health care costs. In 2013, retail sales of prescription and non-prescription medications for dogs and cats was estimated at $7.6 billion.[19] U.S. retail sales of companion animal pet medications are expected to grow to $10.2 billion by 2018, reflecting a compound annual growth rate of 5 percent.[20] U.S. manufacturer sales of companion animal pet medications have been estimated at $3.7 billion to $4 billion annually.[21]

Pet owners appear to be increasingly concerned about the costs associated with pet ownership, particularly pet health care.[22] Most pet owners pay these costs directly, as health insurance coverage for pets tends to be rather limited and most pet owners have not purchased such coverage.[23] The costs associated with pet ownership can be burdensome for many households that currently own pets, and prohibitive for some pet-free households that otherwise might choose to own pets.[24] These costs may result in diminished pet health, fewer pet adoptions, and increased pet abandonments. Therefore, both existing and prospective pet owners have an interest in finding ways to cut pet care costs without significantly undermining the welfare of pets.[25]

B. Retail Options Available to Consumers of Pet Medications

In order to understand marketplace dynamics in the pet medications industry, it is important to recognize the various paths by which pet medications reach consumers.

Historically, nearly all major manufacturers of pet medications distributed their products only to licensed veterinarians or to authorized distributors that sold only to veterinarians. Largely as a result of this exclusive distribution model, consumers purchased virtually all pet medications from their veterinarians, typically at the end of an office visit for the examination and diagnosis of their pet. This is still how most consumers purchase prescription pet medications today.[26] Indeed, consumer surveys indicate that veterinarians remain the most trusted source for pet medications.[27]

Local pharmacists (who are authorized to dispense both human and animal drugs)[28] have always been part of the veterinarian-focused distribution model, but generally only to a limited extent. As several commenters noted, veterinarians have long relied upon local pharmacies to fill prescriptions for drugs that the veterinarians do not ordinarily stock, particularly human generic drugs dispensed for use in animals.[29] In addition, veterinarians typically have maintained relationships with local compounding pharmacies to ensure their ability to meet the needs of pets requiring specialized concentrations, sizes, or flavors of medications.[30]

Over the last decade, coinciding with increased consumer demand for pet medications, there has been a significant increase in the number of retail pharmacies and other retail outlets that compete with veterinarians to sell pet medications.[31] In the late 1990s, online pharmacies began selling pet medications, often at discounted prices.[32] Many of these online pharmacies are owned and operated by licensed veterinarians and focus solely on filling veterinary prescriptions. More recently, brick-and-mortar big-box retail stores, supermarkets, and chain retail pharmacies have begun selling some of the largest volume pet medications, and many of these retailers advertise even greater discounts than online pharmacies.[33] As is discussed in more detail below, however, it is not always clear how these drugs reach non-veterinarian retailers in light of historic manufacturer exclusive distribution policies that remain common today.[34]

As a result of the emergence of alternative retail outlets, many consumers no longer view veterinarians as the sole source for pet medications.[35] It also appears that veterinary practices have lost some portion of their pet medication revenues to these emerging competitors. As one veterinarian stated, "[i]n the past, we've seen little competition for our clients' hearts and pocketbooks. Consumers didn't shop competitively for most products, and the profession enjoyed a prescribing and dispensing monopoly. But that's changing . . . [as] several retail outlet pharmacies are hoping to take that business away by actively seeking pet owner prescriptions" and offering low prices on pet medications.[36] According to one estimate, in 2014 veterinarians accounted for 58 percent of sales of pet medications, with brick-and-mortar retailers accounting for 28 percent and Internet/mail order retailers accounting for 13 percent.[37]

C. Regulations Concerning Pet Medications: Federal, State and Industry Self-Regulation

Participants in the pet medications industry are subject to federal and state regulations, as well as various forms of industry self-regulation. Regulations may govern veterinarians, manufacturers, distributors, pharmacists, pharmacies, or the drugs themselves.

The American Veterinary Medical Association ("AVMA") describes the veterinarian-client- patient relationship ("VCPR") as the basis for interaction among veterinarians, their clients, and their patients.[38] The importance of the VCPR is generally recognized throughout the pet health industry.[39] Under prevailing ethical guidelines for the practice of veterinary medicine, a veterinarian must establish a VCPR before prescribing or dispensing a prescription pet medication. A VCPR typically exists when: (1) a veterinarian assumes responsibility for making clinical judgments regarding the health of the animal and the need for medical treatment, and the client agrees to follow the advice of the veterinarian; (2) the veterinarian has sufficient knowledge of the animal to diagnose the medical condition of the animal, which typically means that the veterinarian has examined the animal; and (3) the veterinarian is readily available, or has arranged for emergency coverage, for follow-up evaluation in the event of adverse reactions or failure of the treatment regimen. A VCPR also typically requires that veterinarians maintain medical records of their patients.[40]

Veterinarians are licensed, regulated, and disciplined by state government agencies and state- authorized independent boards, such as state veterinary boards. The AVMA and individual state veterinary medical associations not only provide professional and ethical guidance to veterinarians, but also influence state regulations and policies regarding veterinarians. For example, several states have formally incorporated the AVMA's ethical codes regarding the VCPR into statutes or regulations.[41] Similarly, pharmacists are licensed, regulated, and disciplined by individual state boards of pharmacy, with support from the National Association of Boards of Pharmacy ("NABP").[42]

The distribution, sale, and dispensing of pet medications is generally governed by state veterinary and pharmacy laws and regulations, which vary by state,[43] but also have some general similarities. For example, all states require that prescription pet medications be dispensed with prior authorization from a prescribing veterinarian. In all 50 states, veterinarians have the authority to dispense pet medications for patients with whom they have established a valid VCPR.[44] All 50 states also permit pharmacists to dispense both human and animal prescription drugs pursuant to a valid prescription.[45] However, there are also some divergent provisions in state regulations, for example, concerning the provision of portable pet medication prescriptions by veterinarians,[46] as well as the dispensing and distribution of pet medications.[47]

In addition to state and federal regulations regarding pharmacy operations, third-party accreditation organizations have promulgated voluntary pharmacy standards that are widely viewed as "best practices" within the industry.[48] For example, the NABP established the Veterinary Verified Internet Pharmacy Practice Site ("Vet-VIPPS") program in 2009 to accredit online pharmacies that dispense pet medications and are properly licensed under and compliant with state and federal laws and regulations.[49] Vet-VIPPS accreditation requirements incorporate criteria specific to veterinary pharmacies, and are designed to protect the health and well-being of pets.[50] At present, 23 online veterinary pharmacies have received Vet-VIPPS certification.[51] Both the AVMA and the FDA recognize Vet-VIPPS accreditation as a helpful factor in evaluating the quality of an online pharmacy selling pet medications.[52] In addition, the Pharmacy Compounding Accreditation Board ("PCAB") has also adopted a set of requirements specifically for compounding pharmacies.[53] PCAB accreditation requires a pharmacy to comply with additional accreditation requirements, beyond the standard licensure requirements in individual states.[54] The AVMA recognizes PCAB accreditation as a helpful tool for evaluating compounding pharmacies.[55] Several online and brick-and-mortar retailers also claim to have internal processes to ensure product pedigree for medications purchased through secondary distribution.[56]

Most of the pet medications available to U.S. consumers can be classified into four areas: (1) parasiticides (e.g., flea/tick/heartworm); (2) vaccines; (3) anti-infectives (e.g., antibiotics); and (4) anti-inflammatory (e.g., non-steroidal anti-inflammatory drugs, "NSAIDs").[57] Pharmaceutical products for companion animals are regulated by the FDA under the Federal Food, Drug and Cosmetic Act. These products may be labeled for OTC or prescription use. The FDA also allows veterinarians to prescribe extra-label use for animals of certain approved human drugs under the Animal Medicinal Drug Use Clarification Act of 1994.[58] Extra-label drug use occurs when a veterinarian prescribes a medication for use in a way other than the label dictates, or when a veterinarian prescribes a human medication for treatment of a pet.[59] Biological products for companion animals, including vaccines and diagnostics, are regulated by the U.S. Department of Agriculture under the Virus-Serum-Toxin Act. Pesticides for companion animals, including flea and tick topical products, are regulated by the Environmental Protection Agency under the Federal Insecticide, Fungicide, and Rodenticide Act.[60]

In situations where controlled substances are prescribed for animals, veterinarians must comply with U.S. Drug Enforcement Administration ("DEA") regulations and any applicable state laws. Direct dispensing by veterinarians, as well as written, faxed, and oral prescriptions provided by the veterinarian, are allowed under all state regulations for Schedule III, IV, and V controlled substances. Schedule II controlled substances must either be dispensed directly by the veterinarian, or prescribed in writing and dispensed by a pharmacy.[61]

D. Overview of Key Issues Analyzed in this Report

As noted above, FTC staff's study of the pet medications industry focused on three questions related to prescription portability and pet medication distribution practices. These issues are explored in detail in Sections III and IV below. However, because of the interdependence of prescription portability and distribution practices, an overview is provided here.[62]

1. Prescription Portability: Overview

To purchase prescription pet medications from a retail pharmacy, a consumer must first obtain a "portable" prescription from her veterinarian. This may take the form of a written prescription that is provided to the client, who can then present the prescription to a retail pharmacy of her choice. Alternatively, a veterinarian may transmit a prescription to a retail pharmacy on behalf of a client via telephone, facsimile, or other electronic means. A veterinarian may also verify a new prescription or refill request received directly from a retail pharmacy, provided a VCPR exists and use of the medication is deemed appropriate.[63] Consumers may purchase OTC pet medications, which are predominantly flea and tick control products, from veterinarians or retail outlets without a prescription.

Observers agree that many veterinarians provide portable prescriptions to clients upon request and, in some instances, may affirmatively offer portable prescriptions to clients. Indeed, the AVMA Principles of Veterinary Medical Ethics state that its members should honor client requests for prescriptions whenever appropriate, although this guidance is neither binding nor does it require veterinarians to affirmatively offer prescriptions or inform clients of the option of requesting a portable prescription. Some states require that veterinarians provide prescriptions to clients upon request or provide notice to clients that they may request a portable prescription.[64] Yet, complaints persist that some veterinarians do not always comply with requests for prescriptions,[65] and the extent to which these requirements are enforced by state veterinary boards is unclear. Furthermore, anecdotal evidence indicates that some consumers either are not aware that they can receive a portable prescription upon request from their veterinarian, or may be uncomfortable asking for one.[66]

As discussed at the FTC workshop, to address these concerns, federal legislation was introduced in 2011 to require veterinarians in all states to provide portable prescriptions for every medication they prescribe, regardless of whether the client requests it. H.R. 1406, titled the Fairness to Pet Owners Act,[67] was modeled after the Fairness to Contact Lens Consumers Act,[68] ("FCLCA") and was intended to enable pet owners to shop for the best prices for pet medications.[69] Comparisons have been drawn between the pet medications industry and the contact lens industry, despite some clear differences,[70] as both involve medical professionals who prescribe and dispense products, and both are affected by the issues of prescription portability and exclusive distribution.[71] Although H.R. 1406 was not enacted, it sparked a debate among industry stakeholders regarding the need for automatic prescription release and whether it should be mandated by the federal government. Similar bills were reintroduced in 2014 and 2015 in both the House and Senate.[72]

2. Industry Distribution Practices: Overview

Nearly all major manufacturers of pet medications appear to maintain formal policies that restrict sales of pet medications to veterinarians or veterinary distributors.[73] Some stakeholders report that despite these stated policies, large retail pharmacies and stores have been able to purchase pet medications directly from the manufacturers, although no manufacturers have confirmed that they engage in this practice.[74] While some distribution through non-veterinary retailers occurs, retail pharmacies and other retail stores expressed the view that it remains difficult to purchase pet medications directly from manufacturers or their authorized distributors. Often, these non-veterinarian retailers must rely on secondary suppliers of pet medications, who typically purchase excess product from veterinarians.[75] The existence of this secondary distribution system likely results in lower prices than would otherwise prevail if exclusive distribution were being strictly enforced. As discussed in greater detail below, this secondary distribution system nevertheless has been described as inefficient, and may result in higher prices than would prevail absent any constraints on sales by manufacturers to non-veterinary retailers.[76] On the other hand, some commentators have suggested that secondary distribution may raise safety concerns involving the pedigree of products distributed outside of the authorized veterinary channel,[77] although no recent evidence of counterfeit or otherwise unsafe products sold through secondary distribution has been presented to FTC staff.

In addition, it appears that some manufacturers and distributors enter into exclusive dealing agreements, whereby a distributor is contractually prohibited from selling either branded (also referred to as "pioneer") or generic pet medication products that compete with the manufacturer's products. Some industry stakeholders point to these types of agreements as a primary reason for the limited availability of generic pet medications.[78]

3. Interdependence of Prescription Portability and Distribution

Prescription portability and product distribution are related. The availability of portable prescriptions to consumers from their veterinarians is unlikely to have any significant effect on competition for pet medication purchases if non-veterinary retailers lack adequate access to pet medications to fill the prescriptions. Likewise, increasing distribution of pet medications to non- veterinary retail outlets is unlikely to affect competition if consumers are unable or unlikely to obtain prescriptions from their veterinarians.[79] Any reduction of supply through restrictive distribution may also affect consumer demand for those alternative sources of supply, especially if consumers perceive that non-veterinarian retail sources are unreliable or slow to fill orders. In addition, several stakeholders suggested that a financial conflict of interest arises when the exclusive legal right to prescribe is combined with de facto exclusive authorization to dispense,[80] which could cause veterinarians to be reluctant to provide portable prescriptions to consumers.

Some stakeholders downplay the likely impact of limits on prescription portability and exclusive distribution. They claim that veterinarians already are legally and/or ethically bound to provide prescriptions whenever clients request them, and that pharmacies and retailers "can and do advertise their ability to provide products and fill prescriptions, and products are readily available" to non-veterinary retailers.[81] Thus, they argue, "current distribution practices do not limit or impact prescription portability" and consumers already have many viable choices for purchasing pet medications.[82]

E. Competitive Dynamics of the Industry

1. Current State of Competition for Pet Medications

During the workshop, in written comments, and in other information gathered by FTC staff, industry stakeholders offered differing views of the current state of competition in the pet medications industry. Some believe the market has become increasingly competitive, and that market forces will continue to correct any remaining market inefficiencies. Others believe that competition has long been and remains constrained, leading to higher prices and a market that is less responsive to consumers.

At least to some extent, the current state of competition reflects historic distribution practices that developed before the emergence of new retail outlets for pet medications. According to one veterinarian, "current dispensing and pharmacy models were developed long before most of us even considered veterinary medicine as a career. We were a closed market dealing with a relatively captive audience, and our markups were pretty much what we thought the market would bear."[83] Another stakeholder asserted, "The veterinary profession has enjoyed nearly total isolation from competition on drug sales for decades. The pioneer drug manufacturers have facilitated that isolation to their pecuniary benefit. Competition is seldom welcomed into such an environment."[84]

Retailers and consumer advocates argue that although the secondary distribution system for pet medications has provided some degree of competition, it remains constrained in ways that undermine the competitive process.[85] First, non-veterinary retailers suggest that unreliable distribution and other inefficiencies of secondary distribution increase their costs, resulting in prices for consumers that are at least five to ten percent higher than they would be if pet medications were available to all sellers through the primary distribution system.[86] Second, they claim that lack of adequate and reliable inventory also harms the ability of non-veterinarian retailers to fill the orders they receive from customers. Third, retailers maintain that their inability to satisfy customer demand reliably discourages customers from seeking pet medications in the non-veterinary channel in the first place.[87] They argue that, collectively, these factors inhibit the effectiveness and growth of competition from non-veterinary retailers, potentially resulting in higher prices and lower levels of service for customers than would otherwise exist.

Those who argue that the pet medications industry is less competitive than it could be also point to the limited availability of generic animal drugs. It is well-established in the human drug market that consumers can secure significant cost savings when they are able to substitute generic drugs for branded drugs.[88] For the most part, purchasers of pet medications have not reaped similar benefits from lower-priced generic animal drugs – either because there have been relatively few generic pet medication entrants,[89] or because available generic alternatives are not typically distributed by veterinarians and are not easily accessible otherwise. Greater competition from generic pet medications would likely result in consumer savings[90] and increased product innovation, as is typically seen in human pharmaceutical markets when generic drugs are expected to take significant market share from pioneer drugs.[91]

A number of manufacturers, distributors, and veterinarians counter that the pet medications market is highly competitive, pointing to consumers' ability to purchase both prescription and OTC pet medications from online and brick-and-mortar retailers, veterinary clinics, and other sources.[92] Some of these industry participants suggest that large retailers would not offer these products if they did not have a reliable supply chain.[93] Others also argue that current distribution practices do not impair innovation in the pet medications market and that manufacturers "continu[e] to invest in developing new and improved products."[94] Some of these stakeholders also frequently argue that market forces – including consumer demand for lower prices and greater convenience, and increased price competition between veterinarians and other retailers – already have benefitted consumers and improved access to competitively priced pet medications, rendering legislation or other types of government intervention unnecessary.[95]

2. Effects of Non-Veterinary Retail Competition on Pet Medication Prices

Despite an extensive record compiled by FTC staff, publicly available data do not permit an empirical analysis of the differences, if any, between prices offered by non-veterinary retailers and those offered by veterinarians.[96] Nevertheless, numerous retailer stakeholders claim that the availability of pet medications from non-veterinary retail outlets offers the potential for consumer cost savings, greater convenience, and improved service.[97] Similarly, industry analysts attribute the growth of the retail channel to lower prices and greater convenience when purchasing products from non-veterinary retail outlets.[98] Several consumer comments indicated that cost savings are possible when purchasing pet medications from retail outlets rather than veterinarians.[99] Various pet industry and consumer publications specifically suggest that pet owners consider purchasing pet medications from retail outlets in order to save money.[100]

Volume-related purchasing efficiencies may permit large retail pharmacies to receive more advantageous pricing than small veterinary clinics.[101] Such lower costs may, in turn, allow large non-veterinary retailers to offer lower prices to consumers.[102] Administrative efficiencies also may contribute to the ability of large non-veterinary retailers to offer lower prices than small veterinary clinics.[103]

Consumer savings do not, however, appear to be limited to purchases through non-veterinary retail channels. As pet medications have become more widely available through alternative retail outlets, the veterinary profession has faced increased competition, which may have driven down prices even for consumers who continue to purchase their pet medications from veterinarians.[104]

Some industry stakeholders argue that many veterinarians already have responded to the competitive pressure by monitoring competing retailers and, for example, offering comparable prices to online pharmacies.[105] Indeed, during the course of FTC staff's interviews with veterinarians, many represented that their pricing for pet medications is very competitive with non-veterinary retailer pricing. Several stakeholders indicate that, despite the claims of some retailers, the prices of pet medications currently do not vary between veterinary clinics and alternative retail outlets.[106]

Thus, it appears that competition from non-veterinary retail outlets may already have resulted in lower prices charged by veterinarians, at least for some consumers and some product categories.

The benefits of price competition could be especially significant for spot-on flea and tick control products and heartworm preventatives, the two largest categories of pet medications.[107] These are the products for which consumers are most likely to comparison shop for the best price, and which consumers most often purchase from alternative retailers.[108] They tend to be the lowest margin products for veterinarians based on survey data collected by the AAHA, which indicates that, in 2012, the average veterinary mark-up was 78.5 percent for flea/tick products and 82.9 percent for heartworm preventatives, compared with 121.6 percent for other prescription drugs.[109]

These findings suggest that consumers may already benefit to at least some extent from price competition in the pet medications industry between veterinarians and alternative retailers. Nevertheless, continued growth of retail distribution could increase competition and lead to lower prices for pet medications in both veterinary and retail channels.

3. Comparison of Animal Drug Industry to Human Drug Industry

There are important differences between the human and animal drug industries with respect to prescription portability, distribution channels, and the availability of generics. Some comparisons between the two markets may help to illuminate the current state of competition in pet medications.

In the human medications marketplace, patients typically receive portable prescriptions from their prescribing physicians without having to request them and with no conditions attached.[110] Consumers almost always purchase their human medications from someone other than the prescribing physician.[111] In contrast, unlike most human doctor's offices, veterinary clinics typically function as one-stop providers of pet care, including not just examination and diagnosis, but also hospitalization and the dispensing of pet medications. Given this important distinction in the role veterinarians play, there does not appear to be any significant objection in the industry to continuing the practice of allowing veterinarians to maintain the right to dispense pet medications,[112] as consumers may prefer in some cases to purchase medication directly from the care provider, especially for acute care and specialty medications.[113]

Some stakeholders are very concerned, however, about the inherent conflict of interest that arises when the only authorized prescriber of medications is also the only authorized dispenser of medications. They claim this conflict of interest is exacerbated when manufacturers offer financial incentives to veterinarians for prescribing or recommending their products, and point out that these types of incentives are illegal in human medicine.[114] Some stakeholders have suggested that the American Medical Association's ("AMA") Code of Ethics provides an appropriate basis for comparing the standard of care owed to patients when prescribing and dispensing human drugs versus animal drugs,[115] as well as potential guidance regarding resolution of conflicts between the physician's financial interest and the physician's responsibilities to the patient.[116]

With respect to human medications, once a portable prescription has been received, it can be filled at a patient's pharmacy of choice, where the patient frequently has access to low-priced generic drugs. Both state law requirements and health insurance policies may compel generic substitution when feasible, which exerts further downward pressure on prices for human medications. In contrast, there are very few generic options for pet medications, and limited regulatory or other mechanisms to encourage their use.[117]

At the wholesale distribution level, there are other important differences between human and animal medications that may affect competition. Retail pharmacies have direct access to reliable supplies of human medications through established channels of distribution. In contrast, as explained above, most drug manufacturers have exclusive distribution policies that aim to restrict distribution of pet medications to veterinary channels – even when these same manufacturers do not impose similar distribution policies for human medications. Indeed, many consumers order their human prescription medications from online pharmacies, which have direct access to the medications and ship products to consumers' homes.

With respect to filling pet prescriptions online, some non-veterinary retailers question why this should be any more dangerous or inappropriate than filling human prescriptions in the same way, especially if the online pharmacy is staffed by veterinary experts.[118] More generally, with respect to the filling of pet prescriptions by pharmacists rather than veterinarians, proponents argue that manufacturers should be no more concerned about pharmacists dispensing pet medications than they are about pharmacists dispensing human medications because, in both instances, the pharmacist is merely dispensing medications as prescribed by a physician or veterinarian.[119] They ask whether and, if so, why a higher standard of care is owed to animal patients than to human patients – especially when, in the human medications context, any purported health and safety concerns clearly have been resolved overwhelmingly in favor of prescription portability and pharmacist dispensing.

Opponents of automatic prescription release for pet medications argue that their positions are justified primarily by unique health and safety concerns that weaken any analogies between the human and pet medication markets. As discussed in greater detail below, pharmacists historically have received little or no education in animal physiology or pharmacology; therefore, some argue, pharmacists are inadequately trained to provide counseling to pet owners, detect dosing errors, or flag potentially harmful drug interactions.[120] In addition, some stakeholders expressed concern that directing an increased volume of pet medication prescriptions to pharmacists could exacerbate the problem of pharmacist error, posing health risks for both humans and animals.[121] Some of these concerns may be more pronounced with respect to traditional retail pharmacies that primarily dispense drugs prescribed for human use than for specialized online veterinary pharmacies that only dispense drugs prescribed for animal use.

It is unclear whether evidence supports veterinarians' claims about dispensing errors by retail pharmacists. Although there has been some empirical research regarding human medication errors,[122] there do not appear to be comparable studies regarding the incidence of pharmacist dispensing errors for pet medications. Likewise, FTC staff has found no information on the frequency of dispensing errors by veterinarians and their technicians, which might enable comparisons to the frequency of pharmacist errors.[123] Even if dispensing errors occur, some stakeholders have suggested that veterinarians may be just as likely to make prescribing and dispensing errors as human doctors and pharmacists.[124] In 2008, the FDA's Center for Veterinary Medicine ("CVM") began to more closely monitor medication error reports involving animals. The CVM formally established its Veterinary

Medication Error Program in 2010, and has learned that errors may occur at veterinary clinics, pharmacies, and in households when pet owners administer medications to their pets.[125] The FDA stated that it has not received specific adverse event reports involving intentional alteration of prescriptions by pharmacists without verification from prescribing veterinarians.[126]

Stakeholders who favor expanded retail distribution of pet medications also dispute the validity of concerns about counterfeit products and fraudulent online vendors, claiming that these problems are no greater for pet medications than for human medications. If non-exclusive distribution and automatic prescription release are appropriate policies for human medications, they say, then these policies should be equally appropriate for animal medications.[127] FTC staff's inquiry did not yield evidence suggesting that counterfeiting or consumer fraud are more significant problems for animal medications than for human medications.[128]

With this overview in place, the next two sections of this report provide a more thorough explanation of FTC staff's findings regarding prescription portability and distribution practices.

III. PRESCRIPTION PORTABILITY

To purchase prescription pet medications from retail pharmacies, consumers must first obtain portable prescriptions from their veterinarians. Consumers are more likely to request prescriptions when seeking refills of preventative medications or long-term therapeutic treatments for chronic conditions, as opposed to treatments for acute conditions.[129] For example, anti-inflammatory drugs and heartworm preventative medications are more commonly "shopped" by consumers seeking to save money on the long-term use of such products.[130] Some consumers may find it more convenient to purchase pet medications from alternative retailers, such as online pharmacies or the retail pharmacies where they normally shop for other items. On the other hand, some consumers may prefer the convenience of leaving the veterinary clinic with the necessary medications, especially if their veterinarian is matching prices available at retail outlets.

It should be noted that under some circumstances, it may not be appropriate for consumers to obtain portable prescriptions, particularly for acute care and specialty medications that can only be practically dispensed by veterinarians.[131] For example, in emergency care situations, it could be medically inappropriate to delay treatment so that pet owners could comparison shop for the lowest priced medications if the animal requires immediate short-term treatment. Also, consumers may be less likely to realize a significant benefit from comparison shopping in these situations because of the sense of urgency and because there are unlikely to be recurring medication costs.[132] Indeed, H.R. 4023 and S. 2756 appear to have acknowledged this distinction, and would have exempted acute care drugs from the automatic prescription release requirements.[133]

If prescription release were "automatic," veterinarians would be required to provide portable prescriptions for all prescribed medications, regardless of whether clients request them. Industry stakeholders have expressed different views about the need for, and potential impact of, automatic prescription release mandated by federal or state law, or by industry self-regulation. This section of the report synthesizes FTC staff's findings regarding the availability to consumers of portable prescriptions, as well as the arguments supporting and opposing automatic prescription release.

A. Current State of Prescription Portability

1. State Laws and Veterinary Codes of Ethics

Currently, 31 states have statutes, rules, or policy statements that require veterinarians to provide their clients with a portable prescription upon request in some circumstances.[134] In addition, California and Arizona mandate certain aspects of notice and prescription release, even if not initiated by the client. California law requires that veterinarians offer their clients a written prescription; clients may then elect to have the prescription filled by either the prescribing veterinarian or the pharmacy of their choice, and veterinarians must provide clients with written notice that this option exists.[135] Arizona law requires veterinarians to notify pet owners that some prescription-only drugs and controlled substances may be available at a retail pharmacy, but Arizona does not require veterinarians to provide a portable prescription to the client.[136]

The AVMA Principles of Veterinary Medical Ethics hold that veterinarians should honor a client's request for a prescription in lieu of dispensing, but they do not mandate notice to the client of the right to request one.[137] Although the Principles on their own are not enforceable, several states have expressly incorporated the Principles into their disciplinary standards; in other states, the Principles may be used by state veterinary boards to determine what constitutes unprofessional conduct.[138] The AVMA argues that the threat of disciplinary action gives veterinarians an incentive to comply with client requests for portable prescriptions,[139] although it is unclear whether veterinarians perceive that threat as significant.[140]

Beyond the potential for disciplinary action, some veterinarians argue that market forces are enough to incentivize veterinarians to provide portable prescriptions: if a veterinarian refuses to provide clients with portable prescriptions upon request, any alienated clients will simply choose to take their pets to another veterinarian.[141] Other stakeholders suggest, however, that switching costs may deter clients from choosing another veterinarian solely because they are discouraged from seeking or denied portable prescriptions.[142] The likelihood of switching may be even lower for consumers who are unaware of the availability of portable prescriptions or who have limited alternatives – for example, in rural areas with few veterinary practices.

2. Veterinarian Attitudes towards Prescription Release

Anecdotal evidence and some survey data suggest that many veterinarians provide portable prescriptions to their clients, either at the clients' request or on their own initiative, in at least some circumstances.[143] For example, in a study commissioned by the American Veterinary Distributors Association ("AVDA"), veterinary prescription data for the 12-month period of July 2010 through June 2011 showed that more than 45,000 veterinarians (over 70 percent of total veterinarians in the United States) provided in excess of four million prescriptions to pet owners to be filled outside of the veterinarian's office.[144] One commenter stated that recent IMS audit data show that over 6 million prescriptions are written by veterinarians each year and filled by retail pharmacies.[145] Although this data indicates that many veterinarians do provide portable prescriptions to their clients, more information is necessary to draw conclusions about the overall prevalence of veterinarian prescription release and the circumstances in which it occurs.[146]

The AVMA has expressed support for a pet owner's ability to obtain a portable prescription upon request, and encourages its members to comply with such requests.[147] Some industry stakeholders applaud the efforts of the AVMA to promote compliance with its Principles of Veterinary Medical Ethics and individual state rules regarding prescription portability,[148] and believe that many veterinarians who may have been reluctant to provide prescriptions in the past have changed their behavior.[149] Some have argued that the long-term viability of a veterinarian's practice can be impacted by the manner in which a veterinarian handles client requests for portable prescriptions.[150] The AVMA has stated that it is unaware of any data suggesting that veterinarians do not currently provide prescriptions upon request.[151]

In contrast, some commenters have suggested that veterinarian practices vary considerably in their willingness to provide portable prescriptions to clients upon request:

> Certainly, there are veterinarians who adhere to very high ethical standards and provide prescriptions to their clients upon request. However, there are frequently barriers to consumers obtaining a prescription. For example, our client has identified: (1) a general reluctance from clients to "demand" a prescription in deference to the veterinarian as a professional; (2) veterinarians putting up barriers to receiving a prescription, e.g., front-office staff stating a policy of not issuing prescriptions and/or insisting that the animal be brought in for a check up even though sufficiently current laboratory results are in the animal's file; (3) veterinarians calling and attempting to change a client's mind about obtaining drugs from other sources; and (4) veterinarians indicating that they are not familiar with the products sold into the retail pharmacy and thereby instilling doubts about safety or efficacy of those products.[152]

FTC staff did not identify any comprehensive data sources regarding the extent to which veterinarians provide portable prescriptions. Some state veterinary medical associations have surveyed veterinarians on this issue, however, and the survey responses revealed that some veterinarians refuse to provide prescriptions to clients when requested, even in states having policies requiring them to do so.[153] Consistent with these findings, anecdotal evidence presented in written comments and other publicly available sources indicates that some veterinarians refuse to provide prescriptions to clients when requested.[154] Furthermore, some veterinarians may try to actively discourage clients from filling prescriptions elsewhere by providing misleading information about non-veterinary retailers, requiring waivers of liability that exaggerate the dangers of purchasing from non-veterinary retailers, or requiring extra fees for portable prescriptions.[155]

During the FTC workshop and in the public comments, several veterinarians offered statements that suggested a tension between their willingness to provide portable prescriptions, on the one hand, and their views of the appropriate role of the retail pharmacist in dispensing pet medications, on the other. For example, some veterinarians stated that they always give a client a prescription when asked and, in fact, will affirmatively offer a client a prescription if they know it will save the client money. Also, some veterinarians indicated that they prefer for retail pharmacists to dispense certain medications that they choose not to carry because of low demand, compounding requirements, or human abuse potential. Yet, the same veterinarians also stated that they are uncomfortable providing prescriptions because they cannot be sure about the level of care the client receives after leaving their office, and because they have serious safety concerns about the products dispensed by retail pharmacists.[156] Some commentators suggest that these positions are contradictory, because presumably veterinarians would not willingly provide any portable prescriptions to clients if they believed doing so would jeopardize the health and safety of animals.[157] Some of these veterinarians may only be providing portable prescriptions to clients because they are required to do so by state regulations or ethical guidelines.

Some veterinarians commented that although they are comfortable providing prescriptions to their clients when requested, they are uncomfortable when they receive prescription verification requests from online and local pharmacies rather than directly from their clients.[158] This situation may arise when a client attempts to purchase pet medications from a pharmacy without first contacting the prescribing veterinarian, prompting the pharmacy to contact the veterinarian directly. In response, the veterinarian may need to review the pet's medical records and determine whether the medication is appropriate or an examination is necessary in order to either verify or deny the prescription.

According to some veterinarians, differences in the regulation of physicians and veterinarians might cause confusion when pharmacists – who are more accustomed to dealing with doctors and human prescriptions – are presented with veterinary prescriptions. For example, doctors are required to include their National Provider Identifier ("NPI") number on every prescription they write, but veterinarians are not eligible to have NPI numbers, which can lead to confusion when clients bring their pet medication prescriptions to retail pharmacies.[159] In these situations, some pharmacies purportedly request veterinarians' DEA numbers as an alternative way to track veterinarians in their electronic pharmacy systems. Some veterinarians stated they are uncomfortable providing their DEA numbers for non-controlled drugs, and therefore may be reluctant to verify prescriptions for these pharmacies.[160] Indeed, the DEA advises veterinarians not to provide their DEA license numbers for non-controlled substances, but instead should provide their veterinary license numbers.[161]

3. Consumer Awareness of Prescription Portability and Effectiveness of "Upon Request" Regulations and Policies

In evaluating the effectiveness of existing "upon request" regulations and policies, it is important to consider whether they promote consumer awareness of prescription portability, such that consumers have accurate information upon which to exercise available choices in the marketplace.

Some industry stakeholders have suggested that many consumers may be unaware of their ability to obtain portable prescriptions for pet medications. In particular, they suggest that this lack of awareness may be perpetuated by the fact that, historically, veterinarians were the only viable source for these products.[162] While state regulations or policies may require veterinarians to provide prescriptions upon request, these stakeholders argue that an "upon request" mechanism, by itself, provides no assurance that pet owners will know the option is available to them.[163] These stakeholders argue that, for such unaware consumers, automatic prescription release would provide "the most effective, most efficient means of creating a consciousness of choice."[164]

Information available to FTC staff suggests that even when consumers are aware that they can request a portable prescription, some may be reluctant to do so for fear of offending their veterinarian.[165] At the workshop and in written comments, stakeholders expressed the view that consumer comfort levels vary with respect to requesting prescriptions.[166] They suggest that affirmatively asking for a prescription can be intimidating to consumers, and that this intimidation factor can be amplified when veterinarians require waivers of liability, make disparaging statements about non-veterinary retailers (e.g., suggesting that the product may be counterfeit), or require extra fees for prescriptions.[167] They further suggest that pet owners do not want to feel that they have somehow degraded or compromised their relationship with their veterinarian, even when they know the veterinarian has a clear economic interest in selling pet medications.[168] Some FTC workshop participants support automatic prescription release to help ensure that all consumers receive a portable prescription when they would like one, but are too afraid or uncomfortable to ask.[169]

In response to these arguments, many veterinarians and manufacturers contend that most consumers are aware that they can request and obtain portable prescriptions, in part because widespread advertising has educated consumers regarding the many online and other retail sources of pet medications.[170]

B. Merits of Automatic Prescription Release

Some stakeholders and policymakers have concluded that current "upon request" policies are inadequate to ensure that consumers are aware of their ability to obtain portable prescriptions for pet medications. This perspective has motivated efforts to reform the current state of prescription portability. Notably, proposed legislation at both federal and state levels would require automatic prescription release for pet medications.[171] Several industry stakeholders support legislative efforts to mandate automatic prescription release.[172] Many veterinarians and other stakeholders have raised concerns regarding automatic prescription release, however, particularly if mandated by federal law.

This section summarizes areas of agreement between proponents and opponents of automatic prescription release, as well as the main arguments for and against automatic prescription release raised by the AVMA, individual veterinarians, retailers, consumer advocates, and other stakeholders.

1. Areas of Agreement between Proponents and Opponents of Automatic Prescription Release

FTC staff notes at the outset that there does not appear to be any dispute between proponents and opponents of automatic prescription release on some overarching principles. First, it seems widely accepted that veterinarians should only be required to provide portable prescriptions for medications that they deem medically appropriate and would have been willing to dispense to the client directly. No mandate is needed for medications that the veterinarian would be unwilling to dispense to the patient themselves. Moreover, there is broad consensus that veterinarians should retain the right to require all necessary examinations and diagnostic tests that would enable them to prescribe treatment regimens that are medically appropriate, within the context of the VCPR, regardless of where the medications are purchased. Furthermore, there is agreement that veterinarians should not be required to verify prescriptions with pharmacies that are not properly licensed or accredited.[173]

2. Arguments in Favor of Automatic Prescription Release

Based on the workshop record and additional information compiled by FTC staff, it appears that entry and expansion by non-veterinary retailers already have increased competition and likely lowered pet medication prices for some consumers.[174] As discussed below, conventional economic theory suggests that greater prescription portability (including via automatic prescription release) would increase consumer awareness about their options for purchasing pet medications from non-veterinary sources, and thereby enhance consumers' ability to evaluate and exercise choices in the pet medications marketplace. This, in turn, could foster additional competition for the sale of pet medications and further benefit consumers.

a. Potential Benefits of Automatic Prescription Release

Advocates of state or federal policies mandating automatic prescription release frequently argue that it would benefit consumers by expanding their access to pet medications prescriptions.[175] In addition to the potential for greater competition and lower prices, they argue automatic prescription release will better enable consumers to choose the most convenient purchase location for their needs at any given time, which may be their veterinarian, the Internet, or their local retail pharmacy.[176] They also contend that automatic prescription release would help to ensure that consumers can obtain competitively priced products, including generic animal drugs, and would spur new product innovation.[177]

Alternative approaches have been suggested to promote the awareness and ability of consumers to obtain pet medications prescriptions, and mitigate some of the alleged burdens of automatic prescription release on veterinary practices. One such approach would require veterinarians to provide clients with notice that they may obtain portable prescriptions in lieu of dispensed medications upon request. For example, veterinarians might be required to post a sign in the veterinary clinic lobby, hand a written disclosure statement to the client, or provide notice verbally. This approach might address the concern that some consumers are unaware of the option to obtain a prescription from their veterinarian and have it filled elsewhere.

Some stakeholders have argued, however, that consumers would obtain even greater benefits if veterinarians were required to offer portable prescriptions to clients, regardless of whether a portable prescription has been requested. As already noted, this kind of mandatory release would address the concern expressed by some stakeholders that consumers may feel intimidated when requesting prescriptions from their veterinarians, regardless of whether veterinarians do anything to intentionally cause the discomfort.[178] Therefore, automatic prescription release might be more effective than notice requirements in raising consumer awareness and mitigating the intimidation a consumer may feel when requesting a portable prescription. Furthermore, some stakeholders have suggested that automatic prescription release may help to resolve the apparent conflict of interest associated with a veterinarian having the power to both prescribe and sell pet medications.[179]

b. Consumer Benefits of Prescription Portability: Lessons from Eyewear Industry and Implications for Pet Medications

Although the FTC has not previously studied prescription portability with respect to pet medications, the FTC has expertise regarding prescription portability in other contexts. Consistent with the FTC's opposition to laws and regulations that inhibit competition by impeding informed consumer choice, the FTC has a long history of supporting efforts to promote prescription portability for eyeglasses and contact lenses, other markets where prescribers also dispense the products.[180] The FTC's experience with the eyeglasses and contact lens industries reinforces the basic principle that prescription portability is generally beneficial to consumers.[181] At the FTC's pet medications workshop, there was a general consensus that prescription portability, as mandated by the FCLCA, enabled consumer choice and thus fostered a more competitive market for the sale of contact lenses,[182] although panelists disagreed as to whether increased competition following the passage of the FCLCA resulted in better prices for consumers.[183] One workshop participant claimed that separating exclusive prescribing power from exclusive dispensing power "promotes healthy results, and it brings value to consumers."[184]

For similar reasons, the elimination of current constraints on prescription portability in the pet medications industry would likely enhance competition to the benefit of consumers. Those benefits might include lower prices, increased service, and greater convenience. The ASPCA, which offered an animal and consumer welfare perspective at the FTC workshop, argued strongly in favor of expanded prescription portability for pet medications. Veterinary and general health care costs are frequently cited as prohibitive factors to pet ownership. The ASPCA has a vested interest in lowering the costs of pet ownership so that fewer pets will be abandoned and more people will adopt animals from shelters.[185] For these reasons, the ASPCA believes that "[v]eterinarians and policy-makers should take every available opportunity to make pet care as affordable as possible. Prescription release is a small but logical part of the solution."[186]

Specifically, the ASPCA contends that "having unfettered access to their pets' prescriptions gives consumers a choice about where they buy pet medications. As with many markets, more choice encourages competitive pricing. Lower prices for pet medications ease the financial burden on pet owners and ultimately benefit pets."[187] The ASPCA argues that this downward pressure on prices is particularly important for price-sensitive consumers who are looking for ways to reduce the costs of pet ownership, and for whom the affordability of preventative medicines is critical to protect against conditions that may be difficult and expensive to treat.[188] Also, for consumers that own pets with chronic conditions requiring maintenance drugs, the ASPCA estimates that the potential cost savings would be substantial.[189]

Although the pet medications industry appears to function in a similar manner as the contact lens industry before the FCLCA passed and manufacturer restrictive distribution practices were eliminated, there are also some notable differences that may limit the comparison that can be drawn between market conditions of these two industries. Several stakeholders observe that the pet medications industry encompasses many different formulations and dosages of drugs administered to a wide variety of animal species, while the contact lens industry encompasses a single-use commodity product dispensed in pre-packaged boxes for human use. Furthermore, they claim that there are much greater health and safety concerns associated with the dispensing of pet medications versus contact lenses, and that for these reasons, it is inappropriate to compare these industries.[190]

3. Arguments Opposing Automatic Prescription Release

While expressing general support for the ability of pet owners to obtain a portable prescription, the AVMA and several other organizations in the veterinary industry have strongly opposed mandatory automatic prescription release.[191] They have taken the position that federal legislation is unnecessary and redundant, arguing that veterinarians already are encouraged to provide prescriptions to clients upon request, and that pet owners already have the ability to fill prescriptions at the pharmacy of their choice. To the extent that prescription portability is not being fully realized, the AVMA argues that state boards of pharmacy and veterinary medicine are fully capable of resolving any outstanding issues.[192] Indeed, several critics of the proposed federal legislation argue that it would encroach upon state jurisdiction,[193] and some stakeholders who support efforts to promote prescription portability believe that implementing such policies on a state level would be a better approach.[194] Based on public comments received in connection with the FTC workshop, individual veterinarians overwhelmingly appear to oppose any legislation that would mandate automatic prescription release, whether at the federal or state level.[195] Some of the primary reasons for this opposition are discussed below, along with responses offered by supporters of automatic prescription release.

a. Effect of Prescription Portability on the VCPR

Opponents of automatic prescription release argue that dispensing medications provides an important "touch point" between veterinarians, clients, and patients, such that mandating prescription portability would threaten the integrity of the VCPR.[196] According to this view, all decisions regarding a pet's health care should be collaborative in accordance with the VCPR, and voluntary.[197] Furthermore, veterinarians argue that pet owners are more likely to comply with treatment regimens if the veterinarian dispenses the medications.[198]

The AVMA has expressed support for the ability of a pet owner to choose where to fill prescriptions,[199] and provides this guidance to veterinarians on how to handle client requests for prescriptions:

> (1) Drug therapy, when medically indicated, should be initiated by the attending veterinarian in the context of veterinarian-client-patient relationship. Clients that wish to purchase their prescription drugs from a pharmacy rather than the veterinarian should be advised to first obtain a prescription from their veterinarian before contacting a pharmacy. The veterinarian may choose to either issue the prescription in writing for the client, or contact the pharmacy electronically or by phone.
>
> (2) Veterinarians should honor client requests to prescribe rather than dispense a drug (AVMA Principles of Veterinary Medical Ethics). The client has the option of filling a prescription at any pharmacy.
>
> . . . .
>
> (4) Veterinarians asked by pharmacies to approve prescriptions they have not initiated should do so only if the prescription is appropriate and a veterinarian- client-patient relationship exists.[200]

Based on this guidance, it seems that while veterinarians may dispense pet medications within the context of a VCPR, a valid VCPR need not always include the dispensing of medications. At the same time, the AVMA has taken the position that a federal law mandating veterinary prescription writing in all cases "would negatively affect the strong bond of trust that veterinarians have earned with their clients."[201]

In response, supporters of automatic prescription release argue that the VCPR is not undermined when a veterinarian does not actually dispense the pet medication because the veterinarian remains the only individual with the legal authority to prescribe the pet medication. They note that pharmacists are already legally allowed to dispense pet medications in every state and argue that this does not undermine the VCPR. In particular, they note that pharmacists are legally required to dispense medications exactly as prescribed. Some pharmacy stakeholders claim that the VCPR is important at the point at which the pet medication is prescribed, but is unlikely to be jeopardized if the prescription is dispensed outside the veterinary channel.[202] They argue that even with automatic release, veterinarians would still maintain most of the major touch points associated with the VCPR, including examining and diagnosing the animals; determining treatment regimens and prescribing medications; and providing follow-up care to pets[203] – all services that may only be provided by veterinarians.

b. Safety Issues Regarding Retail Pharmacists

Although state laws permit pharmacists to dispense both human and animal drugs,[204] many veterinarians have expressed concerns regarding the ability of retail pharmacists to dispense pet medications safely.[205] Many of these concerns relate to pharmacists' training and knowledge, while others relate to the quality of products available to pharmacies through the secondary distribution system.

A principal argument voiced by opponents of automatic prescription release is that pharmacists typically lack training in veterinary pharmacology, rendering it impossible for pharmacists to validate the dosing information included on a prescription for pet medications.[206] Some pharmacists themselves acknowledge discomfort in dispensing pet medications when they do not have a strong working knowledge of veterinary pharmacology.[207] It is unclear to what extent continuing education programs could mitigate these purported safety risks. There do appear to be opportunities for pharmacists to augment their knowledge of veterinary pharmacology,[208] which may enable more pharmacists to confidently and safely dispense pet medications.[209] If demand for pharmacist-dispensed pet medications were to increase, pharmacists may be more inclined to secure additional training.[210] Indeed, this may already be happening to a certain degree.[211] Some commentators believe that basic continuing education for pharmacists should be sufficient,[212] while others believe that more is necessary.[213] Some stakeholders also suggest that informational product inserts can be provided by the manufacturers of pet medications to assist pharmacists,[214] and pharmacists can contact the prescribing veterinarian if they have any questions.[215]

Opponents also argue that retail pharmacists routinely alter pet prescriptions without authorization from the prescribing veterinarian or otherwise make dispensing errors, and may provide inaccurate information to pet owners regarding administration techniques, dosing, side effects, and potential drug interactions.[216] Some state veterinary medical associations have recently attempted to collect information regarding alleged instances of pharmacist errors when dispensing pet medications.[217] It does not appear, however, that this information has resulted in any substantiated claims or formal actions taken by state pharmacy boards.[218]

Proponents of automatic prescription release have responded that pharmacists are highly regulated, trained professionals who understand that they are legally required to dispense medications exactly as written.[219] Pharmacists know that they must obtain authorization from a veterinarian before making changes to a pet prescription, just as they would obtain authorization from a doctor before making changes to a human prescription.[220] Some stakeholders pointed out that existing regulatory mechanisms (namely, oversight by the state pharmacy boards and NABP) already address unauthorized alterations of prescriptions and other dispensing errors.[221]

They suggest that when veterinarians believe a pharmacist has incorrectly dispensed medications to their clients, the veterinarians should file a complaint with the appropriate state board and avail themselves of this regulatory process.[222] Opponents of automatic prescription release have argued, however, that veterinarians rarely file complaints with state pharmacy boards[223] because the process is difficult and veterinarians may be confused about whether pharmacy boards or veterinary boards have jurisdiction.[224]

Some commenters also suggest that alleged safety concerns regarding the capabilities of retail pharmacists have been exaggerated, and that pharmacists are qualified to safely and effectively dispense pet medications.[225] Some workshop participants argued that the health risk arguments raised by veterinarians are very similar to arguments raised by eye care professionals during the contact lens antitrust litigation[226] and in opposition to the FCLCA, and should be treated with skepticism. These commenters emphasized that, if health care concerns are valid, the regulatory system should address them directly, and that this is preferable to industry participants limiting access to portable prescriptions.[227]

Commenters on both sides acknowledged that communication between veterinarians, pharmacists, and clients can potentially address many of these concerns. When in doubt about dispensing pet medications, pharmacists can consult with the prescribing veterinarian, as is the standard practice when dispensing human pharmaceuticals.[228] Although some commenters expressed concerns about retail pharmacists' ability to provide adequate follow-up care to pet owners – particularly in the event of an adverse reaction[229] – there do not appear to be significant obstacles preventing veterinarians themselves from providing information and follow-up care to pet owners after a prescription is dispensed by an alternative retailer.[230]

The AVMA is working with the NABP and other pharmacy stakeholders to help pharmacists better "understand their roles and responsibilities for counseling and educating clients when filling a veterinary prescription, including verification with the prescribing veterinarian should the pharmacist have any questions about the medication or dosage."[231] In addition, some state veterinary medical associations and boards of pharmacy are coordinating to resolve these issues by, for example, instructing pharmacists to encourage pet owners to contact their veterinarians with any questions about medications or follow-up care.[232] Information regarding administration techniques, dosing, side effects, and potential drug interactions could still be provided by veterinarians at the time of the examination or office visit, or through the use of printed instructions.

A second, distinct area of concern relates to the quality of the pet medications dispensed by retail pharmacists. Some veterinarians claim that the integrity of products dispensed outside the veterinary channel cannot be trusted because these medications often are procured through the secondary distribution system, thereby increasing the risk that the products could be counterfeit, adulterated, or otherwise compromised.[233] The FDA has issued a warning to consumers about purchasing pet medications from unscrupulous online pharmacies that operate illegally. The FDA states that it "has found companies that sell unapproved pet drugs and counterfeit pet products, make fraudulent claims, dispense prescription drugs without requiring a prescription, and sell expired drugs."[234] Therefore, it recommends that consumers purchase pet medications only from Vet-VIPPS accredited pharmacies to ensure product quality.[235]

These types of concerns may cause some veterinarians to be reluctant to provide portable prescriptions to clients.[236] However, the AVMA acknowledges that there should not be any serious product safety concerns if retail pharmacists procure and dispense pet medications in an appropriate and legal manner.[237] Other industry stakeholders suggest that limiting prescription portability does not protect consumers from illegal counterfeit products. Rather, they suggest, this problem would be better addressed by making pet medications readily available in retail pharmacies that are equipped to identify and eliminate counterfeits.[238]

c. Administrative Burdens and Cost of Compliance

Many industry stakeholders have expressed concern that veterinary practices, some of which may already face economic pressures, will face substantial administrative burdens and additional costs to comply with automatic prescription release legislation.[239] The AVMA and many veterinarians claim that there is administrative burden associated with writing a prescription for each medication, regardless of whether the client opts to fill it elsewhere. In further describing this burden, the AVMA claims that writing, calling in, or faxing a prescription adds a few minutes to every appointment, or more when patients require more than one medication. The verification requirement for every prescription, including follow-up phone calls from pharmacies, may further increase the time, cost, and burden placed on a veterinary practice.[240] For clients who decide to have their prescriptions filled by the veterinarian, the AVMA claims that extra measures would be needed to store or properly dispose of superfluous written prescriptions, in accordance with state laws, so as to prevent misuse of any prescription.[241] The AVMA further argues that the cumulative time required for prescription writing and verification activities for all patients would substantially impact the scheduling of appointments in veterinary practices, as well as the allocation of support staff duties and other office resources. As a result, a veterinarian might need to extend office hours to ensure sufficient patient volume to keep a practice running, which would increase costs.[242]

In response, other stakeholders contend that the administrative burdens and additional costs of complying with automatic prescription release legislation would be minimal.[243] Human health care practitioners are expected to write and verify prescriptions for their patients, and some use time-saving measures such as automated dispensing devices, personal digital assistant ("PDA") devices, and tablet computers to more quickly generate prescriptions for patients and their medical files and reduce errors. It is possible that existing or evolving technologies, particularly those already used in the human medical field, could help reduce the administrative burdens and compliance costs for veterinarians, while helping them adapt to the changing pet medications marketplace.[244]

Furthermore, it appears that automatic prescription release requirements could be reasonably tailored to avoid imposing any unnecessary administrative burdens on veterinarians. For example, if the client opts to have the veterinarian dispense the medication, the veterinarian does not need to provide a written copy of the prescription.[245] When clients do opt for a portable prescription, they could choose to receive it in writing, or have it transmitted by telephone or in an electronic format.[246] Some clients may prefer the convenience of having a prescription directly transmitted to the retail pharmacy of their choice, rather than having to physically deliver a written copy. It may not be necessary, therefore, to require that written prescriptions be prepared and physically handed to a client in every instance.[247] This would be consistent with emerging practices in the human medications industry, where written prescriptions are increasingly less common.[248]

Some veterinarians have argued that they need to assess fees for issuing portable prescriptions to cover their administrative costs.[249] Concerns have been raised, however, regarding veterinarians' imposition of fees as a precondition to providing clients with a portable prescription. In particular, some observers have expressed concern that veterinarians are requiring such fees as a way to discourage consumers from requesting and obtaining portable prescriptions, rather than for legitimate business reasons.[250] Prescription fees may be economically justified if they represent reasonable compensation for the actual cost of providing portable prescriptions, which in some cases might include reviewing patients' medical files, verifying prescriptions, and answering pharmacists' questions.[251] Some stakeholders have suggested, however, that the procompetitive goals of prescription portability would be better served, and clients would face fewer real or perceived barriers to receiving portable prescriptions, if veterinarians simply charged clients a single professional services fee that encompassed all administrative activities, including providing prescriptions.[252] Of course, that would shift costs to those clients who are not obtaining a prescription drug or those who purchase directly from the veterinarian.

d. Veterinarian Liability Issues

Some veterinarians have expressed concerns about possible liability when pet medications are dispensed by retail pharmacists. In particular, they question whether a veterinarian will be held responsible if a pharmacist dispenses an incorrect, counterfeit, or otherwise adulterated pet medication; therefore, some veterinarians may require clients to sign a waiver of liability before providing them with a portable prescription.[253] Some veterinarians have expressed concern that proposals to prohibit the use of such waivers could potentially expose them to liability for the mistakes of pharmacists, as well as the costs of litigating such claims.[254] Some commentators have also suggested that veterinarians might face legal liability if they prescribe a human generic drug rather than a veterinary-label drug in an effort to save their clients money.[255]

Based on the workshop record and additional research, these concerns do not appear to be founded. FTC staff received no information regarding any instances where a veterinarian has been held liable for a pharmacist's dispensing error. Some pharmacy boards have expressly indicated that pharmacists are responsible for any prescription misfills, not veterinarians.[256] Thus, it is unclear that such waivers are, in fact, necessary to protect veterinarians from legal liability. Available information suggests that as long as an animal is properly examined and diagnosed, and a prescription is written properly, it is unlikely that liability would attach to a veterinarian in the event a retail pharmacist incorrectly dispenses a medication.[257] Likewise, FTC staff is unaware of any evidence that veterinarians have faced legal liability for prescribing human generic drugs for use in companion animals when a veterinary-label drug is available.

Some proponents of automatic prescription release have questioned the motivations of veterinarians who require liability waivers as a precondition for issuing a portable prescription. In their view, it is likely that they do so for the purpose of discouraging consumers from requesting portable prescriptions and that this dampens competition.[258] In any event, restrictions or prohibitions on waivers of liability need not prohibit veterinarians from providing medical advice to clients, which may include truthful information about non-veterinary sources of pet medications.[259]

e. Increased Potential for Prescription Fraud and Abuse

Some veterinarians expressed concern about the potential for increased fraud and abuse if automatic prescription release were mandated by federal or state legislation, asserting that it may result in a surge of written prescriptions given to clients. Veterinarians speculate that this may increase the likelihood that individuals will fraudulently and illegally procure prescription drugs for abuse by humans, and that veterinarians may need to employ enhanced anti-fraud measures to mitigate this risk.[260] It is unclear, however, why the potential for this type of abuse would be worse if prescription portability were enhanced and clients filled prescriptions using a non- veterinary drug source rather than the veterinarian. Either way, the client would obtain the prescribed drug and the veterinarian would have no way to control whether the client uses it appropriately.

Veterinarians also expressed concerns about an increase in inappropriate drug requests – for example, when clients request a drug even though necessary blood work has not been performed on the animal.[261] It is unclear to what extent this problem would be affected by mandating automatic prescription release. With or without a mandate, presumably veterinarians will only prescribe medications when it is appropriate to do so.

C. Impact of Automatic Prescription Release on Veterinary Income and Service Fees

A common theme that emerged during the workshop and in related comments is that many veterinarians fear that automatic prescription release could lead to a significant erosion of their revenues. Commenters have made various assertions regarding the importance of revenue from pharmaceutical sales to current veterinary practice business models, as well as the potential effects of automatic prescription release on clients' total out-of-pocket costs. They have also suggested that veterinarians might seek to increase their service charges to compensate for lost prescription revenues.

Although FTC staff's research allows for a qualitative description of the possible effects of and strategic responses to automatic prescription release, as is discussed in greater detail below, data currently available to staff do not permit a reliable quantification of the likely economic impact of automatic prescription release on veterinarians and consumers. We note at the outset, however, that the seemingly widespread concern among veterinarians that increased prescription portability would lead to a significant loss of revenue appears to be inconsistent with their arguments that prescription portability is not currently constrained and that their prices for pet medications have already been adjusted to account for retail competition. With respect to portability, if most consumers are already aware of and exercise their ability to obtain prescriptions, and veterinarians already provide these prescriptions without any limitations, then it would seem that proposed legislation mandating automatic prescription release should not result in any significant loss of revenues beyond what has already occurred.

1. Importance of Pet Medication Revenues to Veterinary Practices

Veterinarians have long relied upon pet medication sales as a source of revenue.[262] Currently, pet medication sales comprise approximately 20 percent of the total income for a typical primary care veterinary practice.[263] Some commenters speculate that if the prices currently being charged by veterinary practices for prescription drugs are higher than the prices charged by non-veterinary retailers, mandatory automatic prescription release may lead more clients to purchase pet medications from retail pharmacies, thereby reducing veterinary practice revenues.[264] Veterinarians may respond to this additional retail competition by reducing their own pharmaceutical prices to retain sales, which would result in a loss of revenue, even if sales volumes remained constant. Several commenters have further alleged that some veterinarians may actively resist providing written prescriptions to clients due to concerns over revenue loss.[265]

Yet, it is unclear whether automatic prescription release would cause veterinarians to lose a significant amount of pharmacy revenue.[266] Presumably, many clients would prefer to continue filling prescriptions with their veterinarian rather than a retail pharmacy because they consider it more convenient, particularly for acute care products.[267] It also may be the case that consumers who are interested in obtaining portable prescriptions and comparison shopping for pet medications are already doing so, and automatic prescription release would not result in veterinarians losing significant additional sales. In addition, veterinarians likely would continue to sell OTC medications that do not require prescriptions, thereby retaining at least some of this portion of pharmacy revenues.

2. Veterinarian Claims Regarding Increased Service Fees to Offset Loss of Prescription Drug Revenues

For several reasons, it is difficult to determine the likely economic impact of mandatory automatic prescription release on veterinary practices and consumers based on the workshop record and publicly available data.[268] Many veterinarians have stated that prescription drug revenues help to offset the significant costs associated with running a veterinary practice, thereby allowing veterinary practices to charge lower service and examination fees than they otherwise would.[269] They have suggested that if veterinary practices lose a significant portion of their pharmacy revenues to other retailers, they would need to charge higher service fees to compensate for the lower revenues, and that this may deter consumers from seeking care for their pets.[270] Furthermore, they fear that higher service fees could result in an erosion of trust in veterinarians,[271] and that increased price competition for sales of pet medications could degrade beneficial collaboration that has developed over time between veterinarians and pharmacists.[272]

There is some evidence suggesting price sensitivity for veterinary care. For example, there appears to have been a decline in visits to companion animal veterinary clinics in recent years likely due, in part, to a decline in consumer income during the economic recession and the perception among pet owners that veterinary care is too expensive.[273] However, this trend appears to be reversing as the economy recovers.[274] Nevertheless, given that many veterinarians lost some portion of pet medication revenues to alternative retail outlets, even in the absence of automatic prescription release requirements,[275] some have expressed concern that requiring automatic prescription release could accelerate the loss of pharmacy revenues and increase the likelihood that veterinarians would need to increase the prices of their services.[276] In this respect, they argue that automatic prescription release would not lead to consumer cost savings, but would actually increase the cost of pet care.[277]

Consultants and experts often recommend that veterinarians adjust their practice models to decrease their reliance on pharmacy sales versus service revenues, regardless of any automatic prescription release requirement,[278] and this adjustment may already be happening to some degree.[279] The AVMA indicated that, over the past 25 years, drug sales have been a decreasing source of veterinary practice revenues, while physical exams, vaccines, laboratory tests and other diagnostics have become a more significant source of veterinary practice revenues.[280] Similarly, one veterinary consultant has suggested that veterinarians could compensate for lost pharmacy revenues by identifying and filling gaps in animal health care and improving compliance with treatment regimens. She reasons that educating pet owners about unmet needs and improving compliance serves everyone's interests, and suggests that if veterinarians "can grow the market even a small percentage, we can more than make up for the difference in those buying [medications] outside the veterinary channel."[281]

Economic theory alone does not support the argument that veterinarians are likely to increase their prices for services if they must comply with an automatic prescription release requirement. Presumably, veterinarians already set their prices for services and medications at profit- maximizing levels commensurate with their costs, the degree of competition they currently face and the nature of consumer demand. For them to have an incentive to charge a different price, some factor that affects their profit-maximization would need to change. Thus, it is possible that veterinarians may not be able to increase their prices for examinations and other services to offset any additional loss of pharmacy revenues, without losing significant business.[282]

Accordingly, whether automatic prescription portability would result in higher fees for veterinary services depends on the nature of competition for these services, and the degree to which a loss of revenue from dispensing pet medications would affect this competition. If veterinarians set the prices for services and prescription drugs independently, then greater prescription portability may only affect their prescription drug pricing.[283] While automatic prescription portability could change the intensity of the competition veterinarians face for the sale of prescription drugs, under this assumption of independence it would have no immediate and direct effect on the degree of competition that veterinarians face for other services. Thus, it is possible that veterinarians' prices for other services are not dependent on the degree of prescription portability.

Nevertheless, there may be circumstances in which mandating automatic prescription portability could result in a change in the prices for veterinary services. If the loss of prescription drug sales were to reduce the profitability of veterinary practices so much that it significantly diminished their ability to cover their fixed costs, then it is possible that some practices might close, leading to a reduction of competition in affected local markets.[284] Veterinarians facing less local competition might have an incentive to increase service prices. The likelihood of such an effect would depend on whether profits from veterinarians' prescription drug sales cover any fixed practice costs and on the degree to which greater prescription portability would affect veterinary pharmacy profits.

Another possibility is that veterinarians consider anticipated profits from future pharmaceutical sales when they set the prices for services. If anticipated profits from pharmaceutical sales are significant, veterinarians may compete more intensively on service prices in order to attract customers in the first place.[285] If automatic prescription release leads to a reduction in the profits from pharmaceutical sales, veterinarians may have less incentive to accept lower margins on services in order to establish a customer relationship that could potentially lead to future pharmacy sales. Under this latter scenario, it is possible that current veterinary pharmaceutical prices are above the competitive level, and service prices are below the competitive level, as compared to a situation where pharmaceuticals and services are sold by separate sellers. This potential cross-subsidization between products and services could result in an allocative inefficiency,[286] although whether it would in practice is uncertain. Assuming this cross-subsidization were currently happening, the ASPCA argues consumers would be better off with a pricing model that provides sufficient information to support informed choices about services and medications respectively.[287]

3. Professional and Ethical Issues Associated with Pet Medication Revenues

Some veterinarians have suggested that mandating prescription release might affect the economic incentives of veterinarians in other ways that could increase overall service costs for consumers. For example, some veterinarians might try to recover potential pharmacy revenue losses by providing unnecessary or more expensive services, such as requiring complete physical examinations for all prescription refills (which may not be the typical practice for many medications), or by writing prescriptions for more expensive injectable medications that can only be administered by a veterinarian.[288] These tactics may enable veterinarians to maintain or increase their revenues without having to increase their specific service fees, albeit with no offsetting quality improvements for clients or animals. Although the incentive to engage in such tactics could be exacerbated by the loss of pet medication revenues due to automatic prescription release, this may raise ethical concerns and it would seem that less scrupulous veterinarians already have the incentive to do this, regardless of whether prescription release is mandated. Indeed, the AVMA Principles of Veterinary Medical Ethics advise veterinarians not to engage in this kind of behavior.[289]

Some observers have argued that there is already an inherent conflict of interest when veterinarians recommend and prescribe medications they also sell.[290] The fact that veterinarians have a personal financial interest in selling pet medications has caused some to question veterinarians' incentives to provide the lowest prices to customers.[291] In particular, some observers argue that such a conflict of interest can be exacerbated when pharmaceutical companies offer financial incentives to veterinarians for recommending or dispensing their products, a practice they suggest may lead consumers to question the veterinarian's prescribing choices.[292] For example, economic self-interest might lead some veterinarians to be biased towards over-prescribing medications or recommending more expensive categories of medications, in an effort to generate greater revenues. Moreover, small veterinary clinics that cannot practicably stock a full pharmacopeia might have an incentive to prescribe the limited set of drugs they do stock, possibly leading to lower quality outcomes. Some consultants have recommended such tactics to prevent the loss of pet medication sales and maximize revenues.[293] However, many veterinarians strongly deny that these financial incentives have any impact on what products they recommend or prescribe to their patients.[294] Notably, the AVMA Principles of Veterinary Medical Ethics advise veterinarians not to accept financial incentives from pharmaceutical companies.[295]

D. Analytical Framework for Evaluating Possible Limitations on Prescription Portability and Proposals to Eliminate Such Restrictions

To evaluate the competitive impact of possible limitations on prescription portability imposed by veterinarians on consumers, as well as proposals for reform that would promote greater prescription portability, FTC staff recommends that policymakers consider several factors, including:

- The existence and extent of any current limitations on prescription portability;
- The degree to which any such limitations impede competition and have adverse consequences for consumers;
- Whether purported health and safety concerns cited in support of any such limitations (e.g., perceived risks of harm to animals) are genuine and supported by evidence, or are instead pretextual or speculative;
- Whether any limitations on prescription portability being imposed by market participants are narrowly tailored to eliminate genuine risks of harm, or are instead greater than necessary to do so; and
- The potential costs and benefits of any remedial measure that would mandate greater prescription portability.

FTC staff generally believes that the competitive process should determine output and pricing, including for pet medications and veterinary services. FTC staff notes its preference for a market-based approach, driven primarily by the interaction of suppliers and well-informed consumers. Essentially, staff adopts a presumption in favor of competition – here, the unimpeded availability of portable pet medication prescriptions – absent a plausible rationale for how consumer interests would be better served by any limitations on the competitive process.

From the workshop record and related staff research, it appears that consumers have increasingly been able to secure prescriptions and purchase their pet medications through non-veterinary retail channels, but only to a degree. Substantial concerns were expressed that, for a variety of reasons already discussed, many consumers either may be unaware of their ability to secure a portable prescription or are otherwise inhibited from doing so. Both perspectives support the proposition that prescription portability for pet medications has the potential to yield significant procompetitive benefits for consumers, including lower prices, improved service, and greater convenience.

Based on the record of the workshop and additional information regarding the pet medications industry, observations from other industries, as well as the relevant economic literature, FTC staff believes that currently there are constraints on prescription portability and that these constraints likely are limiting competition between veterinarians and retailers in the sale of pet medications, which may result in harm to consumers. While the workshop and comments identified some possible rationales for limiting access to prescription portability, these rationales were not supported by evidence sufficient to rebut the basic presumption in favor of competition, and at least some of the limitations appear to be greater than necessary to address the concerns expressed. Staff notes that the health and safety concerns being expressed by some veterinarians to support limitations on prescription portability are likely being exaggerated or are pretextual, at least in part. Moreover, there may already be sufficient regulatory measures to address any legitimate safety concerns.[296] Although the precise degree of access to portable prescriptions, as well as the magnitude of any harm from restricted access, are unknown, FTC staff concludes that competition in the pet medications market likely would be enhanced by, and consumers of pet medications likely would benefit from, greater prescription portability.

However, the workshop record and publicly available data do not enable staff to quantify the economic impact of automatic prescription release proposals on veterinarians or consumers, including administrative burdens, the benefits of increased competition, and potential increases in service fees to compensate for any reductions in prescription revenues.

IV. Distribution Practices in the Pet Medications Industry

The FTC workshop also examined various distribution practices that may have an impact on competition in the pet medications industry. These practices include manufacturer exclusive distribution policies that require their products to be sold only through veterinary practices and exclusive dealing agreements between manufacturers and distributors that prevent distributors from carrying competing products from other manufacturers.

A. Exclusive Distribution and the Secondary Market

1. Manufacturer Justifications for Exclusive Distribution Practices

Most of the major manufacturers of pet medications in the United States have adopted formal policies to distribute their products exclusively through veterinarians.[297] These policies generally apply to both prescription and non-prescription pet medications. Manufacturers claim that exclusive distribution policies promote a number of business objectives, such as ensuring product quality, reducing dispensing errors, protecting the VCPR, realizing distribution efficiencies, and increasing incentives for product promotion and innovation. However, the primary justification cited by manufacturers for exclusive distribution policies is ensuring the safe use of their products,[298] which presumably would reduce their products liability exposure.

The Animal Health Institute ("AHI"), a trade association representing the interests of animal health product manufacturers, points out that "many manufacturers have invested tremendous resources to educate veterinarians about their products" so that they are better equipped to counsel clients on the proper use of these products. Furthermore, the AHI states that veterinarians are the "primary monitors of patient use of medication including evaluation for interactions in adverse events" and that this "should not be discounted, as many in our industry believe that the safety and efficacy profiles for certain animal health products are positively impacted by the comprehensive role of the veterinarian."[299]

Manufacturers also cite safety concerns about retail pharmacists as the basis for their exclusive distribution practices. Pfizer Animal Health (now known as Zoetis), another major manufacturer of pet medications, stated that dispensing pet medications through retail pharmacists "creates inherent risks because, unlike veterinarians, such pharmacy staff have no formal training on the nuances of animal drug interactions or the potential challenges associated with administration."[300] Pfizer believes "this could raise potential consumer protection issues and potentially compromise animal health."[301]

Manufacturers, like some veterinarians, assert that dispensing medications is a critical component of the VCPR. They argue that veterinarians should be primarily responsible not just for the examination, diagnosis, and treatment regimen of companion animals, which would include prescribing medications that are medically appropriate, but also for the dispensing of medications – both prescription and OTC. Thus, they seek to protect the VCPR through distribution practices intended to restrict dispensing to veterinarians.[302]

Finally, many manufacturers argue that exclusive distribution makes the most sense from an operations standpoint, as well as for furthering the research and development of new products. Historically, manufacturers relied upon veterinarians to promote and dispense their animal products. Many of them argue that this is still the most efficient method for distributing pet medications, especially when launching new products, as this is a cost-effective way to market products to consumers and to ensure that the medications will be used properly. They claim that extending distribution to other retail channels would require additional sales and marketing costs that could result in higher prices for these products or reduced product innovation.[303] Indeed, some suggest that exclusive distribution spurs product innovation.[304]

Some non-veterinary retailers suggested that there may be an element of horizontal coordination with respect to these exclusive distribution practices,[305] analogous to what occurred in the contact lens industry in the mid-1990s. As previously noted, both veterinarians and eye care professionals are allowed to prescribe and dispense products. During the contact lens antitrust litigation, attorneys general from 32 states alleged horizontal collusion between eye care professionals and contact lens manufacturers. They established that eye care professionals and their trade associations collectively coerced contact lens manufacturers to adopt exclusive distribution policies by threatening to boycott manufacturers who distributed their lenses to alternative retail sellers such as online companies, pharmacies, and big-box retailers.[306] Some retail stakeholders in the pet medications industry allege that veterinarians and drug manufacturers may have a similar relationship.[307] Veterinarians appear willing to express their displeasure with manufacturers who do not honor exclusive distribution policies.[308] But beyond such general accusations, FTC staff is not aware of any specific evidence to support a claim of industry-wide collusion between veterinarians and drug manufacturers.

Absent horizontal collusion between manufacturers and veterinarians, economic theory predicts that manufacturers would only continue to have exclusive distribution policies if they are efficient and profit-maximizing. There could be legitimate, efficiency-enhancing justifications for each firm's independent adoption of these practices, which would explain why they are still common across the industry.[309] If a manufacturer could increase profits by selling through non-veterinarian retail channels, then it would be in the manufacturer's interest to choose this method of distribution. Still, the potential for exclusive distribution practices to result in consumer harm may be greater if the practices are widespread across the industry because the manufacturers are engaging in coordinated behavior.

Notwithstanding the benefits of exclusive distribution asserted by most of the major manufacturers, not all manufacturers have chosen exclusive distribution policies.[310] At least one major manufacturer recently abandoned its exclusive distribution policy in favor of selling through both the veterinary and retail channels. Until recently, Bayer Animal Health had an exclusive distribution policy similar to all the other major manufacturers of pet medications. Then, in March 2010, Bayer became the first major drug manufacturer to begin selling pet medications directly to non-veterinary retailers in an effort to address the unauthorized sale (also sometimes called "diversion") of its products outside of the veterinary channel.[311] Bayer also pointed to ways in which the market for pet medications is changing, with pet owners increasingly shifting their purchases to the retail channel, as justification for its decision.[312] Bayer now sells its OTC products to pet specialty retail stores and all of its animal health products, including prescription medications, to licensed online veterinary pharmacies.[313] Although some industry observers expected other manufacturers to follow suit and abandon their exclusive distribution policies, for the time being, all of the other major manufacturers continue to market their products exclusively through the veterinary channel.[314]

2. Non-Veterinary Retailer Concerns about Exclusive Distribution

Some industry stakeholders have sought to criticize exclusive distribution practices for pet medication by suggesting that they are primarily intended to create and maintain favorable relationships with veterinarians by protecting veterinary practices from potential sources of retail competition in the sale of pet medications. However, economic theory offers some commonly accepted justifications for exclusive distribution practices, i.e., that exclusivity provides dealers with the incentive to learn about and promote the manufacturer's products. Although exclusive distribution practices may reduce or eliminate "intrabrand" competition between firms that would normally sell the same brands of drugs, they are often thought to enhance "interbrand" competition between brands precisely because of this added incentive to promote.[315] In the pet medications industry, some non-veterinary retailers nevertheless argue that these practices are simply mechanisms used by manufacturers to increase price, and not mechanisms to induce dealer support and increase interbrand competition.[316] Furthermore, it would seem that veterinarians should already have an economic and ethical incentive to learn about and promote pet medications that are effective in treating their animal patients, regardless of whether they receive the additional incentive of exclusivity.[317]

Economic theory suggests that procompetitive benefits may accrue from exclusive distribution practices. Given the prescribing authority of veterinarians, it is critical for manufacturers to persuade veterinarians to recommend and prescribe their products.[318] Certainly, educating veterinarians about the efficacy of their products is a principal way to persuade them to prescribe certain products. But manufacturers may also strategize that, by promising exclusive sales opportunities, they can more effectively incentivize veterinarians to become knowledgeable about their products and recommend and prescribe them,[319] thereby enhancing "interbrand" competition between veterinarians that sell different brands of drugs within the same therapeutic class. Furthermore, some manufacturers offer additional sales incentives to veterinarians and their staff for recommending and prescribing their products.[320] While these incentives may enhance interbrand competition among different drugs within the same therapeutic class, some observers have questioned the ethics of manufacturers offering such incentives to veterinarians, and have suggested it exacerbates a conflict of interest that exists when veterinarians have the exclusive power to both prescribe and dispense pet medications.[321]

Some stakeholders particularly question whether there is any procompetitive basis for restricting the distribution of OTC animal products, which require neither a visit to the veterinarian nor a prescription, although a veterinarian may recommend such products. FDA-approved nonprescription animal drug products are considered safe and effective for their intended use, including administration by pet owners, if administered as directed on the label.[322] Thus, some stakeholders argue that the justifications asserted by manufacturers for restricting the distribution of prescription pet medications do not apply, or at least do not apply to the same degree, for OTC pet medications.[323]

Pharmacy stakeholders similarly question the manufacturers' safety-related justifications for exclusive distribution and contend that qualified pharmacies should not be subject to restricted distribution policies, and should be allowed to purchase pet medications directly from the manufacturers or their authorized distributors.[324] If a retail pharmacy can demonstrate that it is fully licensed and operating legally, they argue, then there should not be significant concern about whether the pharmacy can safely dispense pet medications.[325] Moreover, if a retail pharmacy can demonstrate specific expertise in veterinary pharmacology, stakeholders question why directly distributing pet medications to this type of pharmacy would generate any greater safety risk than distributing these products through the traditional veterinary channel. Some pharmacy stakeholders claim that the safety concerns cited by manufacturers (which are similar to the concerns cited by veterinarians) are frequently exaggerated and, in many instances, unfounded.[326] Some also believe that manufacturers provide false or misleading information to consumers to dissuade them from purchasing pet medications through non-veterinary retail channels.[327]

Furthermore, as previously discussed, a regulatory mechanism already exists to address the concern that pharmacists may dispense medications in a manner other than prescribed by veterinarians,[328] which may further weaken manufacturers' purported safety justifications. Also previously discussed, pharmacy stakeholders argue that non-exclusive distribution would not threaten the VCPR,[329] and therefore manufacturers should not rely on this justification for restricting distribution to veterinarians only. In particular, pharmacy stakeholders have urged drug manufacturers to consider Vet-VIPPS certification when making decisions about the distribution of prescription pet products to online veterinary pharmacies, as this would appear to mitigate any actual or perceived safety risks associated with these pharmacies.[330]

Some non-veterinary retailers have also noted the apparent contradiction that arises when the same exclusive distribution practices do not always apply to central fill pharmacies. Central fill pharmacies provide veterinary practices with a turn-key online pharmacy solution, in which veterinarians can direct their clients to a proprietary website where the client can fill a prescription online or purchase OTC products, and have these products shipped to them at home.[331] The veterinarian selects the products it wants to offer clients and sets the prices for the products, and then pays the central fill pharmacy a service fee for maintaining the website, inventory, payment processing, and shipping operations. Central fill pharmacies claim to "operate as an extension of the veterinarian's pharmacy and to fit within the context of the current veterinary pharmaceutical network."[332] Non-veterinary retailers argue, however, that it is inconsistent for drug manufacturers to sell directly to central fill pharmacies, yet claim that their policy of selling exclusively through veterinarians is based on safety concerns. It appears that pharmacists trained in veterinary pharmacology, not veterinarians, typically dispense pet medications for central fill pharmacies. Indeed, some central fill pharmacies do not appear to have veterinarians on staff.[333] Non-veterinary retailers suggest that some manufacturers sell directly to central fill pharmacies, but not to other types of pharmacies, because veterinarians benefit from these arrangements and the central fill pharmacy's financial interests are aligned with their interests.[334] Of course, to the extent that this central fill system gives veterinarians a greater degree of control or ability to supervise the dispensing and use of the drugs than if the client went to an independent retail pharmacy, then the apparent contradiction may not be as significant.

3. The Secondary Market for Pet Medications

A secondary distribution system for pet medications has emerged over time, in which sales occur outside of the traditional veterinary-exclusive distribution model. This secondary market enables non-veterinary retailers to purchase pet medications despite stated manufacturer restrictions intended to limit distribution to veterinarians. It appears to have developed as a response to long- standing manufacturer policies of exclusive distribution, growing consumer demand for alternatives to purchasing pet medications from veterinarians, and the development of new methods for distribution, such as online retailing.[335] Retail pharmacies that wish to sell pet medications to their customers have stated that they often face difficulty purchasing products directly from manufacturers, and must instead turn to secondary distribution sources.[336] By some estimates, one-quarter of the sales of pet medications were attributable to secondary distribution in 2009, which may have amounted to hundreds of millions of dollars or more.[337] It appears that a significant volume of pet medications, particularly OTC flea and tick medications, continues to be diverted to non-veterinary retailers.[338]

The secondary distribution system functions in a number of observed ways.[339] Typically, wholesale distributors that are not specifically authorized by manufacturers to distribute their products (i.e., "unauthorized distributors") solicit veterinarians to purchase excess pet medications from manufacturers or authorized distributors, and then sell them a portion of their inventory.[340] These unauthorized distributors, in turn, aggregate these product supplies and re- sell them to non-veterinary retailers for ultimate sale to consumers.[341] This practice is often referred to as "diversion."[342] It remains unclear how many veterinarians are involved in the diversion of pet medications, but it is thought to be substantial. Generally, the veterinary community regards product diversion as unethical,[343] and many manufacturers with stated exclusive distribution policies publicly criticize the practice. Perhaps as a result, some wholesale distributors and the retail pharmacies that purchase inventory from them appear to take steps to protect the identities of veterinarians who sell products into the secondary market.[344]

Manufacturer efforts to address veterinary diversion appear varied. Some observers believe that manufacturers may be complicit in supporting the secondary distribution system, despite public claims to the contrary. They allege that manufacturers and distributors are, to a large extent, involved in the diversion of pet medications, and that manufacturer sales representatives are often encouraged to divert product in order to meet their sales quotas.[345] To the extent that this is true, it may indicate that the benefits of exclusive distribution have been overstated, and that some industry participants are moving away from exclusive distribution through veterinarians towards more multi-channel distribution strategies. At least one manufacturer states that it has generally given up trying to stop diversion, but continues to try to prevent counterfeit products from reaching the market.[346] Other manufacturers state that they implement measures to try to stop veterinary diversion, although such measures may not be totally effective.[347] It appears that many veterinarians are skeptical of claims by manufacturers that they do not support product diversion.[348]

It has been reported that pet medication manufacturers may refuse to guarantee their products if they are not purchased from a veterinarian.[349] Indeed, veterinarians sometimes tout this as a reason that consumers should purchase products only from them.[350] However, it appears that manufacturer policies about whether to guarantee products purchased from non-veterinary retailers vary, and that some manufacturers actually do guarantee their products, regardless of where they are purchased.[351]

Veterinary diversion (i.e., veterinarians who sell pet medications to wholesale distributors or non-veterinary retailers) may arguably be inconsistent with some state laws and policies relating to the distribution of pet medications.[352] At the FTC workshop, some industry stakeholders argued that veterinary diversion of prescription pet medications is almost always illegal.[353] Conversely, some industry stakeholders argue that veterinary diversion of prescription and OTC pet medications may be legal in some states, particularly where veterinarians are allowed to obtain wholesale distributor licenses, or that legality is uncertain.[354] Even where these practices appear to violate state laws, the workshop and additional research produced scant evidence of significant enforcement efforts by the states,[355] despite claims within the veterinary community that veterinary diversion of pet medications is widespread. For those veterinarians who engage in diversion, therefore, the profitability of diversion apparently outweighs any concerns about prosecution or sanctions. This may be particularly true for the diversion of OTC products, which appear to account for a large portion of the secondary market and for which the risk of prosecution may be lower than for the diversion of prescription products. For purposes of this report, FTC staff does not take a position as to whether veterinary diversion of pet medications is legal. Instead, FTC staff recognizes the fact that a secondary market for pet medications exists and analyzes the relevant competitive implications.

4. Competitive Impact of Secondary Distribution

Secondary distribution systems are often viewed as procompetitive, and responsive to consumer demand.[356] In the pet medications industry, the secondary distribution system facilitates increased competition between veterinarians and other retailers, resulting in additional purchasing options and potentially lower prices for consumers, particularly for OTC flea and tick products. However, several industry stakeholders argue that there are significant inefficiencies associated with this secondary distribution system that result in less access and higher prices for consumers when compared to a system in which non-veterinary retailers could procure an inventory of pet medications through primary distribution.[357] As discussed in more detail below, these claimed inefficiencies include a longer distribution chain, unstable supply, and greater inventory requirements.

Workshop participants explained how in a direct distribution system, pet medications typically pass from the manufacturer to an authorized distributor to the veterinarian before being sold to the consumer. In a secondary distribution system, pet medications may pass through two additional entities before reaching the consumer, including an unauthorized wholesale distributor (sometimes called an "aggregator") and a non-veterinary retail outlet.[358] Thus, the secondary distribution system typically involves additional price mark-ups that would be taken at both the wholesale distributor and the non-veterinary retailer levels. These additional steps and mark-ups may result in higher costs to retailers, and ultimately higher prices to consumers.[359]

Although it has been noted that many non-veterinary retailers currently offer lower prices for certain pet medications than some veterinary clinics, some of these retailers have claimed that they could offer prices that are even lower if they could procure products through a more direct and efficient system that did not involve these additional steps.[360] For example, some non-veterinary retailers expected to pay lower prices for Bayer's products once they became available for direct distribution.[361] This assumes, of course, that the manufacturers would not change wholesale prices in the event of a change in distribution strategy. Also, if exclusive distribution motivates veterinarians to sell the manufacturers' products, eliminating the exclusivity could cause the quantity sold to decrease, notwithstanding any price reduction. In other words, price reductions may not increase consumer welfare if veterinarians would be less inclined to promote and prescribe newly developed pet medications that have benefits for consumers and their pets.

Non-veterinary retailers complain that another problem with secondary distribution is unstable product supply. There may be times when retailers are unable to procure certain products, which limits their ability to fill prescriptions for consumers.[362] Compounding pharmacies are particularly concerned about their ability to procure reliable product supplies.[363] Due to this instability, non-veterinary retailers may be compelled in some instances to purchase large quantities of product in advance whenever it becomes available. This may require significant up- front capital and inventory space, which may also add extra costs. Some of these costs may be passed on to consumers.[364] Several retail stakeholders allege that all of these inefficiencies result in higher prices for consumers, and may restrict the consumer's ability to access pet medications from non-veterinary retail outlets. Retail pharmacies have stated that consumers may face longer wait times when purchasing pet medications from a retail pharmacy that must rely on secondary distribution, which may not always make products available on a reliable and predictable basis, thereby impeding consumer access to these products.[365] One retailer suggests that inconsistent supply may deter some retail pharmacies from entering the market, thereby depriving consumers of the benefits of this additional competition.[366]

Some workshop participants expressed the opinion that the market for pet medications is very dynamic and as it continues to evolve, many of these inefficiencies are being resolved. For example, some manufacturers have embraced the retail channel voluntarily.[367] Other participants disagreed, stating that they are still subject to arbitrary supply decisions made by manufacturers.[368] These non-veterinary retailers claim that they are left with many prescriptions on file that cannot be filled as a result of these manufacturer decisions.[369] Although manufacturers did not directly comment on this situation as part of the FTC's record, as is discussed in the next section of the report, it is possible that they would have legitimate justifications for these refusals to supply, such as maintaining the integrity of a distribution system that is optimal for their business operations.

5. Product Pedigree and Safety Issues Associated with Secondary Distribution

Many concerns have been raised about the quality and integrity of pet medications distributed through secondary distribution and dispensed by retail pharmacists. Several stakeholders contend that secondary distribution for pet medications creates substantial risk of adulterated or counterfeit compounds being introduced into the supply chain.[370] Furthermore, they contend that without proper regulatory oversight, products are less likely to be stored and shipped according to manufacturer recommendations.[371] Concern also has been expressed about the lack of transparency in the chain of custody (sometimes referred to as the product's "pedigree") for pet medications that are procured through secondary distribution. Without a traceable product pedigree, it becomes more difficult for pharmacists and consumers alike to verify the authenticity (and thereby the safety and efficacy) of pet medications.[372] Under these conditions, when a treatment failure occurs, it is challenging to determine whether it is the result of an adverse reaction to a legitimate product or whether the product did not perform properly because it was adulterated or counterfeit.[373] For these reasons, pharmacists and retailers state that they would prefer to purchase pet medications directly from a manufacturer or through an authorized distributor.[374]

The NABP has described the "normal" distribution chain that exists for human prescription medications, in which drugs move directly from the manufacturer to the wholesale distributor to the pharmacy or practitioner. In a closed distribution system such as this, the NABP has a high level of confidence in the integrity of the products sold by retail pharmacies because the distribution pedigree can be established definitively. At the FTC workshop, a representative of the NABP explained that this type of system has not been developed for animal drug distribution through retail pharmacies.[375] The NABP would prefer a "normal" distribution chain for prescription pet medications sold by retail pharmacies as opposed to a secondary distribution system in which it can be difficult to determine a product's distribution pedigree and be assured of the product's quality and integrity.[376]

However, it should be noted that products sold through secondary distribution are not necessarily unsafe. Most Vet-VIPPS accredited pharmacies obtain their products from secondary wholesale distributors, and they are required to demonstrate that these products are authentic and originated with the manufacturer.[377] Furthermore, several retail pharmacies stated that they have adopted measures to ensure that these products have been handled and stored appropriately while in the distribution chain.[378] Other observers state that problems with product safety are not limited to non-veterinary retailers who rely on secondary distribution, and can occur at veterinary clinics and retailers alike.[379]

Several non-veterinary retailers who must purchase products through secondary distribution expressed the belief that implementation of the same type of distribution system that exists for human medications, whereby all retailers purchase pet medications directly from manufacturers or authorized distributors, would help to eliminate existing inefficiencies associated with the secondary market. They argued this would ensure the safety, authenticity, and efficacy of products sold by non-veterinary retailers. Indeed, retail pharmacists already purchase human medications from most of the same manufacturers that market pet medications. Direct sales to non-veterinary retailers, they maintained, would also address many of the concerns expressed by veterinarians surrounding secondary distribution.[380] For instance, veterinarians expect assurances that the products their clients purchase from non-veterinary retailers have a known pedigree and have been handled properly.[381] Having a distribution system in which legitimate retailers could purchase pet medications directly from the manufacturer or an authorized distributor would seem to provide this assurance.

Non-veterinary retailers also asserted that having direct relationships with pet medication manufacturers would allow them to access valuable product information and technical support. Typically, manufacturers provide training and educational materials to veterinarians and authorized distributors regarding the proper use and handling of their products.[382] Under the current system of exclusive distribution, however, retail pharmacists typically do not receive this training and information from manufacturers and it is unclear whether secondary distributors provide it. To the extent that manufacturers could offer product guidance and education to non-veterinary retailers if they had direct relationships with them, many safety concerns associated with secondary distribution could be further alleviated.[383] Certainly, this is an advantage that Bayer has touted since establishing direct relationships with non-veterinary retailers.[384]

Some manufacturers respond to these arguments by reiterating the benefits of exclusive distribution and their preference for maintaining their relationships with veterinarians as the best way to promote their products and ensure their safe and effective use. They suggest that it could be cost prohibitive for them to provide all retailers with product training and support similar to what they provide veterinarians, and could ultimately increase the prices of certain products for consumers.[385] Ultimately, if it were in the manufacturers' interest to abandon their exclusive distribution policies, economic theory suggests they would consider doing so. At some point, the potential for increased sales opportunities in the non-veterinary retail channel, combined with increasing consumer demand for purchasing pet medications from these retailers, may ultimately provide manufacturers with sufficient incentive to change their policies.[386]

B. Distribution Practices and Other Factors Affecting the Development of Generic Animal Drugs

1. Limited Consumer Access to Generic Animal Drugs

In the human drug industry, generic drugs have proven to be a source of significant price competition, saving consumers, businesses, and taxpayers billions of dollars every year on drug costs.[387] Similarly, generic animal drug stakeholders argue that their products could provide cost- effective alternatives to name brand pioneer animal drugs and carry the potential for significant savings to consumers.[388] Yet, there are very few generic pet medications currently available,[389] despite an established FDA pathway for approving generic animal drugs.[390] As a result, the kinds of savings realized on the human drug side have not occurred for pet medications. Industry analysts cite several factors that may be limiting the development or success of generic animal medications.

Generic animal drugs have not had the same penetration levels as human generic drugs because there has only been a recent focus on developing companion animal specific medications and there are no "intervening insurance and employer programs mandating the selection of generic alternatives when available."[391] But some industry analysts believe that generic animal drugs have strong market potential, given that many of the patents on branded animal drugs have expired and FDA review of a generic animal drug often takes less than five years.[392]

In a recent survey, veterinarians who are willing to purchase, prescribe and dispense generic drugs indicated that they do so to ensure that pets get the needed course of medications and because of concern for pet owners' ability to afford high-priced branded drugs.[393] Other potential benefits to veterinarians of offering generic animal drugs to their clients may include "higher markups and increased margins, increased prescribing options, and improved compliance since generic drugs cost pet owners less."[394] However, industry analysts contend that prescribing generic animal drugs could actually lower veterinarians' profits or lead to a further shift to the non-veterinary retail channel.[395] Thus, some veterinarians may be reluctant to prescribe generic animal drugs to their clients. If a significant number of veterinarians view generics as less profitable, manufacturers may perceive lower potential demand, which could discourage further development of generic products.

Absent significant demand for generic products in the veterinary channel, generic manufacturers appear skeptical of their chances for attaining a sizeable share of animal drug sales. Although generic manufacturers could try to rely on alternative retail outlets, such as online and brick-and- mortar retail pharmacies, the sales opportunities available through these retailers is lower than through veterinarians, particularly for prescription drugs.[396] Furthermore, there are approximately 25,000 veterinary clinics that treat companion animals in the United States,[397] and these practices are diverse in terms of geography and size.[398] From some manufacturers' perspectives, the only effective way to penetrate the fragmented veterinarian channel is to rely on distributors who have established sales forces that service a large number of veterinary practices. This is especially true when launching new products.[399]

Small generic animal drug manufacturers, in particular, claim that they cannot afford to distribute products themselves or support national sales and marketing forces, and therefore access to distributors is critical to their success. However, nearly all of the large pioneer drug companies utilize distributors and these drug companies represent a significant portion of the distributors' business. Stakeholders claim this gives the pioneer drug companies substantial influence over distributors that can be used to restrict generic manufacturers' access to distributors.[400] As a result, the ability of veterinarians and consumers to purchase generic animal drugs may be limited,[401] which in turn may reduce the incentives for generic animal drug manufacturers to develop them.

2. Exclusive Dealing Agreements May Have an Effect on Generic Entry

Some generic manufacturers claim that at least some pioneer drug manufacturers are impeding competition from generic entrants by entering into exclusive dealing agreements with distributors that prohibit them from also distributing generic drugs that might be substituted for their own branded products. The evidence at the FTC workshop on the existence and effect of such agreements, however, was contradictory.[402] It was suggested by some that exclusive dealing agreements are not common within the pet medications industry. Yet others claimed that they are prevalent at least for the top brands. One explanation for this inconsistency may be that there are two types of exclusive dealing agreements that have been used in the pet medications industry – those preventing distributors from carrying competing pioneer products and those preventing distributors from carrying generic versions of pioneer products.

Several stakeholders agreed that the first type of exclusive dealing agreement, in which, as a condition for carrying a manufacturer's branded products, distributors agree not to carry competing branded products, is no longer common due to the high level of consolidation that has occurred among distributors.[403] It may be the case that there are currently so few distributors, that the exclusive agreements prohibiting distributors from carrying competing pioneer products no longer make economic sense for a variety of reasons. The second type of exclusive dealing agreement, in which pioneer manufacturers prohibit distributors from carrying generic versions of their products, may exist, but it is not clear how common the practice may be. Representatives of generic drug manufacturers point to examples of these agreements and describe how they create barriers to generic entry in the animal drug market.[404] Alternatively, they argue, the pioneer manufacturers may "limit the fees and/or margins earned by the distributor if the distributor offers generics. These restrictive agreements are unique to animal health distribution channels [as compared to human health distribution channels]."[405] In response, a distributor representative argued that these types of exclusivity agreements are not common, and do not raise any competitive concerns.[406]

If such agreements are in effect, they may not only impact generic manufacturers' ability to enter the animal drug industry, but also the ability of larger pioneer manufacturers who decide to launch generic versions of animal drugs. For example, Novartis launched a generic version of a blockbuster product, that it claimed provided superior efficacy at a lower price and was well received by the veterinarians that tried it. Novartis claimed that it was unable to capture more than two percent of the market, however, because distributors refused to carry the product. Novartis presumed that this was due to exclusive dealing agreements that distributors had with the pioneer manufacturer of the blockbuster product, but could not confirm this. To the extent that exclusive dealing agreements protect manufacturers from generic competition, Novartis expressed the belief that they are anticompetitive.[407]

3. Restricted Distribution Practices May Have an Effect on Consumer Access to and Innovation for Generic Animal Drugs

Some generic manufacturers claim to have discontinued research and development programs for generic pet medications because they did not believe they could achieve sufficient market penetration to justify the investment. They state that this was due to the combined effect of manufacturers' exclusive dealing with distributors and exclusive distribution practices with veterinarians:

> Knowing that pioneer drug companies can control a major share of the market via distribution deters developing generic drugs. Developing a generic drug and taking it through the FDA approval process requires significant investment that can cost millions of dollars and take many years. Generic companies are typically much smaller than pioneer companies and have fewer resources and therefore, every product has a significant impact on the bottom line. Furthermore, business owners and investors are reluctant to fund development of generic drugs if they are unable to get their products to the majority of the market.
>
> When generic drug manufacturers are blocked from ensuring that their products reach significant numbers of customers and that their development costs are recouped, they are likely to determine the costs of development outweigh the potential return on investment. The company may choose not to pursue the generic drug, and perpetuate the limitations on the number of generic drug options available to veterinarians and pet owners.[408]

These stakeholders argue that pioneer drug manufacturers use restrictive distribution practices to deter competition from generic animal drug manufacturers. "By cutting the pharmacy out of the supply chain, pioneer animal drug manufacturers have largely denied generic companies the ability to provide their more affordable products to consumers and thereby maintained their higher prices."[409] Likewise, they claim that by offering veterinarians the exclusive sales opportunity for branded pet medications, and thereby ensuring a higher profit margin for the veterinarians, the drug manufacturers reduce the threat of generic competition because veterinarians will support the branded products and will be less likely to prescribe generic products.[410] They note that in the distribution model created by the pioneer manufacturers, there is no incentive for any player (manufacturer, distributor, or veterinarian) to inform consumers that substitutable equivalent generic animal drugs may be available at their local retail pharmacies for lower prices. In addition, there is no third party payer pressure to substitute generic products in an effort to reduce prices. "As a result, one does not see the same degree of competition and savings for generic animal drugs as we see for generic human drugs."[411]

Generic drug stakeholders also claim that the absence of generic competition may reduce the incentives of pioneer manufacturers to develop innovative new pet medications. They explain how branded companies are incentivized to develop new and improved human drugs when they know they will face generic competition after their patents expire. They argue that in the animal drug industry, however, "the absence of generic competition allows pioneer companies to continue to raise prices on and market drugs whose patents have expired, decreasing their incentive to innovate."[412] These statements may be inconsistent, however, with evidence of increased product innovation and growth in the pet medications industry.[413]

4. Prescription Portability May Have an Effect on Consumer Access to Generic Animal Drugs

Some have argued that automatic prescription release would increase consumer demand for affordable pet medications, and that this market pressure would result in increased demand for and hence the supply of generic animal drugs. As described above, consumers may not be aware of their option to receive a portable prescription. If they were more aware of that option, and hence more inclined to seek cost savings by shopping for pet medications, demand for low cost generic drugs might also increase.[414] Generic drug stakeholders argue that without this market pressure and the resulting consumer demand for generic pet medications as manifested in portable prescriptions, it is unlikely that retail pharmacies will stock these products.[415] Furthermore, they state that:

> Veterinarians and pioneer drug companies have set up a distribution and dispensing system that prevents competition and restricts consumer choice. Without a federal law requiring prescription portability and disclosure of the consumers' options, pet owners are unlikely to ever enjoy the cost savings that FDA-approved generic animal drugs provide.[416]

5. Automatic Substitution Might Increase Consumer Access to Generic Animal Drugs

One workshop participant identified an important difference between the human and animal drug industries that may have contributed to the slow adoption of lower-priced generic animal drugs – the lack of automatic generic substitution for pet medications.[417] In the human medications industry, all 50 states permit pharmacists to automatically substitute generic versions of branded drugs, if they are available, resulting in significant cost savings to consumers. At the time of the workshop, these types of regulatory schemes did not exist in many states with respect to animal medications. To the extent that this is still an issue, there appear to be some regulatory and legislative measures that, if implemented, could facilitate automatic substitution for generic animal drugs. The FTC has taken the position that laws facilitating human generic drug substitution benefit consumers.[418] Although the FTC has not studied this issue with respect to animal generic drug substitution, some of the same underlying principles may apply.

The FDA lists all approved human drugs in a publication commonly referred to as the "Orange Book," and all approved animal drugs in a publication known as the "Green Book."[419] One generic animal drug representative claimed that there are some discrepancies between the Orange Book and the Green Book that, if resolved, may help facilitate automatic substitution for generic animal drugs. For example, the Orange Book contains therapeutic equivalence codes used by pharmacists to determine which human generic and human pioneer drugs are interchangeable, and some states have adopted these codes as the sole standard for determining when a pharmacist may substitute any generic drug for any pioneer drug. Because approved animal drugs are not listed in the Orange Book, pharmacists in these states may be prohibited from dispensing generic animal drugs when a pioneer animal drug is prescribed.[420] This generic animal drug representative argued that providing therapeutic equivalence codes in the Green Book and allowing this to serve as the standard for automatic substitution of generic animal drugs could improve consumer access to generic pet medications.[421] Currently, the FDA does not include therapeutic equivalence codes in the Green Book.[422]

Generic manufacturers may also need to address the dissemination of potentially misleading information regarding the effectiveness of generic animal drugs. One workshop participant claimed that veterinarians disparage the quality of generic animal drugs, the FDA approval process, and whether these products really are equivalent to their pioneer counterparts. He noted that these are the same issues the generic drug industry faced with medical physicians 15 to 20 years ago, and that it will require an educational effort that may take some time.[423] Several comments received from veterinarians suggest that they may question the effectiveness of generic pet medications.[424]

V. CONCLUDING REMARKS AND TOPICS THAT MIGHT BENEFIT FROM ADDITIONAL STUDY

A. Summary of Conclusions Regarding Prescription Portability, Industry Distribution Practices, and Generic Animal Drug Development

FTC staff believes that improved consumer access to portable prescriptions would likely enhance competition in the pet medications industry. Many consumers are already aware of their ability to receive portable prescriptions from their veterinarians and many veterinarians already provide portable prescriptions. It appears that there are still many consumers, however, who are either unaware of their ability to obtain portable prescriptions from their veterinarians or are inhibited from requesting them. Likewise, it appears that some veterinarians refuse to provide portable prescriptions to their clients or engage in behaviors intended to discourage clients from requesting portable prescriptions and filling them elsewhere. Legislative and regulatory efforts to mandate aspects of prescription release have the potential to enhance consumer awareness about the ability to purchase pet medications from non-veterinary retail outlets and improve consumer access to portable prescriptions, but FTC staff does not have sufficient data to evaluate the overall economic effect of any specific proposal. FTC staff will continue to monitor legislative and regulatory developments, and evaluate the need for and effects of greater prescription portability in the pet medications industry.

Many stakeholders argue that exclusive distribution and exclusive dealing practices by pet medication manufacturers are prevalent in the pet medications industry to the detriment of pet medications consumers. Although these types of practices can sometimes have adverse effects, they may also benefit consumers, and pet medications manufacturers claim to have legitimate business reasons for engaging in these practices. The increasing availability of pet medications at alternative retail outlets indicates that the market may be in a period of transition and that market forces may already be addressing some of the competitive concerns raised by certain stakeholders, at least to some degree. Ultimately, these restrictive distribution practices could come under increasing competitive pressure in the marketplace and may be difficult to sustain, particularly if portable prescriptions become more widely available and retail pharmacies continue to compete to fill them. FTC staff is interested to see how this industry continues to develop, in light of consumer demand for safe, low-priced pet medications. Industry stakeholders are encouraged to continue expressing their views regarding exclusive distribution and exclusive dealing practices to FTC staff, so that we can consider their effects on competition for the sale of pet medications.

Finally, increased availability of low-priced generic animal drugs would likely result in significant consumer cost savings. There appear to be multiple factors dampening the incentives of generic manufacturers to develop and market generic pet medications. Legislative and regulatory proposals designed to improve incentives for drug manufacturers to develop and market generic animal drugs could be considered by policymakers, and further study may help to support such proposals. Furthermore, efforts to empower pharmacists with the information and authority necessary to substitute generic animal drugs for pioneer animal drugs also could be considered.

B. Topics That Might Benefit from Additional Study

There remain a number of issues that could benefit from further study that would contribute to a better understanding of the competitive dynamics of the pet medications industry. In particular, we note that at present, there is little systematic empirical research on (1) the pricing of pet medications across different channels of distribution, (2) the rate of errors in pet medication dispensing by retail pharmacists and veterinarians, (3) the need for and impact of automatic prescription release requirements, and (4) details regarding the secondary distribution system for pet medications.

1. Pet Medications Pricing

Currently, there appears to be a lack of empirical evidence on the degree of price variation among the different retail distribution channels (e.g., veterinary practices, online retailers, brick- and-mortar retail stores and pharmacies) in which prescription and OTC pet medications are sold, and whether changes in the competitive environment have had any impact on prices. For example, it is possible that veterinarians have responded to competitive pressure from online and brick-and-mortar retail outlets by reducing their prices, at least for certain categories of products. Any such pricing effects may be different for prescription versus OTC products. FTC staff recognizes that it may be difficult to identify publicly available data to analyze pet medications pricing across distribution channels, but maintains that comprehensive empirical research in this area would be beneficial in further considering the issues addressed in this report.

2. Pet Medications Dispensing Errors

Several industry participants defended limitations on prescription portability on the ground that retail pharmacists who are untrained in veterinary pharmacology are more likely to commit pet medication dispensing errors than veterinarians. As noted earlier, some state veterinary medical associations have begun to track alleged medication errors by retail pharmacists, and the FDA appears to have established a process for tracking alleged pet medication dispensing errors made by retail pharmacists and veterinarians. It remains difficult, however, to identify substantiated instances of pet medication dispensing errors. Continued systematic monitoring of this issue might be useful in understanding the frequency of pet medication dispensing errors by retail pharmacists as compared to veterinarians, and ultimately, whether safety concerns about retail pharmacists' qualifications to dispense pet medications are justified.

3. Automatic Prescription Release Requirements

At present, there does not appear to be comprehensive data regarding consumer awareness of their ability receive a portable prescription from a veterinarian. Neither does there appear to be data of the degree to which this awareness may vary by state according to the regulatory requirements for prescription release. Furthermore, there is only limited data available on the frequency of veterinarians' refusals to provide a written prescription upon request or other efforts to discourage consumers from requesting portable prescriptions. A consumer survey might be able to shed light on these types of questions surrounding the need for a regulatory requirement for automatic release of pet medication prescriptions.

Continued monitoring of state legislative efforts regarding prescription release for pet medications might help to identify natural experiments that would permit empirical analysis of the likely effects of any national policy change, such as the ones proposed by H.R. 4023 and S. 2756. As already noted, several states have adopted policies requiring veterinarians to provide prescriptions to clients upon request, while other states have not. If additional states adopt automatic prescription policies, or other policies that change consumers' ability to obtain a portable prescription, there may be an opportunity to study the effects of such changes on the behavior of consumers and veterinarians.[425] For example, it would be helpful to know whether such policies have any impact on consumer awareness of their ability to comparison shop for pet medications at both veterinary practices and retail pharmacies, and whether such awareness has any impact on consumers' purchasing decisions. Also, it would be helpful to know whether veterinarians alter their prices for pet medications in response to increased competitive pressure resulting from these policy changes, or whether they alter their inventory decisions or prescribing habits in any way. Lastly, such policy changes may also provide an opportunity to examine the effect of greater prescription portability on the medication sales of veterinary practices and the pricing of their services, as well as the pricing of medications available from retail outlets.

4. Secondary Distribution System

Some industry stakeholders have attempted to estimate the size of the secondary distribution system. Nevertheless, it would be useful to have more systematic information on the actual size of the secondary market, in terms of both dollar and unit sales, although FTC staff acknowledges that it may be difficult to collect data that would permit such an analysis. Other details that might be helpful to know, but difficult to ascertain, include the cost structure of the secondary distribution system for pet medications, including any inefficiencies that may result in higher prices to consumers relative to more direct distribution. In addition, it could be valuable to know more about the frequency of adverse events that occur in animals that take pet medications distributed through the normal distribution chain (i.e., purchased from veterinarians) versus the secondary distribution chain (i.e., purchased from non-veterinary retail outlets). This information would allow an analysis of the claimed economic and product safety concerns associated with the secondary distribution of pet medications.

WORKSHOP TEAM AND REPORT CONTRIBUTORS

Andrew I. Gavil, Former Director, Office of Policy Planning*
Tara Isa Koslov, Deputy Director, Office of Policy Planning
Stephanie A. Wilkinson, Office of Policy Planning, Principal Author
Christopher Bryan, Office of Policy Planning
Christopher M. Grengs, Office of Policy Planning
Daniel J. Gilman, Office of Policy Planning
Elizabeth A. Jex, Office of Policy Planning

Joel L. Schrag, Bureau of Economics
Kelly Signs, Bureau of Competition

*At the time of the October 2012 Pet Medications Workshop and subsequent report drafting, Andrew I. Gavil was the Director of the Office of Policy Planning. Mr. Gavil departed from the Federal Trade Commission in December 2014.

APPENDIX A: PUBLIC COMMENTS CITED IN THE REPORT

The Federal Trade Commission received over 700 public comments in response to our request for comments related to the pet medications workshop.[426] To assist readers of this report, below is an alphabetical list of the 77 comments that are cited in the report. All names and affiliations were self-reported.

Comment Name	Full Name of Commenter
AAHA Comment	American Animal Hospital Association (AAHA)
AHI Comment	Animal Health Institute (AHI)
S. Anderson (Ass'n for Veterinary Clinic Success) Comment	Scott Anderson, Association for Veterinary Clinic Success
A. Anderson Comment	Ann Anderson, DVM, Quarry Hill Park Animal Hospital
APAW Coalition Comment	Advocacy for Pets and Affordable Wellness (APAW) Coalition
ASPCA Comment	American Society for the Prevention of Cruelty to Animals (ASPCA)
AVDA Comment	American Veterinary Distributors Association (AVDA)
AVMA Comment	American Veterinary Medical Association (AVMA)
Bach Comment	Gregory Bach, DVM
Baragiola Comment	Baragiola (consumer/pet owner)
Black Comment	Black (consumer/pet owner)
Boylan Comment (#255)[427]	Meredith Boylan (consumer/pet owner)
Boylan Comment (#256)	Meredith Boylan (consumer/pet owner)
Bradley Comment	Karen Bradley, DVM, Onion River Animal Hospital
Brady Comment	Kathy Brady (consumer/pet owner)
Brown Comment (#521)	Brown

(Continued)

Comment Name	Full Name of Commenter
Busansky Comment	Busansky (consumer/pet owner)
Carrier Comment	Lee Carrier (consumer/pet owner)
Chesko Comment	Liz Chesko (consumer/pet owner)
S. Clark Comment	Scott Clark (consumer/pet owner)
Coffin Comment	Steve Coffin, DVM, Interbay Veterinary Care Center
Colligan Comment	Suzanne Colligan (consumer/pet owner)
Ellis Comment	Crystal Ellis (consumer/pet owner)
Fankhauser Comment	Fankhauser
J. Forbes Comment	Julie Forbes, DVM, Brea Veterinary Hospital
Foster (F&S) Comment	Race Foster*, DVM, co-founder, Drs. Foster & Smith (F&S)
GADA Comment	Generic Animal Drug Alliance (GADA)
Gay (VetRxDirect) Comment (#576)	William Gay, VetRxDirect
Gonzalez Comment	Denise Gonzalez (consumer/pet owner)
Greeley Comment	Shannon Greeley, DVM
Hamilton Comment	Gayle Hamilton (consumer/pet owner)
Higgins Comment	Cathi Higgins (consumer/pet owner)
Hilton Comment	Hilton (consumer/pet owner)
Hirsch Comment	Robert Hirsch, Light Research (consumer/pet owner)
Holum Comment	Donald Holum (consumer/pet owner)
Indep. Pharmacy Alliance Comment	Independent Pharmacy Alliance
Int'l Bd. of Veterinary Pharmacy Comment	International Board of Veterinary Pharmacy
K&L Gates Comment	K&L Gates LLP (law firm), on behalf of "an affected client"
Kaplan Comment	Jonna Kaplan (consumer/pet owner)
Kordell Comment (#298)	J. Kordell
Kroger Comment	The Kroger Company
Lee Comment	Nathan Lee, University of Tennessee College of Veterinary Medicine (UTCVM)
Loehrer Comment	Marcella Loehrer (consumer/pet owner)
Maddigan Comment	John Maddigan, co-owner, Willamette Valley Animal Hospital
Magee (F&S) Comment	Gordon Magee, Drs. Foster & Smith (F&S)
Maine VMA Comment (#281)	Maine Veterinary Medical Association

Comment Name	Full Name of Commenter
Malon Comment	Erin Malon
Martin Comment	Bernice Martin (consumer/pet owner)
Matter Comment	Sharon Matter, VRS
NACDS Comment	National Association of Chain Drug Stores (NACDS)
Neely Comment	Austin Neely, DVM
Neville Comment	Neville (consumer/pet owner)
Novartis Comment	Novartis Animal Health US, Inc.
Oregon VMA Comment (#422)	Oregon Veterinary Medical Association
Oregon VMA Comment (#175)	Oregon Veterinary Medical Association
Pedersen Comment	Stacey Pedersen, DVM, Capitaland Animal Hospital
PetCareRx Comment	PetCareRx, Inc.
Pfizer Comment (#329)	Pfizer Animal Health
Pieper Comment	Martha Pieper, Smart Love Press (consumer/pet owner)
Powers (F&S) Comment	John Powers*, executive vice president, Drs. Foster & Smith (F&S)
Rafalow Comment	Trish Rafalow (consumer/pet owner)
Rodgers Comment	Amy Rodgers (consumer/pet owner)
Roth Comment	Juliana Roth (consumer/pet owner)
Shaprut Comment	Avi Shaprut, DVM, Kearny Mesa Veterinary Center
Sherman Comment	D Sherman (consumer/pet owner)
N. Smith Comment	Nate Smith*, formerly in charge of retail strategy for Walmart's pet department
Stangl Comment	Mira Stangl (pharmacy technician)
Stevens Comment	Terry Stevens, University of Tennessee College of Veterinary Medicine (UTCVM) Pharmacy
SVHP Comment	Society of Veterinary Hospital Pharmacists (SVHP)
B. Taylor Comment	Beth Taylor, DVM
Valley Vet Supply Comment	Valley Vet Supply
Washenfelder Comment	Marc Washenfelder , DVM
Webb Comment	Catherine Webb, DVM, Lindquist Veterinary Care Ctr.
West Comment	Harvey West (consumer/pet owner)
Wilson (Priority Veterinary Mgmt. Consultants) Comment (#475)	James Wilson, DVM, Priority Veterinary Mgmt. Consultants
Yoo Comment	Yoo (consumer/pet owner)
Zeidner (1-800 CONTACTS) Comment	R. Joe Zeidner*, general counsel, 1-800 CONTACTS

*Also participated in the workshop as a panelist.

End Notes

[1] This report represents the views of the staff of the Federal Trade Commission. It does not necessarily represent the views of the Commission or of any individual Commissioner.

[2] For purposes of this report, the terms "market" and "marketplace" refer generally to the manufacture and sale of, and consumer demand for, all companion animal pet medications. This report does not purport to identify any relevant product market for antitrust law enforcement purposes.

[3] As discussed in greater detail below, 65 percent of U.S. households own pets, and American consumers spent approximately $7.6 billion on prescription and OTC pet medications in 2013.

[4] *See infra* notes 67 and 72 and accompanying text.

[5] Under Sections 6(a) and (f) of the FTC Act, Congress authorized the FTC "[t]o gather and compile information concerning, and to investigate from time to time the organization, business, conduct, practices, and management of any person, partnership, or corporation engaged in or whose business affects commerce," and "[t]o make public from time to time such portions of the information obtained by it hereunder as are in the public interest." 15 U.S.C. § 46(a), (f).

[6] Information about the workshop is available on the workshop's webpage. *Pet Medications Workshop*, FED. TRADE COMM'N (Oct. 2, 2012), http://www.ftc.gov/news-events/events-calendar/2012/10/pet-medications- workshop. A transcript of the proceedings is also available. Transcript of Pet Medications Workshop, Fed. Trade Comm'n (Oct. 2, 2012), http://www.ftc.gov/sites/default/files/documents/public_events/pet-medications- workshop/ petmedtranscript-1.pdf [hereinafter Workshop Tr.].

[7] The FTC held a public comment period from June 29 to November 1, 2012. All comments received are posted on the FTC website. *List of Public Comments Regarding Pet Medications*, FED. TRADE COMM'N, http://www.ftc.gov/policy/public-comments/initiative-433. The FTC received over 580 comments from veterinarians and veterinary hospitals; approximately 70 comments from consumers and consumer advocate organizations; approximately 35 comments from the American Veterinary Medical Association ("AVMA") and state veterinary medical associations; approximately 14 comments from retailers and pharmacies that sell pet medications, as well as pharmacy trade organizations; 3 comments representing the interests of branded manufacturers of pet medications; 2 comments representing the interests of generic manufacturers of pet medications; and 2 comments from optometry industry stakeholders. This report often relies upon statements made by the AVMA as a proxy for views commonly expressed by state veterinary medical associations and individual veterinarians.

FTC staff also received public comments and other information related to prescription pet food, as well as medications for equine and production animals. *See, e.g.*, Boylan Comment (#256); Rodgers Comment; Hamilton Comment; Pieper Comment; Bach Comment. While FTC staff did not study these other products in depth, we note that they raise prescription portability and distribution issues similar to those for companion animal medications.

[8] The terms "retailers," "alternative retailers," and "retail outlets" are used throughout this report to refer to the non-veterinary retail distribution channels that have emerged in the pet medications industry, including online and brick-and-mortar pharmacies and stores.

[9] Price may not be the only factor that consumers consider when choosing where to purchase a particular pet medication. Relevant factors, which may vary significantly among online pharmacies, brick-and-mortar pharmacies, and veterinarians include search costs, shipping costs, and wait times for prescription fulfillment and delivery. When choosing where to make purchases, consumers may face a tradeoff between price and other factors, and different preferences regarding this tradeoff will likely lead different consumers to make different choices.

[10] *See Pet Industry Market Size & Ownership Statistics*, AM. PET PRODUCTS ASS'N, http://www.americanpetproducts.org/press_industrytrends.asp [hereinafter *APPA Statistics*]. The APPA estimates that 54.4 million households own at least one dog (approximately 77.8 million dogs) and 42.9 million households own at least one cat (approximately 85.8 million cats).

[11] *Id.*

[12] *See* GEORGE PURO, PACKAGED FACTS, PET MEDICATIONS IN THE U.S. 20 (3d ed. 2014) [hereinafter PACKAGED FACTS REPORT 3D] ("Recent surveys have consistently found that a large majority of U.S. pet owners consider their pet to be a part of the family, and this human/animal bond is one of the most important factors behind pet owners' willingness to spend generously on pet health products and services."). The Packaged Facts report examines the consumer market for prescription and non-prescription medications for dogs and cats, with a primary focus on flea, tick, and heartworm medications, but also covering a wide range of therapeutic treatments. Medications for production animals and horses are excluded from this analysis, as are nutritional supplements for horses and companion animals. *Id.* at 1. *See also* Bill Ward, *Fidocare Isn't Catching On*, STAR TRIBUNE (Aug. 13, 2013), http://www.startribune.com/printarticle/?id=219448061 (citing the humanization of pets as children as a contributing factor to increased veterinary expenditures); Press Release, Animal Health Inst., Spending on Animal Healthcare Products on the Rise in 2010 (Nov. 16, 2011), http://www.ahi.org/archives/2011/11/2010-annual-sales/ ("America's love for their companion animals also fueled growth in the animal healthcare sector."); Steve Henderson, *Spending on Pets: "Tails" from the Consumer Expenditure Survey, Beyond the Numbers, vol. 2, no. 16*, U.S. BUREAU OF LABOR STATISTICS (May 2013), http:// www.bls.gov/ opub/ btn/ volume-2/pdf/spending-on-pets.pdf; AM. VETERINARY MED. ASS'N, U.S. PET OWNERSHIP & DEMOGRAPHICS SOURCEBOOK at 1 (2012 ed. 2012) (stating that in 2011, 63.2% of pet owners considered their pets to be family members).

[13] The APPA estimates that 2014 sales of pet-related products and services breaks down as follows: $22.26billion for food; $13.75 billion for supplies and OTC medicines; $15.04 billion for veterinary care (includes routine veterinary care, prescription medications, and pet insurance, but does not include surgical veterinary care); $2.15 billion for live animal purchases; and $4.84 billion for other pet services (grooming, boarding, training, pet sitting, and miscellaneous). *APPA Statistics*, *supra* note 10.

[14] DAVID LUMERIS, PACKAGED FACTS, PET MEDICATIONS IN THE U.S. 26-27 (2d ed. 2011) [hereinafter PACKAGED FACTS REPORT 2D] ("Pets are living longer because their owners are taking better care of them, both medically and nutritionally, as well as keeping them inside more often, where they are at less risk of getting hit by cars, etc. Even more important perhaps, longer lives mean stronger emotional bonds and thus an increased willingness among pet owners to do whatever it takes to keep their pets healthy and happy."); PACKAGED FACTS REPORT 3D, *supra* note 12 at 25 ("The growing population of older pets means more companion animals are suffering from age-related conditions, including joint, coronary, cognitive, and immune-system-related, as well as diabetes and cancer. Senior- targeted pet products cover all of these needs as well as routine daily concerns, and because of their more specialized health focus, senior products and services are typically priced well above the market average."); AM. VETERINARY MED. Ass'n, *supra* note 12, at 2 (noting that U.S. pets are living longer, perhaps because of better care). *See also id.* at 26-28 (citing obesity as a major threat to the health of pets, leading to higher rates of chronic diseases, as well as higher health care costs); Press Release, Ass'n for Pet Obesity Prevention, Big Pets Get Bigger: Latest Survey Shows Dog and Cat Obesity Epidemic Expanding (Feb. 6, 2012), http://www.petobesityprevention.com/wp-content/uploads/2012/02/APOP-Survey-2011.pdf (showing a 37 percent increase in overweight dogs and a 90 percent increase in overweight cats from 2007 to 2012, which would potentially lead to an increase in chronic diseases).

[15] Novartis Comment at 1 ("Today's therapeutic products provide treatments and solutions that pets did not enjoy decades ago, and reflect the increasingly important role that pets play in our lives."). *See also* Workshop Tr. at 42-44 (Clinton Vranian); PACKAGED FACTS REPORT 3D, *supra* note 12, at 49 (stating that investors recognize the growth potential in animal therapeutics, and "how the devotion of pet owners can drive demand for innovative pet medicines.").

[16] *See* PACKAGED FACTS REPORT 3D, *supra* note 12, at 28; PACKAGED FACTS REPORT 2D, *supra* note 14, at 60 ("In keeping with the broader pet market trend of humanization, whereby human product companies, brands, and product and service styles are crossing over, major pharmaceutical companies are adapting human drugs for pets and developing new ones. The practice of prescribing human medications to pets has grown significantly in the past two decades, with more than 600 human drugs being used 'off-label' to treat pets, and pharmaceutical companies are taking it to the next level by developing pet-specific therapies. Modes of adaptation include reformulating existing drugs, adding new ingredients, altering treatment modes, and offering new delivery systems and packaging forms."); *A Guide to Prescription Drugs for Dogs*, VETINFO, http:// www. vetinfo. com/ prescription-drugs-dogs.html ("Recent advances in the development of drugs for dogs have yielded many new and effective treatments for common dog ailments and conditions. These pet drugs reduce pain, prevent and treat disease and improve the quality of life for millions of dogs each day. Many veterinary drugs are based on successful human drugs including those for arthritis, anxiety and infections."); ANIMAL HEALTH INST., 2013 MARKET RESEARCH REPORT: U.S. ANIMAL HEALTH PRODUCTS INDUSTRY 25, 30, 34 (2013) (research and development expenditures of AHI members steadily increased from $689.7 million in 2010, to $712.6 million in 2011, to $746.8 million in 2012).

[17] *See generally A Guide to Prescription Drugs for Dogs*, *supra* note 16 (noting that recent developments of drugs for dogs has improved the quality of life for millions of dogs); *Industry Statistics*, ANIMAL HEALTH INST., http://www.ahi.org/about-animal-medicines/industry-statistics/ ("Scientists have developed numerous medicines that have resulted in dramatic improvements in the prevention and treatment of animal health issues such as flea and tick infestation, Lyme disease, rabies, diabetes, feline leukemia, and other types of cancers."); Press Release, Animal Health Inst., Animal Healthcare Products Continue Sales Recovery in 2012 (Nov. 22, 2013), http:// www.ahi.org/ archives/ 2013/11/animal-healthcare-products-continue-sales-recovery-in-2012/ (quoting AHI President and CEO Alexander S. Mathews, "The availability of animal medicines . . . allows our pets to live longer healthier lives and improves our enjoyment of them."); Linda J. I. Horspool, *Animal Health Markets and Opportunities: Companion Animal Landscape*, *in* LONG ACTING ANIMAL HEALTH DRUG PRODUCTS: FUNDAMENTALS AND APPLICATIONS 15-16 (Michael J. Rathbone & Arlene McDowell eds., 2013) ("the bond between companion animals and people is continuing to strengthen and with it the market for products, including pharmaceuticals and vaccines, which contribute significantly to the health and wellbeing of these animals."). *But see* PACKAGED FACTS REPORT 3D, *supra* note 12, at 204 (indicating no general trend towards increased use of pet medications); PACKAGED FACTS REPORT 2D, *supra* note 14, at 44-46 (describing risks and criticisms of increased development and use of pet medications).

[18] *See* Tess Vigeland, *How to Set a Price on the Life of a Beloved Pet?*, N.Y. TIMES (Mar. 25, 2013), http://www.nytimes.com/2013/03/26/your-money/costs-and-choices-mount-for-pets-end-of-life-care.html (describing how pet owners have more ethical and financial decisions to make when caring for their pets in light of technological advances in animal medical treatments over the last 10-30 years).

[19] PACKAGED FACTS REPORT 3D, *supra* note 12, at 17. Packaged Facts retail revenues are inclusive of sales through veterinarians, brick-and-mortar retailers, and online retailers. *Id.* In 2011, Packaged Facts estimated U.S. retail sales of pet medications to be $6.7 billion, and this figure was broken down as follows: $2.4 billion in flea/tick control products (36%);

$1.3 billion in heartworm preventatives (19%); $603 million in anti-infectives (9%); $335 million in pain relievers (5%); and $2.1 billion in other categories (31%). PACKAGED FACTS REPORT 2D, *supra* note 14, at 3. In 2012, other industry stakeholders estimated the consumer retail market for pet medications at $6 billion to $10 billion annually. Workshop Tr. at 27 (Paul D. Pion); Advocacy for Pets and Affordable Wellness ("APAW") Coalition Comment at 1.

[20] PACKAGED FACTS REPORT 3D, *supra* note 12, at 43. In 2011, Packaged Facts predicted that growth of pet medications sales would "come from both the pharmaceutical side of the market, as new drugs are launched, and from the retail side of the market, as products and ingredients crossing over from the veterinary channel broaden their retail following." PACKAGED FACTS REPORT 2D, *supra* note 14, at 5.

[21] *See* Animal Health Institute ("AHI") Comment at 2 (estimating 2011 ex-manufacturer sales of companion animal health products to be approximately $3.8 billion); Axxiom LLC, US Animal Health Market Overview for Veterinary and OTC Products 2-3 (2012) [hereinafter Axxiom Market Analysis], *attached to* Am. Veterinary Distributors Ass'n (AVDA) Comment at 16-22 (estimating U.S. companion animal health revenues at $3.7 billion, as measured in ex-manufacturer dollar sales for 2010). "Ex-manufacturer" sales refer to the value of goods sold by manufacturers, with no wholesale or retail margins added, and thus do not reflect the actual retail prices paid by consumers. *See also* PetMed Express, Inc., Annual Report (Form 10-K) 5 (May 27, 2014), http:// www.sec.gov/ Archives/ edgar/ data/ 1040130/000157104914002091/t79402_10k.htm ("The pet medication market that we [PetMed Express] participate in is estimated to be approximately $4.0 billion, with veterinarians having the majority of the market share.").

[22] *See infra* note 185; K&L Gates Comment at 1 ("In recent years, the importance of companion animals in the American household has increased dramatically. As our nation's population begins to age, many households have taken in pets to provide comfort and companionship. New advances in animal drugs and veterinary treatment practices have allowed these pets to live longer and healthier lives. But, these advances come at a cost to pet owners. The cost of responsible pet ownership has skyrocketed and as a result consumers are searching for new ways to reduce those costs."); Indep. Pharmacy Alliance Comment at 1 ("[T]he need to ensure consumer choice and competition for owner's access to pet medications is a significant issue and a growing need for U.S. pet owners."). According to the American Society for the Prevention of Cruelty to Animals ("ASPCA"), new dog owners can expect to pay over $1,500 in pet care costs during the first year alone, and new cat owners can expect to pay over $1,000. Included in these figures is the estimated average annual cost of medical expenses, which is over $230 for dogs and $160 for cats. ASPCA Comment at 1-2. According to the 2015-2016 APPA National Pet Owners Survey, dog owners spent approximately $786 on routine and surgical veterinary visits, while cat owners spend approximately $594. *APPA Statistics*, *supra* note 10. According to the AVMA, total veterinary expenditures for all household pets rose about 15 percent from 2006 to 2011, to approximately $28 billion in 2011. AM. VETERINARY MED. ASS'N, *supra* note 12, at 65, 78, 91, 103, 113 (includes total veterinary expenditures for dogs, cats, birds, horses, and specialty/exotic animals). According to the Bureau of Labor Statistics Consumer Expenditure Survey, each American household spends, on average, over $500 on pets, which amounts to about 1% of total annual spending per household. By way of comparison, this is more than the average household spends on alcohol ($456), residential landline phone bills ($381), men and boys clothing ($404), or reading materials ($115). Henderson, *supra* note 12. However, medical costs could be substantially higher for pets that suffer unexpected illnesses or have chronic conditions that require long-term therapeutic treatments. Furthermore, households with multiple pets will pay proportionately more than households with single pets.

[23] *See* APAW Coalition Comment at 1-2; Indep. Pharmacy Alliance Comment at 1 ("[M]ost individuals [pay] directly for the costs of these medications out of their own pockets as pet

healthcare coverage insurance is fairly limited."); Ward, *supra* note 12 (despite increased spending on veterinary care, fewer than 1 percent of dogs and cats in the United States are insured, as compared to 26 percent in Great Britain and 48 percent in the Netherlands). *But see* PACKAGED FACTS REPORT 3D, *supra* note 12, at 29-30 (describing how pet health insurance is expected to become more prevalent in the future, potentially making pet health care more affordable, and estimating North American pet insurance sales at $618 million in 2013, up almost 15 percent since 2012 and projected to reach $962 million by 2018, with U.S. sales accounting for nearly 87 percent) ("[T]he sharply rising cost of veterinary care remains a potent driver behind increased acceptance of pet health insurance among consumers and veterinarians alike, and one that will continue to spur pet insurance recommendation and adoption in the years ahead"). Even if pet insurance were widespread, however, the price of pet medications would still be important because that would affect the cost of the insurance.

[24] *See* AM. VETERINARY MED. ASS'N, *supra* note 12, at 72, 85 (stating 29.3 percent of households that did not take their dogs to the veterinarian in 2011 and 21.5 percent of households that did not take their cats to the veterinarian in 2011 indicated that the primary reason was because they could not afford it); NAT'L COMM'N ON VETERINARY ECON. ISSUES ("NCVEI") & BAYER HEALTH CARE LLC, ANIMAL HEALTH DIVISION, NCVEI UPDATE/BAYER VETERINARY CARE USAGE STUDY 38, 60 (2011), http:// www. brakkeconsulting.com/files/download/BAYERBCI_VET_CARE_USAGE_STUDY.pdf [hereinafter referred to as NCVEI/BAYER USAGE STUDY] (NCVEI Update is on pages 2-28, Bayer Veterinary Care Usage Study is on pages 29-101) (indicating that 53 percent of pet owners view veterinary costs as higher than expected, and that this results in fewer veterinary visits); AM. HUMANE ASS'N, KEEPING PETS (DOGS AND CATS) IN HOMES: A THREE- PHASE RETENTION STUDY, PHASE I: REASONS FOR NOT OWNING A DOG OR CAT 7 (2012), http://www.americanhumane.org/aha-petsmart-retention-study-phase-1.pdf.

[25] *See* ASPCA Comment at 1-2.

[26] *See* Packaged Facts Report 3d, *supra* note 12, at 197 ("Other than flea/tick and heartworm control products, the top pet medications are antibiotics, pain relief products, allergy relief products, joint/arthritis products, and eye or ear products."); *id.* at 198 (stating that as a general rule, veterinarians are the main source for these types of pet medications with a few exceptions: retail stores are the primary source of insulin and other diabetes medications, and veterinarians and retail stores are equally likely to be the source for nonprescription pain relievers and joint/arthritis medications); *infra* note 31 (noting that consumers are more likely to purchase prescription animal medications from veterinarians). *See generally* Packaged Facts Report 3d, *supra* note 12, at 154 ("Veterinarians have an inherent advantage in that they are the most trusted source of pet health information, with a built-in base of potential pet medications customers. For certain types of prescription medications, moreover, they are at times the only source.").

[27] *See* PACKAGED FACTS REPORT 3D, *supra* note 12, at 207.

[28] *See infra* note 45 and accompanying text.

[29] *See infra* note 58 and accompanying text (discussing veterinarians' extra-label use of human generic drugs for animals). Some human generic drugs commonly dispensed for use in animals include antibiotics, corticosteroids, insulin, epilepsy drugs, thyroid drugs, and pain relief drugs. In recent years, manufacturers have developed branded versions of some of these drugs that are specific to animals. Some clients still prefer the human generic versions, however, because they are often less expensive than the branded animal versions. Generally, it is within the veterinarian's discretion to prescribe human generic drugs or veterinary label drugs for use in companion animals.

[30] Foster (Drs. Foster & Smith (F&S)) Comment at 8 ("For more than fifty years veterinary clinics have relied on local pharmacies to fill certain prescriptions. . . . The practice of pharmacists filling pet prescriptions is normal and widely accepted and has been so for decades."); Nat'l Ass'n of Chain Drug Stores ("NACDS") Comment at 1 (". . . working in

partnership with veterinarians, retail pharmacists have historically dispensed human medications for use in pets. Chain pharmacies also provide over the counter (OTC) pet medications and other pet-related items. These are established business practices."); Workshop Tr. at 30 (Paul D. Pion); K&L Gates Comment at 4; Pfizer Comment (#329) at 2 (". . . veterinarians routinely rely on prescribing human drugs that, to some extent, are dispensed at retail pharmacies. Recent [IMS] audit data show that over 6 million prescriptions are written by veterinarians each year and filled by retail pharmacies.") [In January 2013, Pfizer spun off its animal health division into what is now called Zoetis. Pfizer retains about 80 percent of the company.].

[31] *See* PACKAGED FACTS REPORT 3D, *supra* note 12, at 154 ("The range of channels carrying pet medications has broadened considerably, and the shift away from the dominant veterinary channel is ongoing."); *Id.* at 45 (noting that the distinction between the pharmaceutical/veterinary channel and the pet product/retail channel is blurring). In the past, non-veterinary retailers primarily sold OTC products that were supposed to be distributed exclusively through the veterinary channel. In recent years, non-veterinary retailers have begun selling a broad range of prescription products, as well. *See id.* at 160 (noting that PetMed Express's sales of prescription medications increased from 29 percent in 2007 to 40 percent in 2013, while sales of non-prescription medications have fallen from 70 percent to 59 percent). However, consumers still appear more likely to obtain prescription products from veterinarians, even if they are willing to obtain OTC products from non-veterinary retailers. *See, e.g.*, *id.* at 182-83, 195-96 (indicating that 46 percent of dog owners purchase OTC spot-on flea and tick medications from veterinarians, versus 53 percent of dog owners who purchase from retail outlets; whereas 76 percent of pet owners purchase prescription heartworm medications from veterinarians, versus 24 percent who purchase from retail outlets). *See also id.* at 199-201 (showing channel breakdown of other common pet medications).

[32] *See* Workshop Tr. at 30 (Paul D. Pion); Edward Woo, *Analyst Interview: Increased Competition in the Pet Medication Space*, WALL ST. TRANSCRIPT (May 30, 2011), https://www.twst.com/interview/28302 ("Before, about 10 years ago almost all pet medication was sold by the vets. You visited your vet, and you picked up the medication on your way out. Vets controlled the treatment and the maintenance of the animals. And because of that they often controlled the dispensing of the drugs. Pet owners have a very personal relationship with their vets, so they didn't necessarily want to endanger it or offend the vet by not buying his products or not buying the medication from him. The Internet started to change all that. You started to having companies like PetMed Express enter the market. They looked around and realized they could sell the same medications a lot cheaper than what customers were getting from the vets, and that started to get people to start to buy medication away from the vets. It was a popular alternative because these medications can get expensive, so owners started to seek out other places to buy the same product.").

[33] *See* Workshop Tr. at 32 (Paul D. Pion); NACDS Comment at 1 ("At the request of customers, many chain pharmacies have begun to dispense, or are in the process of exploring options to provide prescription pet medications to their customers. We see this as a natural expansion of our current role with customers that are pet owners."); Jeff Siegel, *The New Pet Med Market*, PET AGE, Sept. 2012, at 28, 32 (quoting Daryl Szyska, pharmaceutical consultant: "The more mainstream these products become, the more retailers are going to find ways to sell them. . . . And more people are going to ask their retailers why they aren't selling them."); Woo, *supra* note 32 ("The next wave of change was with the general retailers. Now we have started to see nonprescription products show up in places like Costco (COST), Wal-Mart (WMT), Target (TGT) or even the grocery stores and smaller stores. When they first started, PetMed Express had almost a little monopoly in terms of selling the products online and outside the vet. It may still be the largest exclusive retailer of pet medication online, but it now has plenty of competition both from brick-and-mortar retailers and from other Internet or e-commerce retailers.").

[34] *See infra* Section IV.A.3, The Secondary Market for Pet Medications, at 74.

[35] *See* Workshop Tr. at 32-33 (Paul D. Pion); Dennis Arp, *Pharmacy Options for Veterinary Practices*, VETERINARY PRACTICE NEWS (July 26, 2012), http:// www. veterinarypracticenews.com/June-2012/Pharmacy- Options-For-Veterinary-Practices/ ("From discount online pharmacies to neighborhood drug and grocery stores as well as big-box retailers such as Walmart, Costco and Sam's Club, competitors for pet-medication business abound, chipping at sales that once were solid for veterinary practices."); Workshop Tr. at 60, 62 (Brad Dayton) (noting that 60-65% of Ahold USA's customers shop for pet products at its grocery stores, which is consistent with the number of American households that own pets, and Ahold views pet medications as a "natural offering" for its customers); PetCareRx Comment at 1 ("Most consumers obtain prescription pet medications directly from veterinarians . . . Increasingly, however, consumers have turned to third-party pharmacies like PetCareRx for their pets' prescription medications.").

[36] Michael Paul, *The Real Future of Pharmacy: New Competition and Proposed Prescription Legislation Are Tough Pills to Swallow*, DVM360.COM/VETERINARY ECONOMICS (June 1, 2012), http://veterinarybusiness.dvm360.com/real-future-veterinary-pharmacy.

[37] PACKAGED FACTS REPORT 3D, *supra* note 12, at 154 (noting that "the days of veterinarians having a virtual monopoly on sales of pet medications are a thing of the past, with the days of pet medication distribution increasingly paralleling that of human medications."). By comparison, in 2011, veterinarians were estimated to account for 63 percent of sales, brick-and-mortar retailers 28 percent, and Internet/mail order retailers 7 percent. PACKAGED FACTS REPORT 2D, *supra* note 14, at 11. See also PACKAGED FACTS REPORT 3D, *supra* note 12, at 19 and PACKAGED FACTS REPORT 2D, *supra* note 14, at 22 (indicating that pet care service providers, such as groomers, and all other distribution channels accounted for 1 percent of pet medication sales in 2014, and 2 percent in 2011).

[38] *Principles of Veterinary Medical Ethics of the AVMA*, AM. VETERINARY MED. ASS'N, https://www.avma.org/KB/Policies/Pages/Principles-of-Veterinary-Medical-Ethics-of-the-AVMA.aspx (approved Jan. 2015) (Principle II).

[39] *See, e.g.*, AHI Comment at 3 ("The veterinarian plays a critical role in our industry, particularly related to product selection for companion animals. . . . [T]he veterinarian is the primary source of information about animal health products for pet owners. Veterinarians have typically counseled clients regarding the use of products and many manufacturers have invested tremendous resources to educate veterinarians about their products. Veterinarians also have ongoing close interaction with their clients and have been the primary monitors of patient use of medication including evaluation for interactions and adverse events. They often train clients to administer products that are dispensed. These roles for the veterinarian are understandable as veterinarians are uniquely trained in the physiology and pharmacology for the various species they treat."). *See also* Novartis Comment at 3 ("Prescription medications, by definition, must be administered with regard to their efficacy and their safety for a particular patient. It is therefore essential to ensure that these products are prescribed by trained professionals, educated on the risks and benefits of these innovative technologies. The unique circumstances of a particular pet can impact the administration, efficacy and safety of these medications. Only a veterinary-trained professional can assess these variables and ensure that the client is properly counseled.") [In January 2015, Eli Lilly acquired Novartis Animal Health and merged the Novartis assets with Lilly's existing animal health business, Elanco. As part of the transaction, certain animal health assets in the United States relating to Novartis's Sentinel® canine parasiticide franchise were divested to Virbac.]; AVDA Comment at 5 ("While the traditional human pharmacy has an important role to play in fulfilling certain prescriptions, particularly in those instances where the veterinarian is prescribing a standard human pharmaceutical product or a specialty compounding application, it is equally evident the veterinarian is the only medical professional sufficiently trained to judge the pharmacological agent to be

used, its dosage, the duration of treatment and any other special considerations which may be unique to that species or even a given breed of pet.").

[40] *Principles of Veterinary Medical Ethics of the AVMA*, *supra* note 38 (Useful Terms – VCPR); Workshop Tr. At 22 (Douglas G. Aspros).

[41] Workshop Tr. at 139 (Adrian Hochstadt).

[42] *See generally About the NABP*, NAT'L ASS'N OF BDS. OF PHARMACY, http:// www.nabp.net/ about.

[43] *See* Workshop Tr. at 139 (Adrian Hochstadt); PetMed Express, Inc., *supra* note 21, at 6.

[44] *See* Workshop Tr. at 24 (Douglas G. Aspros).

[45] *See* K&L Gates Comment at 4.

[46] *See infra* Section III.A.1, State Laws and Veterinary Codes of Ethics, at 29.

[47] *See infra* notes 352, 354.

[48] *See* Workshop Tr. at 199-200 (Race Foster).

[49] NAT'L ASS'N OF BDS. OF PHARMACY, FACT SHEET: VET-VIPPS ACCREDITATION PROGRAM (July 2013), http://www.nabp.net/system/redactor_assets/documents/605/Vet-VIPPS.pdf.

[50] *Vet-VIPPS*, NAT'L ASS'N OF BDS. OF PHARMACY, http:// www.nabp.net/ programs/ accreditation/vet-vipps/ ("The Vet-VIPPS program is an expansion of the Verified Internet Pharmacy Practice Sites program, which NABP established in 1999 after a coalition of state and federal regulatory associations, professional associations, and consumer advocacy groups provided their expertise to develop criteria for accredited Internet pharmacies to follow as part of their commitment to public health protection.").

[51] *Find a Vet-VIPPS Online Pharmacy*, NAT'L ASS'N OF BDS. OF PHARMACY, http://www.nabp.net/programs/accreditation/vet-vipps/find-a-vet-vipps-online-pharmacy.

[52] *See* AM. VETERINARY MED. ASS'N, FREQUENTLY ASKED QUESTIONS BY PET OWNERS ABOUT PRESCRIPTIONS AND PHARMACIES 5 (n.d.), https:// www.avma.org/ KB/ Resources/ FAQs/ Documents/Prescriptions-and-Pharmacies- Pet-Owner-FAQs.pdf [hereinafter AVMA FAQS]; *Client Requests for Prescriptions*, AM. VETERINARY MED. ASS'N, https://www.avma.org/KB/Policies/Pages/Internet-Pharmacies.aspx [hereinafter *AVMA Client Requests for Prescriptions*] (Recommendation 3); *Online Pet Pharmacies: Protect Yourself and Your Pet: Be Online Pet Pharmacy A.W.A.R.E.*, U.S. FOOD & DRUG ADMIN., http:// www.fda.gov/AnimalVeterinary/ResourcesforYou/AnimalHealthLiteracy/ucm 203000.htm (last updated June 6, 2014) (encouraging pet owners to look for Vet-VIPPS accreditation before purchasing pet medications from online pharmacies). *See also* PACKAGED FACTS REPORT 3D, *supra* note 12, at 157 ("With the implementation of Vet-VIPPS . . . the Internet has become a more trusted source of pet medications.").

[53] A compounding pharmacy can often concoct drug formulas that are specially tailored to meet the unique needs of patients. For example, drug formulas may be compounded to create liquid versions of medications that are normally available only in solid pill form for patients who cannot swallow pills; to avoid a non-essential ingredient to which the patient is allergic; to obtain the exact doses needed of active pharmaceutical ingredients; or for optional reasons, such as adding flavors to a medication or otherwise altering taste or texture. For information on the PCAB accreditation program, *see PCAB Pharmacy Compounding Accreditation*, ACCREDIT'N COMM'N FOR HEALTH CARE, http://achc.org/ go/achc-pharmacy-compounding-accreditation.

[54] *See For Prescribers*, PHARMACY COMPOUNDING ACCREDITATION BD., http:// www.pcab.org/ prescribers (summarizing accreditation standards). *See also* Foster (F&S) Comment at 2.

[55] *See* AVMA FAQS, *supra* note 52, at 5.

[56] Typically this is accomplished through the possession of original manufacturer invoices displaying product identification numbers and expiration dates that correspond with the pharmacy's product inventory. *See, e.g.*, Kroger Comment at 2; Giselle Smith, *Kroger fills pet prescriptions*, MSN MONEY (Jan. 26, 2012) (confirming that Kroger uses "very strict procedures" to ensure the pedigree of its products, even when purchased from a secondary wholesaler); Edie Lau, *An Inside Look at Parasiticide Product Diversion*, VIN News Serv.

(Apr. 7, 2009), http://news.vin.com/VINNews.aspx?articleId=12583 [hereinafter Lau, *Parasiticide Diversion*] ("Online retailers, for their part, bristle at the suggestion that their goods are any less authentic than those purchased in a veterinary clinic.").

[57] *See generally* Pfizer Comment (#329) at 2 n.1.

[58] *See The Ins and Outs of Extra-Label Drug Use in Animals: A Resource for Veterinarians*, U.S. FOOD AND DRUG ADMIN., http:// www.fda.gov/ animalveterinary/ resourcesforyou/ ucm380135.htm (last updated June 26, 2014).

[59] *See id.* Much of modern veterinary education is focused on understanding the complexities of veterinary pharmacology, and how human drugs can be used to safely treat animal health problems. *See* Workshop Tr. at 29 (Paul D. Pion).

[60] *See generally* AHI Comment at 1-2.

[61] *See generally* AVMA Comment at 2.

[62] We are mindful of experiences in other jurisdictions that might inform policy decisions in the United States. Notably, in April 2003, the United Kingdom Competition Commission also published a report after investigating similar issues for the sale of prescription-only veterinary medicines. U.K. COMPETITION COMMISSION, VETERINARY MEDICINES: A REPORT ON THE SUPPLY WITHIN THE UNITED KINGDOM OF PRESCRIPTION-ONLY VETERINARY MEDICINES (2003), http:// webarchive.nationalarchives.gov.uk/ +/http:/ www.competition- commission.org.uk/rep_pub/reports/2003/478vetmeds.htm#full. This report concluded that effective competition in the retail supply of prescription-only veterinary medicines depends on a number of factors, including the ability of alternative sources of supply to offer effective competition to veterinarians who diagnose animals and recommend prescriptions; the availability of prescriptions from veterinarians; the ability of pharmacies to supply medications on terms that do not prevent, restrict or distort competition with veterinarians; and the provision of transparent information to enable animal owners to understand and compare prices.

[63] *See infra* note 246.

[64] *See infra* Section III.A.1, State Laws and Veterinary Codes of Ethics, at 29.

[65] *See infra* Section III.A.2, Veterinarian Attitudes Towards Prescription Release, at 30.

[66] *See infra* Section III.A.3, Consumer Awareness of Prescription Portability, at 35.

[67] Fairness to Pet Owners Act of 2011, H.R. 1406, 112th Cong. (2011), *available at* http:// www.gpo.gov/fdsys/pkg/BILLS-112hr1406ih/pdf/BILLS-112hr1406ih.pdf. This bill would require veterinarians to provide prescriptions (in written, oral, or electronic form) to pet owners for all prescribed medications, regardless of whether requested. Veterinarians also would have to provide a written disclosure to pet owners that they may fill the prescription through the veterinary practice or through another pharmacy as determined by the pet owner. Veterinarians would not be allowed to charge a separate fee or require pet owners to sign a waiver of liability in exchange for providing a prescription. Furthermore, veterinarians would be required to verify prescriptions that are requested by any person designated to act on behalf of a pet owner, consistent with applicable state laws. As introduced, the bill would have made the Federal Trade Commission responsible for promulgating implementation rules.

[68] Fairness to Contact Lens Consumers Act, H.R. 3140, 108th Cong. (2003), *available at* http:// www.gpo.gov/fdsys/pkg/BILLS-108hr3140enr/pdf/BILLS-108hr3140enr.pdf (enacted Dec. 6, 2003). This act requires contact lens prescribers to provide patients with a copy of their contact lens prescriptions, regardless of whether requested. Contact lens prescribers are not allowed to charge a separate fee or require patients to sign a waiver of liability in exchange for providing a prescription. Furthermore, contact lens prescribers are required to verify contact lens prescriptions in accordance with the Contact Lens Rule, issued by the Federal Trade Commission in 2004.

[69] *See* Daniel R. Verdon, *AVMA Works to Quash Legislation Targeting Veterinary Prescription Sales for Dogs and Cats*, DVM360.COM/DVM360 MAG. (May 10, 2011), http:// veterinarynews.dvm360.com/dvm/Breaking+News/AVMA-works-to-quash-Rx-

bill/ArticleStandard/Article/detail/721946 (citing Representative Matheson's intent in drafting H.R. 1406).

[70] *See infra* note 190 and accompanying text.

[71] *See generally* Statement of Robert Hubbard, Assistant Attorney Gen., Antitrust Bureau, N.Y. Attorney General's Office, for FTC Workshop on Pet Medications at 6-7 (Oct 2, 2012), http://www.ftc.gov/sites/default/files/documents/public_events/pet-medications-workshop/rhubbardstmt.pdf [hereinafter Hubbard Statement]; Zeidner (1-800 CONTACTS) Comment at 1-2; PACKAGED FACTS REPORT 3D, *supra* note 12, at 50-51 (quoting Chairman and CEO of Perrigo, Q3 2013 Perrigo Company Earnings Conference Call, May 7, 2013, expecting the pet medications industry to evolve in a similar manner as the contact lens industry).

[72] Fairness to Pet Owners Act of 2014, H.R. 4023, 113th Cong. (2014), *available at* http://www.gpo.gov/fdsys/pkg/BILLS-113hr4023ih/pdf/BILLS-113hr4023ih.pdf; Fairness to Pet Owners Act of 2014, S. 2756, 113th Cong. (2014), *available at* http:// www.gpo.gov/ fdsys/pkg/BILLS-113s2756is/pdf/BILLS-113s2756is.pdf. These bills are similar to H.R. 1406, except that they would not have required veterinarians to provide pet owners with a written disclosure that pet owners may fill the prescription through the veterinary practice or through another pharmacy as determined by the pet owner. They also stated that veterinary prescriptions subject to automatic prescription release would not have included animal drugs administered by veterinarians while providing acute care. On May 6, 2015, legislation identical to S. 2756 was reintroduced in the Senate. Fairness to Pet Owners Act of 2015, S. 1200, 114th Cong. (2015).

[73] *See infra* note 297. For further discussion of the potential benefits and harms of exclusive distribution practices, *see infra* Section IV.A.1, Manufacturer Justifications for Exclusive Distribution Practices, at 66, and Section IV.A.2, Non-Veterinary Retailer Concerns About Exclusive Distribution, at 70.

[74] *See infra* notes 345, 348, and 338 and accompanying text.

[75] These wholesale distribution practices may be limited by applicable state laws, which govern the distribution of pet medications. *See infra* note 354.

[76] *See infra* Section IV.A.4, Competitive Impact of Secondary Distribution, at 78.

[77] *See infra* Section IV.A.5, Product Pedigree and Safety Issues Associated with Secondary Distribution, at 81.

[78] *See infra* Section IV.B.2, Exclusive Dealing Agreements May Have an Effect on Generic Entry, at 86.

[79] *See* Workshop Tr. at 52 (John Powers) ("[T]rue prescription portability cannot exist within the context of restricted distribution"); Powers (F&S) Comment at 3 ("[I]t does no good to encourage prescription portability without ensuring product supply."); Workshop Tr. at 146 (Race Foster) ("In my definition, portability ends with filling the prescription, not just obtaining it."). *See also* Zeidner (1-800 CONTACTS) Comment at 1-2 (suggesting analogous interdependence of prescription portability and distribution practices within the contact lens industry).

[80] *See* Workshop Tr. at 232 (Robert Hubbard) (stating that in markets where the prescriber is the only entity that is allowed to fill a prescription, power is conferred to the prescriber that does not usually exist in competitive markets, whereby they have the ability to restrict consumer access to competitive alternatives and protect their revenues); *id.* at 233 (stating that consumer access to competitive alternatives is restricted even further when manufacturers have the ability to limit access to products). *See also id.* at 114-15, 150 (Nate Smith); N. Smith Comment at 8.

[81] AHI Comment at 4.

[82] *Id.*

[83] Michael Paul, *Leading Off: Find a Winning Strategy in the Big Box Battle*, DVM360.COM/VETERINARY MEDICINE (Mar. 1, 2012), http:// veterinarymedicine. dvm360.com/leading-find-winning-strategy-big-box-battle.

[84] K&L Gates Comment at 12. *See also* Hubbard Statement, *supra* note 71, at 6 ("Veterinarians have the power to withhold or otherwise limit access to the prescriptions necessary for consumers to consider and to use competitive alternatives for pet medications. Moreover, manufacturers of products sold in those markets appear to restrict distribution of their products to those who can prescribe their products, emphasizing profits for veterinarians, rather than value for consumers.").

[85] Workshop Tr. at 88-89 (John Powers). *See also id.* at 192 (Nate Smith).

[86] *Id.* at 190-91 (Race Foster); Foster (F&S) Comment at 9 ("Restricted distribution limits choices and causes consumers to pay more than necessary for prescription and OTC products. Pets may suffer if medications are not readily and economically available. Restricted distribution, in my view, affects both the availability and the cost of prescription and OTC medications to consumers and their pets."); Valley Vet Supply Comment at 1 ("In our opinion, the current veterinary drug distribution system harms animal owners. It limits their choices and costs them more than necessary for veterinary drugs.").

[87] PetCareRx Comment at 3; Kroger Comment at 2.

[88] FED. TRADE COMM'N, GENERIC DRUG ENTRY PRIOR TO PATENT EXPIRATION 9 (2002), http://www.ftc.gov/sites/default/files/documents/reports/generic-drug-entry-prior-patent-expiration-ftc- study/genericdrugstudy_0.pdf; *See* David Reiffen & Michael R. Ward, *Generic Drug Industry Dynamics*, 87 REV. ECON. & STAT. 37 (2005), http:// www.mitpressjournals.org/doi/pdf/10.1162/0034653053327694.

[89] *See About Animal Generics: Facts & Figures*, GENERIC ANIMAL DRUG ALLIANCE, http://www.gadaonline.org/animalgenerics/facts.cfm. According to statistics from the Generic Animal Drug Alliance ("GADA"), 86 percent of FDA-approved animal drugs do not have a generic version. Furthermore, of the top 20 human drugs that lost patent protection between 2005 and 2007, 100 percent went generic, versus only 20 percent of the top 20 veterinary companion animal drugs during the same time frame. *See also* PACKAGED FACTS REPORT 3D, *supra* note 12, at 37 ("In large part because many companion animal specific medications are new, generics have played a relatively minor role in the market thus far compared with their ubiquitous position in human pharmaceuticals, but this is starting to change."); *id.* at 58 ("Currently, with so few companies fielding pet generics, the cost savings are around 20 percent compared with the 80 percent discounts often seen on generic prescription drugs for humans."). Perhaps the most notable generic entry in the pet medications industry occurred when Merial's patent for fipronil (the active ingredient in Frontline) expired in 2010. *Id.* at 55.

[90] *See infra* Section IV.B.1, Limited Consumer Access to Generic Animal Drugs, at 84.

[91] *See infra* note 412 and accompanying text.

[92] *See* Workshop Tr. at 75-76 (Mark Cushing) ("It's simply not correct to say that that marketplace is constricted and somehow works against the consumer."); Axxion Market Analysis, *supra* note 21, at 7 ("US Consumers in the United States have a broad array of options from which to legally purchase regulated pharmaceuticals, vaccines and non-regulated products typically used to insure the general health and welfare [sic] pets and food producing animals. The number of options and competition for consumer spending has accelerated with the expansion of on-line retailing operations serving the animal health market over the past decade."); Workshop Tr. at 188 (Douglas G. Aspros) ("[T]he market is functioning quite well today. It's diverse, there's new products coming on to the market all the time, consumers have choices like never before. The Internet and transparency and pricing has probably been a part of that . . . . [I]t's a very, very vigorous and well functioning marketplace."); AHI Comment at 3 ("The very large number of sales outlets creates an environment of rigorous competition and choice."); Maddigan (Willamette Valley Animal Hosp.) Comment ("[T]here are many more competitors in the marketplace the free market is working . . . .").

[93] *See* Workshop Tr. at 80-81 (Paul D. Pion).

[94] AHI Comment at 3. *See also Industry Statistics*, *supra* note 17 ("Each year, AHI member companies spend 10-12% of their sales investing in new innovations in animal health.") and *Regulation*, ANIMAL HEALTH INST., http://www.ahi.org/about-animal-medicines/regulation/ (estimating that regulatory approval for new animal drugs takes an average of 5-7 years).

[95] Lau, *Parasiticide Diversion*, *supra* note 56 (quoting Bruce Rosenbloom, CFO of PetMed Express, "At the end of the day, the consumers are going to call the shots. . . . The consumer demand is overwhelming. I don't think the veterinarian or the manufacturer is going to get in the way."); Oregon VMA Comment (#422) at 1-2 ("We also acknowledge that pet owners should have the ability to obtain a veterinary prescription from his or her veterinarian to be filled at a retail pharmacy of the client's choosing. In fact, we believe this is already occurring across the country, with market forces ensuring that consumers have access to such medications fairly and without the need of federal legislation. . . . We also are confident that the current marketplace is a fair barometer that ensures the consumer reasonable choice and access to veterinary prescriptions and keeping their pets healthy and safe."); Workshop Tr. at 244 (Link Welborn) ("The veterinary profession is currently experiencing numerous economic challenges. While these challenges intensify during the recession, they certainly predate the downturn in the U.S. economy and will persist even as the overall economy improves. Included among these are the progressive margin compression on veterinary medications that spans more than a decade. While this has reduced the profitability of veterinary practices, it has been beneficial to consumers in that it has reduced the cost of pet medications and it is an example of successful function of the free market. Today, the mark-up for the most commonly prescribed parasite control medication in my practice is about half of what it was ten years ago, even though there is no generic competition for that medication."); *id.* at 245-46 ("Clients commonly request prescriptions for the parasite control medications with the expectation that the cost of these medications will be less from another source. Once again, free market forces have been very effective in the pricing of these medications within most veterinary practices as set based on the prices available through online outlets."); Soc'y of Veterinary Hosp. Pharmacists ("SVHP") Comment at 2 ("SVHP also believes market forces currently in place or evolving will accomplish the inevitable and intended goals of the proposed legislation without the need for its enactment."); Maine VMA Comment (#281) ("The free market is already providing pet owners with competitive pricing of veterinary medicines. . . . Consumers can sort this out, just as the free market is sorting out consumer choices between online veterinary pharmacies and medications purchased through their family veterinarian."). *See also* PACKAGED FACTS REPORT 3D, *supra* note 12, at 32 ("[F]or pet owners as for U.S. consumers in general, economizing or spending optimizing often involves strategic retail behavior including buying across channels and brands, [and] shopping multiple channels for bargains . . ."); *id.* at 108-110 (suggesting that some of the pet medications manufacturers that typically marketed their products only to veterinarians have now begun marketing directly to consumers to help drive demand).

[96] *See, e.g.*, AVMA Comment at 6 ("We do not have data regarding prices charged to consumers by veterinary clinics for comparison to those charged by retailers and are not certain whether quantifying and comparing such data would be feasible. Veterinary business models range from small, single doctor practices to large, multidoctor, multifacility practices as well as from practices that treat only one species to practices that treat multiple species.").

[97] *See, e.g.*, PetMed Express, Inc., *supra* note 21, at 3 (emphasizing the company's ability to "rapidly deliver to customers the same medications offered by veterinarians, but at reduced prices."); PetCareRx Comment at 1 ("While veterinarians and affiliated institutional pharmacies charge substantial mark-ups for prescription medications, third- party pharmacies generally offer more competitive pricing. In some cases, PetCareRx charges customers as much as 50 percent less than a veterinarian may charge for the same medication."); NACDS Comment at 2 ("Retail pharmacy is a highly competitive industry,

operating on razor thin profit margins which average two percent. Consumers benefit from this competition through convenient access, lower prices, and outstanding customer service."); Kroger Comment at 2 (stating that retail drug stores are extremely competitive and customers frequently voice their preference to purchase pet medications from retail drug stores). *See also* Workshop Tr. at 183 (Nate Smith) (noting that prices online are generally lower than in a veterinary clinic); N. Smith Comment at 1 ("The bottom line is that American consumers stand to save hundreds of millions of dollars annually – if steps are taken to inject competition and choice into the marketplace for pet medications and specialty products.").

[98] *See., e.g.*, LHK PARTNERS INC., PET MEDICATION PRICING: WHOLESALE, ONLINE, VETERINARIAN (2009) (concluding that average online prices for pet medications for cats and dogs are less expensive than average veterinarian prices, based on pricing data collected in 2009 from 15 websites offering prescription pet medications and telephone surveys of 1,728 veterinarian offices); PACKAGED FACTS REPORT 2D, *supra* note 14, at 151 (". . . veterinary clients opt to purchase pet medications online for two reasons: price and convenience . . . The lure of lower prices is not restricted to the Internet. Price-based value is one of the key factors behind the projected bright future of pet medications . . . in brick-and-mortar retailers."); *id.* at 42-43 (suggesting that many pet medications are available at retail pharmacies as significant cost savings when compared to veterinary offices, especially if the pharmacy offers a generic discount drug plan); PACKAGED FACTS REPORT 3D, *supra* note 12, at 38 ("More broadly speaking, the retail turf of pet medications continues to expand into heavily price-focused channels. . . . Already, Internet sales of pet medications have cut deeply into veterinary channel sales, and it's no coincidence that Internet sellers charge significantly less for pet medications than veterinarians do. Now, additional price-focused competition is under way, with the top two mass-merchandiser chains – Walmart and Target – tapping more heavily into pet medications."); *id.* at 160, 165-68 (citing examples of retailers that offer pet medications at significantly lower prices than veterinarians).

[99] *See, e.g.*, Carrier Comment; Higgins Comment; Busansky Comment; Kaplan Comment.

[100] *See* Siegel, *supra* note 33, at 30-32 (stating that Walmart, Target, Walgreens, and Kroger are all offering discount pet medications as a way to lure pet owners into their stores, and that regional grocers and pharmacies also see an opportunity in the pet medications market); Smith, *supra* note 56 (describing how Kroger offers hundreds of prescription pet medications at all of its pharmacy locations throughout 31 states, and that many of these products are included in Kroger's generic drug program, through which typical dosages are available for $4 for a 30-day supply or $10 for a 90-day supply); Karla Bowsher, *How to Get $4 Generic Pet Meds*, MONEYTALKS NEWS, (Mar. 1, 2012), http:// www.moneytalksnews.com/2012/03/01/how-to-get-4-generic-pet-meds/ (stating that Target and Kroger offer $4 discount pet medications); *Don't Automatically Get Pet Medicines From the Vet*, CONSUMER REPORTS (Aug. 2011), http:// www.consumerreports. org/cro/magazine-archive/2011/august/money/pet-costs/dont-automatically-get-pet-medicines-from-the-vet/index.htm (suggesting that consumers can save money on pet care costs by shopping for less expensive pet medications at chain drugstores, supermarket pharmacies, big-box retailers, or online veterinary pharmacies). "For one-time prescriptions, you might be willing to pay extra for the convenience of getting the drugs at your vet's office. You might not have a choice in an emergency. But especially for medications that you'll be buying repeatedly for a pet's chronic conditions, you should consider going elsewhere. Ask your vet to quote a price and give you a written prescription, then call around." *Id.* at 33.

[101] *See* PACKAGED FACTS REPORT 3D, *supra* note 12, at 155 (stating that individual veterinarians are forced to compete for sales of OTC and prescription pet medications with large online retailers that have substantial buying clout). Some veterinarians have complained that many retail outlets sell pet medications at prices that are lower than the price at which most small veterinary clinics could purchase these products. It has been suggested that veterinary

clinics could purchase pet medications through veterinary group purchasing organizations ("GPOs") or other buying cooperatives, in an effort to obtain more advantageous volume-based pricing. Indeed, it appears this is may already be happening. *See* Edie Lau, *Group Purchasing Activity on Upswing in Veterinary Medicine,* VIN NEWS SERV. (Feb. 28, 2013), http://news.vin.com/VINNews.aspx?articleId=26218.

[102] *See* AVMA FAQS, *supra* note 52, at 4.

[103] *See* K&L Gates Comment at 7 ("The process of veterinarian dispensing, however, suffers from numerous inefficiencies. Pharmacies are set up to dispense drugs in an efficient, cost-effective and compliant manner. Pharmacies are generally able to stock more products than veterinarian offices and provide better pricing due to the larger volume of drugs that they dispense.").

[104] *See* Lowell Ackerman, Dir., Veterinary Bus. Solutions, Pfizer Animal Health, Remarks at the American Animal Hospital Association Annual Conference: Barbarians at the Gate: Managing the Veterinary Pharmacy in a Time of Extreme Outside Competition (Mar. 16, 2012) (stating that there is increased pressure on veterinary pricing strategies, and that veterinarians must respond accordingly if they want to remain competitively viable); Siegel, *supra* note 33, at 32 (stating that Ron Brakke, a leading pharmaceutical consultant, "maintains that price matching is veterinarians' most effective method for dealing with big-box encroachment, and more of them ought to be doing it."); WENDY S. MYERS, FIGHT FOR YOUR PHARMACY IN A COMPETITIVE MARKET (n.d.), http:// mycomm.fatcow.com/ library/fight_for_your_pharmacy_in_a_competitive_market.pdf (providing advice to veterinarians about how to better compete against retail pharmacies); AM. ANIMAL HOSP. ASS'N, THE VETERINARY FEE REFERENCE 245 (8th ed. 2013) (describing the market pressure that veterinarians face from online and retail pharmacies offering pet medications at reduced prices, and encouraging veterinarians to monitor competing retailers' prices so that they can respond accordingly; "Many practices have lowered their prices to be reasonably competitive with other outlets; it is difficult to charge a great deal more for these products when clients are aware of the prices elsewhere."); Edie Lau, *Target Tests Market for Pet Medications*, VIN NEWS SERV. (Dec. 22, 2010), http:// news.vin.com/ VINNews. aspx?articleId=17307 [hereinafter Lau, *Target Tests Market*] ("Certainly the expanding availability of pet medications beyond the clinic is putting pressure on veterinary hospital owners."); Maddigan (Willamette Valley Animal Hosp.) Comment.

[105] Lau, *Parasiticide Diversion*, *supra* note 56 (providing examples of veterinarians who monitor the prices of online competition and set their prices to be comparable); Workshop Tr. at 245-46 (Link Welborn) ("The reality is that most [veterinary] practices set prices at, slightly above or slightly below the prices of online outlets with many practices matching the lowest price available online."); *id.* at 193 (Douglas G. Aspros) (stressing that pricing offered by veterinarians is competitive with retail channel pricing, due largely to the pricing transparency available through the Internet); Arp, *supra* note 35 (quoting veterinary consultant who suggests that when possible, veterinarians should compete on price, which means knowing what online pharmacies and big-box outlets charge so that veterinarians can respond accordingly; "There's no doubt that veterinarians are feeling the competitive pressure." The article goes on to state that, "Practitioners are selling more units at cheaper prices per unit to keep up with the competition.").

[106] *See* Workshop Tr. at 245-46 (Link Welborn) ("In our practice, clients are often surprised to find that the pricing in our hospital is slightly less than that available from online sources."); *id.* at 38 (Paul D. Pion); Generic Animal Drug Alliance (GADA) Comment at 2 ("Informal surveys and anecdotal information from veterinarians suggest that online retailers do not offer much if any discount over veterinarians' prices."); Ackerman, *supra* note 104 (pointing out that there is not a significant gap between Internet retail prices and vet prices, but noting that big box retailers offer lower prices than Internet retailers).

[107] PetMed Express, Inc., *supra* note 21, at 7 (noting that a significant portion of sales is attributable to the most popular flea and tick and heartworm preventative brands);

PACKAGED FACTS REPORT 3D, *supra* note 12, at 37 ("The most active area of consumer pet medications is the largest one, flea/tick care, especially in the spot-ons (topical) segment."); PACKAGED FACTS REPORT 2D, *supra* note 14, at 50 ("the heartworm segment continues to see increased competition resulting in higher-level marketing support and heightened consumer awareness."); *id.* at 67 ("From a consumer brand perspective, flea/tick care is the most important category in the U.S. market for pet medications, as well as the largest. During 2011, flea/tick care medications rang up over $2 billion at retail, Packaged Facts estimates, with spot-on treatments accounting for the large majority of this amount. Not surprisingly therefore, this has long been the most directly competitive area of the pet medications market, and now all the more so due to channel cross-over and the arrival on the scene of generic versions of fipronil (Frontline) …").

[108] *See infra* notes 129-130 and accompanying text.

[109] AM. ANIMAL HOSP. ASS'N, *supra* note 104, at 245. Veterinary consultants frequently counsel veterinarians to use competitive pricing for these categories of products because they are being competitively shopped by clients. *See, e.g.*, Lowell Ackerman, Dir., Veterinary Bus. Solutions, Pfizer Animal Health, Remarks at American Animal Hospital Association Annual Conference: Keeping Your Eye on the Prize: Increasing Hospital Profitability (Mar. 16, 2012).

[110] By contrast, consumers usually must request portable prescriptions from veterinarians, at which time they may be asked to pay an additional fee or sign a waiver. *See infra* notes 249 and 253 and accompanying text.

[111] *See* Workshop Tr. at 149-50 (Nate Smith). Physicians generally are discouraged from dispensing medications, to avoid any conflicts of interest. *See infra* notes 115 and 116.

[112] *See* Foster (F&S) Comment at 8 ("To be clear, I also am firmly in favor of maintaining the ability of veterinarians to dispense medications, as opposed to the model in human medicine where physicians are generally discouraged from dispensing for profit."); K&L Gates Comment at 7 ("Veterinarian dispensing is still a viable option that should be preserved for those consumers who are willing to pay a higher price for the convenience of receiving their pet's drugs before they leave their veterinarian's office.").

[113] *See infra* notes 131-133 and accompanying text.

[114] Magee (F&S) Comment at 12-13. *See generally infra* note 295 and accompanying text.

[115] AMA Opinion 8.06 regarding the prescribing and dispensing of drugs states that:

(1) Physicians should prescribe drugs, devices, and other treatments based solely upon medical considerations and patient need and reasonable expectations of the effectiveness of the drug, device or other treatment for the particular patient. (2) Physicians may not accept any kind of payment or compensation from a drug company or device manufacturer for prescribing its products. . . . (3). . . Physicians may dispense drugs within their office practices provided such dispensing primarily benefits the patient. (4) In all instances, physicians should respect the patient's freedom of choice in selecting who will fill their prescriptions as they are in the choice of a physician and, therefore, have the right to have the prescription filled wherever they wish. . . . Physicians should not urge patients to fill prescriptions from an establishment which has entered into a business or other preferential arrangement with the physician with respect to the filling of the physician's prescriptions. . . . (6) Patients have an ethically and legally recognized right to prompt access to the information contained in their individual medical records. Since a prescription is part of the patient's medical record, the patient is entitled to a copy of the physician's prescription for drugs or devices, including eyeglassses and contact lenses. Therefore, physicians should not discourage patients from requesting a written copy of a prescription.

Opinion 8.06 - Prescribing and Dispensing Drugs and Devices, AM. MED. ASS'N (June 2002), http://www.ama-assn.org/ama/pub/physician-resources/medical-ethics/code-medical-ethics/opinion806.page (AMA Code of Medical Ethics).

[116] AMA Opinion 8.03 regarding conflicts of interest states that:

Under no circumstances may physicians place their own financial interests above the welfare of their patients. The primary objective of the medical profession is to render service to humanity; reward or financial gain is a subordinate consideration. For a physician to unnecessarily hospitalize a patient, prescribe a drug, or conduct diagnostic tests for the physician's financial benefit is unethical. If a conflict develops between the physician's financial interest and the physician's responsibilities to the patient, the conflict must be resolved to the patient's benefit.

Opinion 8.03 – Conflicts of Interest: Guidelines, AM. MED. ASS'N (June 1994), http://www.ama-assn.org/ama/pub/physician-resources/medical-ethics/code-medical-ethics/opinion803.page (AMA Code of Medical Ethics).

[117] *See infra* Section IV.B.1, Limited Consumer Access to Generic Animal Drugs, at 84; *infra* Section IV.B.5, Automatic Substitution Might Increase Consumer Access to Generic Animal Drugs, at 90. Some consumers have questioned why they pay more for human generic medications when prescribed for use in animals than when they are prescribed for humans. *See, e.g.*, Colligan Comment. However, pet owners may be receiving different dosages and formulations for use in animals that are higher priced. In addition, drugs for human use are usually covered by health insurance, whereas drugs for animal use may not be covered.

[118] Foster (F&S) Comment at 7. Workshop Tr. at 146-48 (Race Foster).

[119] Foster (F&S) Comment at 9.

[120] *See infra* Section III.B.3.b, Safety Issues Regarding Retail Pharmacists, at 45.

[121] *See* AVDA Comment at 12-13; Greeley Comment.

[122] *See, generally* INST. MED., COMM. ON QUALITY OF HEALTH CARE IN AM., TO ERR IS HUMAN: BUILDING A SAFER HEALTH SYSTEM 2 (1999) ("Medication errors alone, occurring either in or out of the hospital, are estimated to account for over 7,000 deaths annually."); INST. MED., COMM. ON IDENTIFYING AND PREVENTING MEDICATION ERRORS, PREVENTING MEDICATION ERRORS (2007) 1-2 ("The committee estimates that on average, a hospital patient is subject to at least one medication error per day, with considerable variation in error rates across facilities.").

[123] *See* Workshop Tr. at 269 (Link Welborn) (stating that he is unaware of any data measuring adverse events or medication dispensing errors occurring at veterinary clinics); JoNel Aleccia, *When Vets Make Mistakes, Pets Pay the Price*, NBCNEWS.COM (Feb. 10, 2010), http://www.nbcnews.com/id/35286379/ns/health-pet_health/t/when-vets- make-mistakes-pets-pay-price/ (claiming that medical errors made by veterinarians, including those involving medications, are not routinely tracked and investigated the way they are in the human market). *See also infra* Section V.B.2, Pet Medications Dispensing Errors, at 93.

[124] *See* James F. Wilson & John A. Rossi, *Medical error and liability: How technology can be a safeguard*, DVM360.COM/DVM360 MAG. (Apr. 1, 2008), http:// veterinarynews. dvm360.com/medical-error-and-liability-how- technology-can-be-safeguard ("The rate of error in human medicine is well documented and staggeringly high. The soaring costs of professional liability insurance for physicians and hospitals is forcing human medicine to take steps to reduce error rates. As veterinarians, it can be assumed that we commit just as many errors and for the same reasons. Reducing them in the interest of better patient care should be a priority."); Aleccia, *supra* note 123 (stating that industry experts believe the occurrence of veterinary medical errors is likely comparable to medical errors in the human market).

[125] *See* U.S. FOOD & DRUG ADMIN., MEDICATION ERRORS HAPPEN TO PETS, TOO (2012), http://www.fda.gov/downloads/ForConsumers/ConsumerUpdates/UCM327172.pdf; *Product Safety Information: Veterinary Medication Errors*, U.S. FOOD & DRUG ADMIN., http://www.fda.gov/AnimalVeterinary/SafetyHealth/ProductSafetyInformation/ucm380574.htm (last updated July 28, 2014).

[126] Telephone Interview with Linda Kim-Jung, Martine Hartogensis, John Baker, Janice Steinschneider, and others from FDA CVM, Office of Surveillance and Compliance (Sept.

11, 2014). CVM's post-market safety surveillance program utilizes pharmacovigilance database applications to monitor for adverse events, lack of effectiveness, product defects and medication errors. CVM can use this information to evaluate trends and relative frequencies of reported adverse drug experiences. However, the adverse event data do have limitations. For any given adverse event report, there is no certainty that the reported drug caused the adverse event or medication error. The adverse event may have been related to an underlying disease, using other drugs at the same time, or other non- drug related causes. The number of reports simply represents the numbers of adverse events received for a particular drug, by species, and route of administration. For additional information on adverse drug experience reports, please refer to: http:// www.fda.gov/ AnimalVeterinary/ SafetyHealth/ProductSafetyInformation/ucm055369.htm. *Id.*

[127] Workshop Tr. at 53 (John Powers). *See also* PACKAGED FACTS REPORT 3D, *supra* note 12, at 171 ("Packaged Facts views the [H.R. 1406] initiative as indicative of the way the pet health market is moving – toward greater parallelism with human healthcare – a natural progression as pets continue to gain status in American society.").

[128] *See* Telephone Interview with Kim-Jung et al., *supra* note 126 (indicating that counterfeit drug issues appear to be a bigger problem for human medications than for animal medications, and that a bigger problem exists for unapproved pet products, which include such products as compounded drugs, medicated shampoos, and vitamins).

[129] *See id.* at 174 (Race Foster); PetCareRx Comment at 1.

[130] Workshop Tr. at 172-73 (Wendy Hauser).

[131] *See* GADA Comment at 2 ("Some treatments take place in the veterinary practices (such as with an injectable medication), while the majority of drugs are dispensed to pet owners for a prescribed treatment regimen (for example, antibiotic tablets to be dosed at home)."); Workshop Tr. at 181 (Deborah Dubow Press) ("When we know that it will result in significant cost savings, we will affirmatively suggest that the prescription be filled elsewhere, and when it will benefit the client and the patient that's what we do. Certain medicines, we can't do this for. They're not available at retail pharmacies."). *But see* Gay (VetRxDirect) Comment (#576) ("There are hundreds of veterinary prescription medications for pets, each with their own indications, contraindications, and side-effects. Some are proven safe (like canine heartworm preventatives) and could be dispensed by a non-knowledgeable pharmacist or pharmacy, but the dispensing of the majority of veterinary prescription medicines require the special knowledge of a veterinarian or the suitable, similar training in veterinary pharmacy and pharmacology of a pharmacist.").

[132] Workshop Tr. at 172-73 (Wendy Hauser); *id.* at 181-82 (Douglas G. Aspros). Other situations in which only veterinarians can practically dispense prescription pet medications may include euthanasia, anesthesia used during surgery, and certain injectables requiring veterinarian oversight.

[133] *See supra* note 72.

[134] According to the AVMA, 21 states have adopted laws, regulations, or policy statements requiring veterinarians to provide their clients with portable prescriptions upon request, and another 10 states have incorporated the AVMA Principles of Veterinary Medical Ethics into their disciplinary rules, which state that veterinarians should honor a client's request for a portable prescription. *See State Summary Report: Client Request for Prescriptions*, AM. VETERINARY MED. ASS'N, https:// www.avma.org/ Advocacy/ StateAndLocal/ Pages/ veterinary-prescription- orders.aspx (last updated May 2014).

[135] CAL. BUS. & PROF. CODE § 4170(a)(6)-(7) (2014).

[136] ARIZ. ADMIN. CODE R3-11-801 (2014).

[137] *Principles of Veterinary Medical Ethics of the AVMA*, *supra* note 38 (Principle II.b.).

[138] *State Summary Report: Client Request for Prescriptions*, *supra* note 134; Workshop Tr. at 139 (Adrian Hochstadt). *But see* Valley Vet Supply Comment at 4 ("In reality, the AVMA position does very little to effectuate written portable prescriptions, or to ensure consumer choice or price competition. That will only happen when mandated by law.").

[139] AVMA Comment at 5 ("Even in states that have not adopted formal laws or regulations in this area, state boards of veterinary medicine could find . . . that failure to honor a client's request for a prescription constitutes unprofessional conduct, leading to discipline against a veterinarian."). *See also* Pfizer Comment (#329) at 3 (noting that "state laws, regulations, policies and veterinary ethical codes of conduct ensure that if a consumer wants a prescription, he or she should receive it.").

[140] Although some veterinarians may refuse to provide portable prescriptions upon request, FTC staff found almost no evidence of disciplinary actions taken against veterinarians by state boards for failure to provide prescriptions (even in California, which has the most stringent prescription portability requirements). It is unclear whether the absence of disciplinary actions indicates substantial veterinary compliance, few consumer complaints, or a lack of active enforcement by state boards.

[141] *See, e.g.*, B. Taylor Comment; A. Anderson Comment.

[142] *See* N. Smith Comment at 8 & Kroger Comment at 1 (describing a situation in which a consumer's only practical choice is to purchase a pet medication from the prescribing veterinarian at an inflated price or switch to another veterinarian who will charge for a second examination before being able to provide a portable prescription).

[143] *See, e.g.*, AVMA Comment at 1 (stating that veterinarians already write prescriptions for clients); AHI Comment at 4 ("It is our view that under current law and practice veterinarians will provide written prescriptions to clients upon request."); Bradley Comment; A. Anderson Comment; Brown Comment (#521). Veterinarian surveys conducted by state veterinary medical associations in Oregon, Washington, southern California, and Iowa suggest that many veterinarians provide prescriptions to their clients upon request. *See* OR. VETERINARY MED. ASS'N, VETERINARY PRESCRIPTIONS & RETAIL PHARMACIES SUMMARY: MEMBERSHIP SURVEY 2 (2012) [hereinafter OR. VET SURVEY], *attached to* Oregon VMA Comment (#175) (Oregon VMA sent a survey to approximately 525 veterinary practices in the state of Oregon and received responses from 21%. The survey indicated that 95% of responding veterinarians honor client requests for prescriptions); WASH. STATE VETERINARY MED. ASS'N, WSVMA PRESCRIPTION MEDICATION SURVEY (2013) [hereinafter WASH. VET SURVEY] (on file with report authors) (Washington VMA sent a survey to 2387 veterinarians, and received 332 responses. The survey indicated that 96% of responding veterinarians honor client requests for prescriptions); S. CAL. VETERINARY MED. ASS'N, SCVMA VETERINARY PRESCRIPTIONS AND MEDICATION SURVEY (2013) [hereinafter S. CAL. VET SURVEY] (on file with report authors) (Southern California VMA sent a survey to 1000 veterinary members and received 108 responses. The survey indicated that 96% of responding veterinarians honor client requests for prescriptions); IOWA VETERINARY MED. ASS'N, IVMA MEMBER SURVEY (2012) [HEREINAFTER IOWA VET SURVEY] (on file with report authors) (Iowa VMA sent a survey to approximately 900-1000 active veterinarians and received 100 responses. The survey indicated that 77% of responding veterinarians honor client requests for prescriptions).

[144] Axxiom Market Analysis, *supra* note 21, at 6. Bureau of Labor Statistics data indicates that there were 61,400 practicing veterinarians in the United States in 2010. *Veterinarians: Occupational Outlook Handbook*, BUREAU OF LABOR STATISTICS (Apr. 29, 2012), https://web.archive.org/web/20120429053206/http://www.bls.gov/ooh/Healthcare/Veterinarians.htm (site snapshot saved on Internet Archive WayBack Machine). Thus, according to the Axxiom Market Analysis, over 70% of veterinarians provided at least one written prescription.

[145] Pfizer Comment (#329) at 2.

[146] The circumstances surrounding these prescription releases remain unclear, making it difficult to draw conclusions about the prevalence of veterinary prescription release. For example, if veterinarians typically offer prescriptions only for products they do not keep in inventory, this data may reveal little about the extent to which veterinarians routinely offer, or provide

upon request, portable prescriptions for products that they do keep in inventory. Furthermore, without knowing the total number of prescription pet medications dispensed by veterinarians and retail pharmacists each year, it is difficult to determine the frequency with which veterinarians issue portable prescriptions based on this data alone.

[147] Workshop Tr. at 179-80 (Douglas G. Aspros); AVMA Comment at 1-2.

[148] *See, e.g.*, Foster (F&S) Comment at 6-7; Workshop Tr. at 178 (Race Foster) ("There's no question that the veterinary profession today is more likely to give out a prescription. I think the American Veterinary Medical Association has done an excellent job of talking to their constituents and educating them."). *See also* PACKAGED FACTS REPORT 2D, *supra* note 14, at 12 ("Well aware of the Internet competition, some veterinarians have been reluctant to write prescriptions for online pharmacies, but the American Veterinary Medical Association ("AVMA") has advised its members that pet owners have a right to shop around, while noting that the Vet-VIPPS designation should help vets and pet owners identify legitimate online pharmacies.").

[149] *See, e.g.*, Gay (VetRxDirect) Comment (#576) ("In my experience, veterinarians are now over the initial shock of losing the exclusive dispensing business and are gradually, if not completely cooperative in providing a prescription to a pet-owning client if requested."); Pedersen Comment (noting that vets have been writing more prescriptions in recent years, regardless of whether clients request them, in order to lower their inventory costs). *See also* Oregon VMA Comment (#175) at 1 ("According to the [veterinary] practices that responded to the survey, a significant majority of them will, at the client's request, write a prescription to be filled outside of the practice. In addition, most veterinary practices DO NOT charge a prescription fee for this service.").

[150] *See* AM. ANIMAL HOSP. ASS'N, *supra* note 104, at 245 ("[Prescription] drugs are available online, and many human pharmacies are offering certain drugs for almost nothing. Clients are aware of this and are asking their veterinarians for cheaper alternatives. Veterinarians have reacted in various ways. Some have switched to drugs that are not available in human pharmacies or are not included in the list of those sold at very low cost. Others recommend to their clients that they buy those drugs at the human pharmacy for the significant cost savings; a great deal of client goodwill can be generated this way, and the long-term bonding of the client to the practice may outweigh the short-term loss of income."); Lowell Ackerman, Dir., Veterinary Bus. Solutions, Pfizer Animal Health, Remarks at American Animal Hospital Association Annual Conference: Promoting Practice Protocols (Mar. 16, 2012).

[151] *See infra* note 191.

[152] K&L Gates Comment at 8 (representing sentiments expressed in other comments and stakeholder interviews). *See also* PetMed Express, Inc., *supra* note 21, at 7 ("Since we began our operations some veterinarians have resisted providing our customers with a copy of their pet's prescription or authorizing the prescription to our pharmacy staff, thereby effectively preventing us from filling such prescriptions under state law. We have also been informed by customers and consumers that veterinarians have tried to discourage pet owners from purchasing from Internet and mail-order pharmacies."); Valley Vet Supply Comment at 2-3 ("It is common for practicing veterinarians to make it difficult or impossible for the client to purchase their prescription products from a source other than the attending veterinarian. . . . Veterinarians use a variety of manipulative tactics to deny the clients the free-market option of filling their prescription at a licensed pharmacy." These tactics include making unfounded claims about the quality of products provided by retail pharmacies, adopting practice policies of not providing portable prescriptions, charging a substantial fee for writing the prescription, suggesting that they will not provide follow-up care if medications are purchased elsewhere, or refusing to provide an open prescription and instead directing clients to an affiliate pharmacy that shares a portion of the revenues with the prescribing veterinarian.); Arp, *supra* note 35 (referencing veterinarians who charge prescription fees of up to $17 or institute policies of not writing prescriptions for any online

pharmacy); MYERS, *supra* note 104, at 2-3 (instructing veterinarians how to discourage pet owners from having prescriptions filled elsewhere).

[153] *See* OR. VET SURVEY, *supra* note 143, at 2 (indicating that 5% of surveyed practices do not honor a client's request to have a prescription filled outside of the veterinary practice and 7% charge a fee when the client fills the prescription outside of the veterinary practice); WASH. VET SURVEY, *supra* note 143 (indicating that 4% of responding veterinarians do not honor client requests for prescriptions and 4% charge a fee); S. CAL. VET SURVEY, *supra* note 143 (indicating that 4% of responding veterinarians do not honor client requests for prescriptions and 7% charge a fee); IOWA VET SURVEY, *supra* note 143 (indicating that 23% of responding veterinarians do not honor client requests for prescriptions and 29% charge a fee).

[154] *See, e.g.*, Foster (F&S) Comment at 7 ("By various methods a minority of veterinarians are putting pressure on their clients to purchase prescriptions only from them, the veterinarian. These methods include requiring consumers to sign waivers and/or pay an 'extra' fee if they choose to fill prescriptions anywhere other than the veterinarian's office."); Magee (F&S) Comment at 8 ("Most veterinarians handle consumer choice well, and follow the AVMA guideline that says written prescriptions should be given when a client asks. Many even offer a written prescription without the client having to ask. . . . However, not all veterinarians handle prescription writing as the majority do."); ASPCA Comment at 2 ("While many veterinarians are happy to provide written prescriptions for clients to fill anywhere they choose, not all veterinarians offer this option.").

[155] We received public comments from several individual consumers raising these types of concerns. *See, e.g.*, S. Clark Comment; Baragiola Comment; Gonzalez Comment; Yoo Comment; West Comment; Ellis Comment; Brady Comment; Chesko Comment; Higgins Comment; Martin Comment; Sherman Comment; Hirsch Comment; Roth Comment; Holum Comment; Loehrer Comment; Hilton Comment.

In addition, several veterinarian comments included in state veterinary medical association surveys indicate that at least some veterinarians are reluctant to provide prescriptions to clients upon request and try to discourage clients from seeking portable prescriptions. *See, e.g.*, IOWA VET SURVEY, *supra* note 143 (Responses to survey question asking whether veterinarians provide prescriptions for clients to fill at an online outlet or retail pharmacy include: "Never been asked and I would charge for that service."; "I do not provide prescriptions for on line pharmacies but I often will call prescriptions in to local pharmacies for medications I do not carry."; "I try to fill all prescriptions in house. For those that go elsewhere I charge a fee."; "We charge $8/script to do this, so we don't get too many"; "Generally i [sic] try and price match, or ask the client why they wish to have their prescriptions filled elsewhere first."; "very seldom"; "We aggressively price match online prices to attempt to keep the clients business, while educating the client of the concern of proper storage, counterfeit product, non US-label product, etc., and the difficulty managing an issue if a problem develops from an unknown compound."; "We do this on a limited basis only"; "Very seldom and very reluctantly"); S. CAL. VET SURVEY, *supra* note 143 ("Usually able to steer clients away from online pharmacies."; "We require that the client picks up a written script to mail into the online retailer. . . . This way it takes almost 2 weeks for them to get the drug and by then they are frustrated and realize its not worth the savings."; "I am concerned with the lack of response/action from the veterinary profession (stricter guidelines/regulations for these outside pharmacies esp online?). Pharmacy is a part of our bottom line and we should do what we can to keep these customers/clients.").

[156] *Compare, e.g.*, Workshop Tr. at 154, 180 (Wendy Hauser) (stating that she routinely offers to write portable prescriptions for clients, especially when significant cost savings are possible), *and id.* at 171-72 (stating that there are many circumstances in which veterinarians will choose not to stock certain medications and will instead choose to write portable prescriptions for the clients to take to retail or compounding pharmacies), *with id.* at 155 (stating that she fails to see how clients and their pets benefit when they are given

portable prescriptions, and that she believes "if H.R. 1406 is enacted, that drug-induced adverse events will occur and will cause harm."), *and id.* at 186 ("You bet I have my clients sign a waiver if they want to order online, and the reason that I do is because I can't guarantee the safety of those drugs.").

Compare AVMA Comment at 3 ("Given that not all veterinarians, particularly mobile practitioners, are able to stock every prescription product they might prescribe for their patients, there is an efficiency associated with pharmacies carrying certain prescription products."), *with id.* ("[T]reatment with medications dispensed directly from a veterinary clinic can be started promptly and there are no anticipated concerns associated with the quality of the drug product. . . . [P]harmacists are not required to have training in animal pharmacology. . . . We have learned that this has resulted in incorrect counseling, wrong dosages, or unauthorized drug substitutions, which could harm animal patients and create the need for additional treatment that would have been unnecessary had the correct medications or information been dispensed initially.").

See also Pedersen Comment (stating that veterinarians are providing more prescriptions in recent years to reduce inventory costs, even when they are not requested, but opposing any requirements to provide prescriptions in all instances due to safety concerns regarding retail pharmacies and potential losses in pharmacy revenues); Neely Comment (claiming to already routinely provide prescriptions to clients to be filled by retail pharmacies, often when they are not even requested, yet also claiming that "[m]ost human pharmacists are not adequately trained to fill pet medications"); Malon Comment ("Veterinarians already provide prescriptions when asked and direct clients to appropriate sources. Human pharmacists are not trained in veterinary prescriptions and can make dangerous or even fatal mistakes . . ."); Hearing on L.D. 676 Before the J. Standing Comm. on Agriculture, Conservation, and Forestry, 215th Leg., 1st Reg. Sess. (Me. 2011) [hereinafter Maine Hearing on L.D. 676] (separate statements from 15 veterinarians opposing L.D. 676) (stating that veterinarians already provide prescriptions upon request and sometimes offer prescriptions to save clients' money, despite their expressed concerns).

[157] *See, e.g.*, N. Smith Comment at 3 ("[I]t is incongruous for veterinarians to claim both that they release prescriptions but that there is a negative health impact when they do release. If there was any quantifiable or realistic health concern with release, the AVMA would have never adopted provisions in its Principles of Veterinarian Medical Ethics stating in an unqualified manner that 'veterinarians should honor a client's request for a prescription in lieu of dispensing.'"). *See also* K&L Gates Comment at 6 ("While it is true that many state-level veterinary practice ethical rules call for veterinarians to provide a prescription upon customer request, these rules fail to take into account the natural trepidation that pet owners feel in requesting a prescription. In actual practice, if the prescribed drug is stocked by the veterinarians, the office staff typically provides the drug at check-out without any mention of the customer's other options. Only when the veterinarian elects not to stock the prescribed drug is the customer typically provided with a prescription. Thus, the veterinarians' reluctance to an *obligation* to provide notice of the availability of a prescription is not based on safety. If it were, veterinarians would presumably stock all necessary drugs and write no prescriptions. Rather, the stated reluctance is based in economics and the potential profits provided by veterinarian-dispensed drugs."). Veterinarians employed by the ASPCA will affirmatively suggest that their clients fill prescriptions elsewhere if they know that doing so will be significantly less expensive. Workshop Tr. at 164 (Deborah Dubow Press). An ASPCA representative confirmed that the ASPCA would not have adopted this policy if the organization believed serious safety concerns existed with respect to retail pharmacies. Telephone Interview with ASPCA representative (Sept. 18, 2012). However, "[t]he ASPCA always counsels clients to avoid purchasing drugs from non-U.S. sources and to purchase drugs from reputable pharmacies, whether on or off-line." ASPCA Comment at 3.

[158] *See, e.g.*, Greeley Comment.

[159] *See Are Veterinarians Eligible to Obtain NPIs?*, CTRS. FOR MEDICARE & MEDICAID SERVS., https://questions.cms.gov/faq.php?id=5005&faqId=8240 (clarification issued by CMS); Email from Or. Veterinary Med. Ass'n & Or. Bd. of Pharmacy to Licensees (May 2014), http://www.oregon.gov/pharmacy/Pages/oboplistserve.aspx (noting that CMS has clarified that veterinarians are ineligible for NPI numbers and stressing that this should not be a barrier to prescription processing).

[160] *See, e.g.*, Greeley Comment; Stevens Comment; Kordell Comment (#298).

[161] *See* Email from Or. Veterinary Med. Ass'n & Or. Bd. of Pharmacy, *supra* note 159 (instructing Oregon pharmacies that dispense veterinary prescriptions to request practitioners' veterinary license numbers rather than their DEA numbers).

[162] *See, e.g.*, K&L Gates Comment at 10 ("Veterinarian dispensing has been the norm for so long that many pet owners may not be aware of the fact that their pet's drugs may be available at a lower price from their local pharmacy."). *See also* Workshop Tr. at 82-83 (Paul D. Pion) (stating that pet owners should be more informed about their ability to obtain a prescription from their veterinarian so that they may choose to purchase pet medications elsewhere, and suggesting that perhaps veterinarians should do more to inform pet owners in this regard, but that "it shouldn't be at the expense of ensuring that the medications are dispensed appropriately with appropriate ability to counsel.").

[163] *See, e.g.*, Indep. Pharmacy Alliance Comment at 2 ("In many states, the practice of obtaining pet medications is governed in veterinarian profession practices law. Not surprisingly, many states give veterinarians great control and/or influence over how pet owners access pet medications. While many states give these owners the right to a prescription, often it is a passive right to request a prescription rather than the automatic requirement that a prescription be generated. And in many states, there is virtually no assurance that a pet owner will know they have the right to obtain a pet medication from a retail pharmacy rather than a veterinarian's office or a veterinary hospital. . . . With these laws allowing veterinarians to essentially control the market of dispensing pet medications, pet owners are not given all of the economic advantages of competition in filling these medications, nor the convenience and choice of when and where to fill these pet medications."); K&L Gates Comment at 11 ("H.R. 1406 would ensure that veterinarians cannot preserve their monopoly by remaining silent and relying on their position of authority to prevent competition.").

[164] Workshop Tr. at 151, 183 (Nate Smith). Smith argues that this principle underlies both the FTC's Eyeglass Rule and the FCLCA. N. Smith Comment at 5. Indeed, the cornerstone of the FTC's Eyeglass Rule and Contact Rule (which implements the FCLCA) is that automatic prescription release helps to ensure the availability of eyeglass and contact lens prescriptions so that consumers can choose among sellers of these products. *See infra* note 180. *See also* Zeidner (1-800-CONTACTS) Comment at 1-2 (stating that "by request" prescription release laws are unenforceable, discriminatory, and ineffective and that automatic prescription release was the best way to raise consumer awareness of their ability to purchase eyeglasses and contact lenses from a retailer other than their prescriber).

[165] *See* Boylan Comment (#255) (describing the awkwardness of requesting a prescription from a veterinarian from the perspective of a pet owner); Maine Hearing on L.D. 676, *supra* note 156 (statement of Curtis Picard, Exec. Dir. of the Me. Merchants Ass'n and pet owner) (describing a recent experience purchasing pet medications from a veterinary clinic: "After the visit with the vet, the assistant came into the exam room, told us we were all set and the prescriptions would be ready for us out front. At no time was I told that I had the option of getting the prescription filled elsewhere nor was I told what the prescriptions would cost. . . . I don't know if the two medications I was prescribed could have been filled elsewhere at a dramatically different price. However, I felt like an uneducated consumer and felt like I had no power in the transaction. The price could have been any amount. I understand only from researching this bill that I could have asked for a prescription and sought to have it filled

somewhere else. I am sure that only a very small percentage of Mainers know that this is permitted and take advantage of it.").

See also PetMed Express, Inc., Annual Report (Form 10-K) 4 (May 29, 2012), http://www.sec.gov/Archives/edgar/data/1040130/000118811212001799/t73684_10k.htm (stating that many pet owners "may be hesitant to offend their veterinarian by not purchasing these products from the veterinarian."); N. Smith Comment at 5-6 ("In any event, when it comes to prescription release, such "by request" provisions do not work. They do not provide pet owners with the same level of knowledge regarding their ability to choose alternatives which automatic release provides. They put the pet owner squarely in the crosshairs of the conflict of interest, placing him or her in the difficult, and often intimidating position of having to ask a health provider for permission to purchase products elsewhere.").

[166] *See, e.g.*, Workshop Tr. at 175-76 (Deborah Dubow Press) (". . . some people are savvier shoppers than others. Some people are more assertive than others when it comes to speaking out and being advocates for themselves. So, some people just may be more comfortable asking questions of their veterinarians than others.").

[167] *Id.* at 176-78 (Race Foster).

[168] *See id.* at 182 (Nate Smith).

[169] *See id.* at 176, 201-02 (Deborah Dubow Press); N. Smith Comment at 5.

[170] *See* Workshop Tr. at 209 (Wendy Hauser); *id.* at 209-10 (Douglas G. Aspros) (stating that 1-800-PetMeds spent more than $200 million on advertising over the past 10 years informing pet owners that they can request prescriptions and have them filled online); *id.* at 245 (Link Welborn) ("Consumer awareness of a large number of online and discount retail sources of pet medications has increased greatly since 2003, as a result of millions of dollars of advertising. As a result, virtually every pet owner that I see in my practice is aware of these options."); Neely Comment; Pfizer Comment (#329) at 2; AHI Comment at 4. *See also* Maine Hearing on L.D. 676, *supra* note 156 (separate statements from 15 veterinarians) (many stating that their clients are already aware that they can request prescriptions and purchase pet medications from retailers; e.g., testimony submitted by Lawrence Buggia, DVM, Annabessacook Veterinary Clinic, suggesting that retailers, not veterinarians, should be responsible for informing consumers about the option of purchasing pet medications from some place other than the veterinary clinic).

[171] *See supra* description of H.R. 1406, at note 67; H.R. 4023 and S. 2756, at note 72. We are also aware of at least two states where similar legislation was proposed, prompting the question of whether automatic prescription release should be mandated by individual state governments. *See* An Act to Enact Requirements Concerning Veterinary Prescriptions, L.D. 676, 125th Leg., 1st Reg. Sess. (Me. 2011), *available at* http:// www.mainelegislature.org/ legis/bills/getPDF.asp?paper=SP0207&item=1&snum=125; An Act Concerning Veterinarians and Supplementing Chapter 16 of Title 45 of the Revised Statutes, S. 2915, 215th Leg., Reg. Sess. (N.J. 2013), *available at* http:// www.njleg.state.nj.us/ 2012/ Bills/S3000/2915_I1.PDF. Both state bills require veterinarians to notify their clients, both orally and in writing, of the option to obtain prescription items from sources other than the veterinarian, and provide written prescriptions to their clients without imposing an additional fee, regardless of whether the client requests it. The Maine bill was introduced on February 17, 2011, and received a unanimous "Ought Not To Pass" committee vote on May 10, 2011. The New Jersey bill was introduced on July 29, 2013, and was referred to the New Jersey Senate Commerce Committee.

See also Maine VMA Comment (#281) (stating that a hearing on the proposed Maine legislation identified the following issues: (1) errors arise when pet medications are dispensed by anyone other than the veterinarian who has the VCPR; (2) veterinary medications are generally not well-suited for substitution; (3) decisions to substitute generic human medications for veterinary medications should be made by the veterinarian; and (4) the free market is already sorting out consumer choices between online veterinary pharmacies, human retail pharmacies, and veterinary practices). A review of the written testimony submitted to the Maine legislature in connection with this hearing reveals that several veterinarians attended the hearing and voiced concerns with the bill. They provided anecdotal examples of pharmacist dispensing errors, although it is unclear whether any of these cases were submitted to the state pharmacy board for investigation and possible disciplinary action. Maine Hearing on L.D. 676, *supra* note 156 (separate statements from 15 veterinarians).

[172] *See* N. Smith Comment at 5; APAW Coalition Comment at 3 ("By extending long-standing prescription release principles found in the distribution of human medications to the marketplace for pet medications . . . the price of pet medications will decrease. . . . Finally, by giving pet owners the right to receive a copy of their pet prescriptions and the ability to choose the place and location for filling these prescriptions, they will be empowered to make more informed choices . . ."); K&L Gates Comment at 9 (supporting automatic prescription release because it promotes consumer choice and would further enable retail pharmacies to compete in the market for pet medications); NACDS Comment at 2 ("NACDS believes the choice of where to obtain pet medications – both OTC and prescription – should be made by the pet owner. For this reason, we support H.R. 1406, the Fairness to Pet Owners Act . . ."); Hubbard Statement, *supra* note 71, at 6 ("Mandatory release of prescriptions for pets will allow owners to choose more easily where to buy those prescription products. The proposed legislation would reduce the costs to consumers of prescription products both by providing an opportunity for comparison shopping by pet owners and by fostering a more competitive market for those products.").

[173] *See* AVMA Comment at 8; AAHA Comment at 2; SVHP Comment at 1 ("[R]equiring verification of prescriptions, regardless of whether the pharmacy is accredited or licensed, places the veterinarian in both a legal and ethical dilemma. At the same time, it puts consumers at risk . . . ."). *See also* A. Anderson Comment (stating that she only verifies prescriptions to Vet-VIPPS certified pharmacies due to the large number of fraudulent Internet sites selling unsafe products and expressing concerns that H.R. 1406 may deny her the ability to protect her clients from fraudulent Internet sites); J. Forbes Comment ("Being forced to provide a written prescription which a consumer can utilize virtually anywhere is disturbing to me. Presently, I try to guide my clients to the most reputable sources I know when they choose to fill a prescription elsewhere.").

[174] *See supra* Section II.E.2, Effects of Non-Veterinary Retail Competition, at 21.

[175] Currently, laws, regulations, and polices governing prescription release for pet medications vary across states. *See supra* note 134 and accompanying text. Some proponents of automatic prescription release believe that a federal law would "harmonize state laws to provide one consistent guideline for veterinarians" and most importantly, "provide a uniform framework to guide consumer expectations." ASPCA Comment at 4. They argue that a uniform federal measure would raise consumer awareness of the ability to purchase pet medications outside of the prescribing veterinary clinic based on the factors most important to them (e.g. price, convenience, service), thereby facilitating consumer choice and competition. *See* ASPCA Comment at 4; APAW Coalition Comment at 2. However, some proponents of automatic prescription release believe that this can be best accomplished at the state level. The Independent Pharmacy Alliance supports state-level prescription portability efforts and urges the FTC "to endorse policies that give pet owners greater choice over access to pet medications and the economic benefits from greater competition than currently exists in the marketplace." Indep. Pharmacy Alliance Comment at 2.

[176] *See* N. Smith Comment at 5 ("Customer value is a function of having choice across comparable products, convenient access, in combination with price. For many (and likely most) the vet clinic will continue to be the best value or place to shop based on immediate access, service and convenience – even if the price is higher. For others, their familiar pharmacy with lower prices will be the best value."); Workshop Tr. at 174 (Deborah Dubow

Press) (noting that access to a veterinary clinic may be limited in certain areas, whereas access to a pharmacy may be more convenient); PACKAGED FACTS REPORT 3d, *supra* note 12, at 154 ("Consumers are clamoring for choice. . . . 59% of pet owners believe they pay more for pet meds at the vet and 87% would like vets to give them all of their options rather than just dispensing the meds in the office.").

Some stakeholders contend that automatic prescription release would not alter consumer purchasing behavior much, because it is more convenient for pet owners to purchase pet medications from the veterinarian at the time of an office visit. *See, e.g.*, *id.* at 175, 180-81 (Wendy Hauser) (about 50 percent of the cost-sensitive clients to whom she affirmatively offers prescriptions choose to purchase pet medications at the time of the veterinary office visit); PetMed Express, Inc., *supra* note 21, at 7 ("Veterinarians hold a competitive advantage over us because many pet owners may find it more convenient or preferable to purchase these products directly from their veterinarians at the time of an office visit."); ASPCA Comment at 3 ("BMAH [Bergh Memorial Animal Hospital, an ASPCA-run facility] does not have data showing the frequency with which clients fill prescriptions outside of the hospital.

However, given the choice to fill their prescriptions elsewhere, most BMAH clients will fill their prescriptions at the hospital dispensary simply as a matter of convenience.").

[177] *See* K&L Gates Comment at 7 ("Because pioneer companies are able to use the current distribution/dispensing system to greatly limit competition from affordable substitutable products, there is less incentive to develop new animal drugs. A portable prescription system would ensure that competition, in the form of generic drugs dispensed at retail pharmacies, would enter the marketplace as soon as all patents on a pioneer drug expire and thus stimulating pioneer companies to develop new and better proprietary products.").

[178] *See* Foster (F&S) Comment at 7 ("However, putting the burden on the consumer creates pressure and intimidation which can be removed by having the veterinarian offer to provide a written prescription."); Magee (F&S) Comment at 15 ("Veterinarians should consider offering written prescriptions rather than waiting until a consumer asks.").

[179] *See, e.g.*, Lau, *Parasiticide Diversion*, *supra* note 56 (quoting a member of the Society for Veterinary Medical Ethics as stating, "It's clearly a conflict of interest to be prescribing and selling the drug at the same time." She suggested two ways for veterinarians to resolve the conflict: not selling medications at all or proactively offering clients a portable prescription that they can take to a pharmacy if they wish).

[180] *See* Ophthalmic Practice Rules, 69 Fed. Reg. 5451, 5453 (Feb. 4, 2004) (codified at 16 C.F.R. pt. 456) ("Because release might not occur in the absence of a federal release requirement and because release of prescriptions enhances consumer choice at minimal compliance cost to eye care practitioners, the FTC has decided to retain the eyeglass prescription release rule. . . . In the absence of automatic prescription release, these consumers may not know to ask for their prescription, or their eye care practitioner may discourage them from requesting it. With automatic prescription release, these consumers will receive their prescription so that they can comparison shop among eyeglass sellers if they choose to do so."); Contact Lens Rule, 69 Fed. Reg. 40,482 (July 2, 2004) (codified at 16 C.F.R. pts. 315, 456); FED. TRADE COMM'N, THE STRENGTH OF COMPETITION IN THE SALE OF RX CONTACT LENSES (2005), http://www.ftc.gov/sites/default/files/documents/advocacy_documents/strength- competition-sale-rx-contact-lenses-ftc-study/050214contactlensrpt.pdf.

[181] *See* FED. TRADE COMM'N, *supra* note 180, at 50 ("The Eyeglass Rule has improved the ability of consumers to comparison shop for eyeglasses. Its prescription release requirement, in particular, continues to benefit consumers by spurring competition and providing consumers with more choices and lower prices.").

[182] *See* Workshop Tr. at 256 (Hubbard) ("So, I want to give as many alternatives as I can to consumers, and the portability of the prescription is one thing that does."); Hubbard Statement, *supra* note 71, at 5 ("Mandating the release of prescriptions by ECPs has fostered a competitive market for the retail sale of eyeglasses and contact lenses. Consumers

have enjoyed ever-expanding and value driven competitive alternatives for purchasing their eyeglasses and contact lenses."); Workshop Tr. at 261-62 (James C. Cooper) ("[M]ore choice is unambiguously good, even if consumers don't use it."); *id.* at 276 (Robert D. Atkinson); *id.* at 226-27 (Clarke D. Newman) ("The Lens Act was a very good thing for the consumer by creating a framework for prescription acquisition that enabled the patient to shop for the best deal on lens prices.").

[183] *See* Workshop Tr. at 240-42 (James C. Cooper) (describing his empirical research, and stating that "I don't really find any evidence [that the prescription release requirement affected prices], but my takeaway from that isn't that it was a bad idea or that consumers didn't benefit."). Dr. James Cooper, Director of Research and Policy at the George Mason University Law & Economics Center, argued that his research shows offline vendors have not lowered their prices for contact lenses in response to increased competition from online vendors. *Id.* Robert Atkinson, President of the Information Technology & Innovation Foundation, argued that contact lens providers have competed on the basis of price since the passage of the FCLCA, and believes there is evidence that offline vendors have responded to price competition from online vendors. Furthermore, he claimed that there are several price benefits enjoyed by consumers that would not have been captured in the study that Cooper conducted. *Id.* At 238-39, 259 (Robert D. Atkinson).

Other panelists stated their understanding that price competition in the contact lens industry increased significantly since passage of the FCLCA, and that consumers have benefitted. *Id.* at 244-45 (Link Welborn); *id.* At 264-65 (R. Joe Zeidner); Zeidner (1-800 CONTACTS) Comment at 4-10 (providing examples of consumer cost savings and product innovation that he claims have resulted from increased competition for contact lenses). *See also* FED. TRADE COMM'N, *supra* note 180, at 41 tbl.9 (finding that on average, independent eye care professionals charged more than other retail vendors, including wholesale clubs, online vendors, and mass merchandisers). On balance, the evidence suggests that consumers have the potential to achieve significant cost savings by purchasing their contact lenses from alternative retailers.

[184] Workshop Tr. at 233-34 (Robert L. Hubbard).

[185] Workshop Tr. at 163-66 (Deborah Dubow Press). *See also* consumer comments stating that the high cost of pet medications is a real deterrent to pet ownership. Neville Comment; D. Sherman Comment; Black Comment; Rafalow Comment.

[186] ASPCA Comment at 4.

[187] *Id.* at 3.

[188] *See* Workshop Tr. at 166 (Deborah Dubow Press); ASPCA Comment at 3.

[189] ASPCA Comment at 3. *See also* Hubbard Statement, *supra* note 71, at 6.

[190] *See* Workshop Tr. at 243-44 (Link Welborn); *id.* at 247-49, 263 (Kent D. McClure); Gay (VetRxDirect) Comment (#576); AVDA Comment at 12; AHI Comment at 4-5. FTC staff has also learned that there may be material differences between the prescriber/vendor models in these industries. For example, it appears that at the time of the FCLCA, various state laws permitted a prescriber to be the only entity that could fill the contact lens prescription. *See* Workshop Tr. at 215 (Sydney Knight). By contrast, pharmacists are legally permitted to dispense pet medications under the laws of all 50 states.

[191] *See* AVMA Comment at 7 ("The AVMA is strongly opposed to HR 1406 and does not believe any amendments should be considered."); AVDA Comment; AAHA Comment; SVHP Comment. *See also* AVMA Comment at 1 ("The AVMA has concerns with mandatory prescription writing for veterinarians."); *id.* at 5 ("We believe that state regulatory mechanisms pertaining to veterinary prescription writing are adequate and that there is no need for a federal mandate. Both veterinary medicine and pharmacy practices have traditionally been regulated by the states. A federal mandate would be a dramatic and unwarranted departure from state professional regulation and should be done only if there is a particular problem that needs to be addressed. We are not aware of consumers widely being denied their requests for prescriptions and see no need for a federal mandate that

would undercut existing state regulation of veterinary medicine and pharmacy practices."); Workshop Tr. at 144 (Adrian Hochstadt); *id.* at 201 (Douglas G. Aspros) (the AVMA is unaware of any data suggesting that there is a problem with veterinarians providing written prescriptions that requires a federal legislative solution, and to the extent that there are any issues, state boards of pharmacy and veterinary medicine are fully capable of resolving them); Am. Veterinary Med. Ass'n, *Action Alert: Take a Stand Against H.R. 1406*, THE PETWORK (May 3, 2011), http://thepetwork.wordpress.com/2011/05/03/action-alert-take-a-stand-against-h-r-1406/ [hereinafter AVMA Action Alert] (encouraging veterinarians to take a stand against H.R. 1406); Verdon, *supra* note 69; *How the Maine VMA Rallied to Help Defeat Adverse Legislation - A Case Study*, AM. VETERINARY MED. ASS'N (May 17, 2011), https:// www.avma.org/ KB/ VMA/ Pages/How-the-Maine-VMA-rallied-to-help-defeat-adverse-legislation---a-case- study.aspx (describing efforts that state VMAs can take to defeat proposed state legislation that would mandate automatic prescription release for pet medications).

[192] *See* AVMA Action Alert, *supra* note 191; Verdon, *supra* note 69; Workshop Tr. at 201 (Douglas G. Aspros) ("If there is any issue, there's certainly no federal recourse required to resolve it. State boards of pharmacy and state boards of veterinary medicine certainly have the tools they need to identify and solve this problem if they decide that there is one.").

[193] *See* AVMA Comment at 8; Am. Animal Hosp. Ass'n ("AAHA") Comment at 2; Workshop Tr. at 74-75 (Mark Cushing); *id.* at 205 (Douglas G. Aspros) ("My license as a veterinarian is governed under state law. Pharmacy is governed under state law. And suddenly we have this overlay of Federal legislation over both of those licensed professions, and it's not clear how that's going to be managed.").

[194] *See* Indep. Pharmacy Alliance Comment at 2 (arguing that the economic benefits of greater prescription portability cannot be achieved at the federal level, and instead consumers would most benefit from automatic prescription release requirements being adopted at the state level).

[195] *See, e.g.*, Gay (VetRxDirect) Comment (#576); Pedersen Comment; Neely Comment. Hundreds of additional comments received from individual veterinarians echo the sentiments expressed in these three examples. *See also* Maine Hearing on L.D. 676, *supra* note 156 (separate statements from 15 veterinarians opposing L.D. 676).

[196] *See* Workshop Tr. at 187 (Wendy Hauser) ("We have had so much fragmentation within our industry, that this is one more way that we're going to lose touch with our patients."); Greeley Comment ("The prescription and fulfillment of medications for animals and the delivery of veterinary services are interwoven in the practice of veterinary medicine and should remain firmly under the authorization of veterinarians.").

See also Novartis Comment at 4-5 ("Veterinarians understand patient history and drug interactions and serve as a control point for dispensing medications, which is key to supporting proper drug usage. Contact points such as treatment, prescription, dispensing and follow up appointments with pets and pet owners create a base of experience and opportunities for feedback that are unmatched. These contacts, and the continuity of care fostered by a strong VCPR, are critical to the effective administration of animal health care. When this continuity is broken, then health and safety of companion animals are threatened. It is our position that nothing should interfere with this relationship or these contact points."); S. Anderson (Ass'n for Veterinary Clinic Success) Comment (expressing the fear that excessive outsourcing of dispensing might break the link between veterinarians and their clients).

[197] *See* AVMA Action Alert, *supra* note 191.

[198] *See, e.g.*, S. Anderson (Ass'n for Veterinary Clinic Success) Comment ("In regard to patient care, our experience indicates that a client is less diligent in following a medication protocol when a veterinarian and veterinary practice are not involved through each step in the process, including the dispensing of medications."); Maine Hearing on L.D. 676, *supra* note 156 (separate statements from 15 veterinarians opposing L.D. 676) (expressing concerns

that clients will be less likely to comply with recommended prescription drug treatment regimens if they do not leave the veterinary clinic with the product in hand).

[199] *See supra* notes 137 and 147 and accompanying text.

[200] *AVMA, Client Requests for Prescriptions*, *supra* note 52. *But see* AVMA Comment at 8 ("The AVMA believes that veterinarians are uniquely educated to provide the best professional guidance and education to pet owners when dispensing prescription products.").

[201] Workshop Tr. at 157-58 (Douglas G. Aspros). *See also* Pfizer Comment (#329) at 3 ("PAH [Pfizer Animal Health] sees no need for legislation, regulation or other government action which might, inadvertently, diminish critical interaction between the veterinarians, patients and clients while putting more pressure on the retail pharmacies that are not properly equipped to meet the challenges.").

[202] Workshop Tr. at 178-79 (Race Foster) ("Remember, you've already had the client-patient relationship, that's at the point where the drug is prescribed. Now we just have to count the pills and fill it."); Magee (F&S) Comment at 15 (claiming that the VCPR relates to the writing of prescriptions, not necessarily the dispensing of medications, and is fulfilled when the patient has been examined and the prescription has been written); Jorgensen (Animal Pharm) Comment.

[203] *See* Valley Vet Supply Comment at 4 ("Certain segments of organized veterinary medicine and veterinary practitioners will oppose a mandate for written, portable prescriptions. These interest groups and individuals argue that veterinary product sales should be limited to the veterinarian's clinic to ensure proper medical care, and client information. But these needs are met in a valid VCPR. . . . And if the customer requires additional guidance in administering the prescription drug, he/she can consult with the prescribing veterinarian.").

[204] *See supra* note 45.

[205] *See infra* notes 216 and 229 and accompanying text.

[206] *See* AVDA Comment at 4-5 (questioning the ability of pharmacists to perform appropriate drug utilization reviews before dispensing pet medications). *See also* AVDA Comment at 3, 11; AAHA Comment at 1-2.

[207] *See* Stangl Comment (pharmacy technician has observed a lack of knowledge about animal products in human pharmacies, and questions whether pharmacists are as equipped to identify mistakes on veterinary prescriptions as they are with human prescriptions). Dr. Elaine Blythe acknowledges that the vast majority of pharmacists do not have any training in veterinary pharmacology and are not comfortable filling pet medication prescriptions. She points out, however, that there are subsets of pharmacists who have sought additional training and education in veterinary pharmacology, some with highly specialized post-graduate veterinary pharmacology training and clinical experience, that have developed positive working relationships with veterinarians within their communities and should be able to safely and confidently dispense pet medications and field common questions related to chronic and preventative medications used in companion animals. Workshop Tr. at 194-96 (Elaine Blythe).

[208] *See* Workshop Tr. at 160-62 (Elaine Blythe) (describing the educational opportunities available to pharmacists who want to learn veterinary pharmacology); *id.* at 196-98 (explaining that roughly 20-25 percent of the 127 accredited pharmacy schools in the U.S. offer courses in veterinary pharmacology; and when this is not an option, pharmacy students and practicing pharmacists may enroll in online courses in veterinary pharmacology; "I think the increase in educational offerings is reflective of the increase in prescriptions that are being outsourced to community pharmacies"); Int'l Bd. of Veterinary Pharmacy Comment ("Veterinary pharmacy continuing education programs taught by ICVP diplomats are available and can fill the knowledge gap for the practicing pharmacist."); SVHP Comment at 1 ("SVHP represents pharmacists actively working in veterinary pharmacy, and our membership is uniquely positioned to educate veterinarians and pharmacists in the safe distribution of prescription products to pet owners through compliance with existing state regulation and the education of all the stakeholders in the drug distribution chain.");

Telephone Interview with Kim-Jung et al., *supra* note 126 (stating that they are aware of some pharmacy schools now offering elective veterinary medicine courses and/or veterinary clinical pharmacy residence programs, and some pharmacies now offering continuing education courses in veterinary pharmacology).

[209] *See* Lau, *Target Tests Market*, *supra* note 104 (quoting Donald Plumb, author of Plumb's Veterinary Drug Handbook, as stating that continuing education courses and access to decent reference materials should provide pharmacists with enough knowledge to dispense pet medications and interact with veterinarians in a professional manner); Workshop Tr. at 82-83 (Paul D. Pion) (stating that these safety issues "can all be overcome by education" and that he has "no doubt that pharmacists can learn this," although he questions whether "big box stores and pharmacies who largely see selling pet medications as a way to increase traffic are going to pay adequate attention to these issues?"); Stevens Comment (arguing that pharmacists should receive proper training in veterinary medicine before automatic prescription release is implemented, and that this might be accomplished by requiring a continuing education course or primary coursework in pharmacy schools); Workshop Tr. at 61 (Brad Dayton) (agreeing that pharmacists are not fully trained in veterinary pharmacology, but that a pharmacist's experience, knowledge, and education can be used to develop working relationships with veterinarians so that retail pharmacists can properly dispense pet medications); NACDS Comment at 1-2 (noting that pharmacists are highly trained healthcare professionals that "have developed additional policies and programs to ensure pet medications are dispensed in a safe manner. Initiatives by chain pharmacies include accredited continuing education lessons on common pet medications, common conditions, counseling, dosing in pets and triage – the recognition of symptoms that require immediate intervention by a veterinarian."); Workshop Tr. at 125 (David G. Miller) (arguing that training should be the responsibility of the pharmacy profession and should be included within the pharmacy curriculum, continuing professional education, and board certification processes).

[210] *See, e.g.*, Terry Chowder, *No. 511: Comment Re: August 2012 Newsletter Article No. 509: Veterinary Prescriptions*, OR. ST. BOARD OF PHARMACY NEWSL. (Or. State Bd. Of Pharmacy, Portland, Or.) Nov. 2012, at 1, http:// www.nabp.net/ publications/ assets/OR112012.pdf ("As community pharmacists increasingly dispense both human and traditional veterinary prescription products for animals it is important that we have the education necessary to best serve our animal patients. . . . Many of us did not receive veterinary pharmacy education when in school, so it is important that we discover this education on our own or encourage our employers to provide access to continuing education. As a suggestion, the education should not only cover the medications used in veterinary pharmacy, but should also consider the perspectives of veterinary practice, legal implications for dispensing to animals, and information regarding how we as pharmacists can best provide support to animal owners and veterinarians.").

[211] *See* PACKAGED FACTS REPORT 3D, *supra* note 12, at 168 (describing how, in response to increased consumer demand for prescription pet medications, Costco implemented a new pet medications initiative that includes a continuing education program for its pharmacists, a veterinary drug handbook, and access to assisting veterinarians).

[212] *See* Workshop Tr. at 199 (Race Foster) (stating that continuing education for pharmacists is "absolutely essential" and should be mandatory for any pharmacist that wants to participate in the field of veterinary medicine, but arguing that the training a pharmacist receives probably does not need to be as extensive as veterinarian training, because they are only dispensing the medications, not prescribing them); Foster (F&S) Comment at 9; *supra* note 209.

[213] *See* AVDA Comment at 5-6 ("A mandated expansion of the role of human pharmacies designed to increase participation in the veterinary prescriptions market would necessitate clinical pharmacists demonstrate the same level of competency for veterinary medicine as currently required for human health."); SVHP Comment at 2 ("Most importantly, SVHP

believes that although pharmacy education is rapidly coming up to speed with regard to veterinary pharmacotherapy that the average pharmacist is not yet ready to dispense and counsel for veterinary prescription drugs with the same level of expertise and accuracy as he/she possesses for human prescriptions. . . . SVHP believes that the average retail pharmacist is currently incompletely prepared to participate in the Veterinary- Client-Patient-Relationship. This training will evolve through continuing education, self-training, and formal education in pharmacy schools and will obviously take years to fully accomplish."); Brown Comment (#521).

[214] *See* Workshop Tr. at 125 (Brad Dayton) ("So, if we have the package insert coming from a manufacturer, we have a better chance to answer questions and dispense medication properly."); *id.* at 95-96 (Michael H. Hinckle) (mentioning the usefulness of FDA-approved informational package insert that a pharmacist can reference).

[215] *See, e.g.*, *id.* at 61-62 (Brad Dayton); *id.* at 95-96 (Michael H. Hinckle).

[216] *See id.* at 78 (Mark Cushing) (stating that there is a "whole series of examples of adverse consequences for pets when there was a decision made by a pharmacist . . . to change dosage, or to swap out the particular prescription for a different drug reflecting a lack of concern or understanding about how the medication would work with a pet when a simple phone call might have made the difference."); AVMA Comment at 5 ("Potential risks associated with prescription filling at pharmacies include those pertaining to lack of formalized veterinary medical pharmacology educational requirements for pharmacists. Untrained pharmacists can unknowingly provide incorrect counseling or substitute inappropriate medications to the detriment of the patient."). *See also* Workshop Tr. at 83 (Paul D. Pion) (claiming knowledge of hundreds of examples where this has been issue, and pointing out that pharmacists should seek proper training and respect veterinary prescription directions to avoid these problems); Maine Hearing on L.D. 676, *supra* note 156 (separate statements from 15 veterinarians opposing L.D. 676) (expressing concerns that retail pharmacists are untrained in veterinary pharmacology and often substitute other products for prescribed products or question the veterinarian's expertise).

[217] *See* Oregon VMA Comment (#422) at 1 ("While we recognize that retail pharmacies are filling prescriptions issued by veterinarians upon the request of their clients, we expect this to be conducted in accordance with state laws and administrative rules of boards of pharmacies. Regrettably, this has not always happened in Oregon – and it has caused serious concerns among our member veterinarians. . . . Since late February [2012] we have monitored this issue and documented specific examples where retail pharmacists have changed dosages of drugs prescribed by veterinarians and even dispensed an entirely different drug to the veterinary client. This has been done without consulting the veterinarian and receiving his or her authorization."); *id.* at 5 (indicating that 35% of responding veterinarians claim to be aware of instances in which a retail pharmacy changed a veterinary prescription without contacting and receiving authorization from the veterinarian; 17% of responding veterinarians claim that this resulted in an adverse health event for the pet);WASH. VET SURVEY, *supra* note 143 (indicating that 38% of responding veterinarians claim to be aware of instances in which a retail pharmacy changed a veterinary prescription without contacting and receiving authorization from the veterinarian; 10% of responding veterinarians claim that this resulted in an adverse health event for the pet); S. CAL. VET SURVEY, *supra* note 143 (indicating that 33% of responding veterinarians claim to be aware of instances in which a retail pharmacy changed a veterinary prescription without contacting and receiving authorization from the veterinarian; 9% of responding veterinarians claim that this resulted in an adverse health event for the pet); IOWA VET SURVEY, *supra* note 143 (indicating that 20% of responding veterinarians claim to be aware of instances in which a retail pharmacy changed a veterinary prescription without contacting and receiving authorization from the veterinarian; 10% of responding veterinarians claim that this resulted in an adverse health event for the pet).

[218] Greg Cima, *Substitution Errors*, J. AM. VETERINARY MED. ASS'N (Sept. 4, 2014), https://www.avma.org/News/JAVMANews/Pages/140901a.aspx (For example, the Oregon VMA forwarded its survey results to the Oregon Board of Pharmacy, although this information did not result in any substantiated claims or formal disciplinary actions. Gary Miner, Compliance Director of the Oregon Board of Pharmacy, stated that the survey did not provide sufficient details to allow the Board to investigate the alleged incidents of pharmacist error. Since the time of the survey, the Board has received additional reports of pharmacist error that have been investigated, and some have resulted in disciplinary fines being imposed. Miner stated, however, that most of these reported incidents are related to accidental changes rather than deliberate substitutions, and that such mistakes are unfortunate but normal occurrences in pharmacies.).

[219] *See* K&L Gates Comment at 7-8 ("Pharmacists are trained professionals who operate within very stringent state law requirements concerning the dispensing of drugs. Pharmacists routinely communicate with medical doctors about the human drugs they prescribe. There is no reason to believe that pharmacists could not, or would not, similarly communicate with veterinarians when it is necessary to do so. In fact, pharmacists already safely dispense significant numbers of animal drug products and human drugs for animal patients. The assertion that animal drugs can only be safely dispensed by a veterinarian is simply unsupportable and runs counter to reality."). *See also* Workshop Tr. at 95-96 (Michael H. Hinckle) (stating that the large volume of pet prescriptions filled by retail pharmacies suggests that for the most part, they already properly and safely dispense pet medications, exactly as prescribed by veterinarians).

[220] Indep. Pharmacy Alliance Comment at 2 ("Since both the practice of veterinarian medicine and pharmacy are licensed professions in all states, ensuring policies that mandate prescriptions for pet medications and an affirmative freedom of choice for the owner in when and where to fill this prescription does not jeopardize pet health treatment or the need for veterinarian medical diagnoses decisions. As with human medication therapy, no pharmacy can fill a pet medication that is contrary to the medical decision of the prescribing professional. Indeed, state pharmacy practices laws require compliance with treatment directions of any prescriber for a living being, either human or animal.").

[221] *See* Valley Vet Supply Comment at 2 (the inspection, certification, and licensing by the state boards of pharmacy and the NABP ensure high levels of competency in the retail pharmacies that wish to dispense pet medications); PetCareRx Comment at 3 ("PetCareRx is not aware of any safety issues posed by licensed, Vet- VIPPS-accredited pharmacies' dispensing pet medications pursuant to verified prescriptions. States heavily regulate the practice of pharmacy, and the NABP actively monitors for compliance with accreditation criteria and standards as well as legal requirements. More than sufficient oversight exists to address any safety concerns."); Workshop Tr. at 126 (David G. Miller).

[222] *See* Workshop Tr. at 126 (David Miller); *id.* at 256 (Robert L. Hubbard) ("If there is an adverse health consequence, that's something that the regulatory system should address, and that should be discussed with evidence, and we should go forward from there.").

[223] AVDA Comment at 7-8 ("It is important to note that changes for script medications by the pharmacist absent consultation with the issuing practitioner is illegal and subject to disciplinary action or even prosecution by state authorities and the boards of pharmacy. Yet, these types of incidents generally go unaddressed, leaving unsuspecting pet owners subject to further abuse at the hands of perhaps well intended but grossly ill-informed pharmacists."); Brown Comment (#521) (claiming to have had pharmacists substitute inappropriate medications on written prescriptions on three separate occasions, but not reporting these instances to state pharmacy boards, and therefore believing that this is likely a more widespread problem than what is reflected in complaints to state pharmacy boards). *See also* AVMA Comment at 4 (arguing that state authorities need to better enforce rules relating to prescription drug sales to ensure that the decision for use of prescription drug in an animal is made by a veterinarian within the confines of a VCPR, not a pharmacist).

[224] *See* Workshop Tr. at 127-28 (Mark Cushing); *id.* at 129 (Paul D. Pion).

[225] *See, e.g.*, K&L Gates Comment at 10 ("These [safety] allegations are without merit. Human drugs have been safely and effectively dispensed by pharmacists based on physician prescriptions for decades. The pharmacy environment is efficient and safe. The veterinarian is not abdicating the veterinary-patient relationship to the pharmacist any more than a physician would abdicate the physician-patient relationship to the pharmacist in the human context. If the pharmacist has a question about a prescription or a dose, they would call the veterinarian, just as they would call a physician about a human prescription. Responsible pet drug manufacturers provide pharmacists with educational material and programs to ensure than pharmacists are equipped to counsel consumers about their product. The FDA-approved product insert that accompanies each animal drug also provides information about species, weight and potential metabolic issues as well as concerns about dosing. There is simply no supportable argument for the position that pharmacies cannot safely dispense animal drugs. In fact, pharmacies are generally better suited to dispensing drugs than veterinarians. Pharmacies are routinely inspected by the state Boards of Pharmacy and have developed highly efficient inventory and dispensing systems to minimize errors. While errors by pharmacists are cited in the comments, it goes without saying that veterinarians also make mistakes. Obviously, veterinarians can also safely dispense drugs and there will always be a place for vet-dispensed drugs.").

Some retail pharmacies claim to have implemented internal processes to ensure that their pharmacists dispense pet medications safely. *See* Kroger Comment at 2 (stating that pharmacists are well-suited to accept prescriptions from veterinarians, and Kroger is "very satisfied with the tools that have been developed for our pharmacists, by vets and vet drug references, to help pharmacists practice the same drug utilization review (DUR) skills used in every day practice of human med dispensing, and apply them to pet prescriptions."); PetMed Express, Inc., *supra* note 21, at 3 (noting that pharmacists and pharmacy technicians are required to verify all prescriptions with the prescribing veterinarian before an order can be processed); PetCareRx Comment at 2 ("After a veterinarian has examined a customer's pet and prescribed a particular medication, the customer calls PetCareRx or visits the company's website to place an order for the prescribed product. . . . PetCareRx then contacts the prescribing veterinarian to confirm that a valid prescription exists. After the prescribing veterinarian provides the prescription to PetCareRx, one of the company's licensed pharmacists dispenses the medication in accordance with applicable legal requirements . . . PetCareRx dispenses prescription pet medications only after confirming the existence of a valid prescription with the customer's treating veterinarian. Our business model provides pet owners with a safe, convenient, and often less expensive alternative to purchasing the medications their pets need.").

[226] *See* In re: Disposable Contact Lens Antitrust Litigation, No. MDL 1030 (complaints filed M.D. Fla. 1994). During this litigation, the attorneys general of 32 states and a certified class alleged that eye care professionals engaged in an organized effort to prevent or hinder consumers from obtaining their contact lens prescriptions. The complaints named Johnson & Johnson, Bausch & Lomb, CIBA Vision, the American Optometric Association, and individual optometrists as defendants. The complaints alleged two conspiracies: (1) that the practitioners and their trade associations conspired to prevent the release of contact lens prescriptions to consumers, and (2) that the manufacturers, practitioners, and trade associations, including the American Optometric Association, conspired to eliminate sales of contact lenses by pharmacies, mail order, and other alternative sellers. According to the complaints, the conspiracy severely restricted the supply of contact lenses available to alternative sellers, which hampered the growth of such sellers, decreased the supply of lenses to consumers, and increased the price of lenses. The parties reached settlements, the last of which the court approved in November 2001. As part of these settlements, defendant manufacturers agreed to sell lenses via alternative distribution channels. *Id.*

[227] *See, e.g.*, Hubbard Statement, *supra* note 71, at 8-9. *See also* Workshop Tr. at 234-36 (Robert D. Atkinson) ("I've been writing and speaking about this issue of intermediary resistance to e-commerce since 2000, and it's been amazing to watch the proliferation of industries and professions that fight back against consumer choice. They all use exactly the same logic and argumentation. This is car dealers, wine wholesalers, lawyers, realtors, undertakers, optometrists, and now veterinarians. They engage in this through three principal ways. "). The three principal ways include: (1) collusion with producers, (2) limiting access to key resources, and (3) supporting passage of state laws that restrict access. *Id.*

[228] Indeed, surveys conducted by some state veterinary medical associations suggest that this already occurs to a significant degree. *See* Oregon VMA Comment (#422) at 3; WASH. VET SURVEY, *supra* note 143; S. CAL. VET SURVEY, *supra* note 143.

[229] *See* Workshop Tr. at 35-36, 82-83 (Paul D. Pion) (veterinarians have concerns about the ability of retail pharmacists to provide information regarding administration techniques, dosing, side effects, and potential interactions); *id.* at 157-58 (Douglas G. Aspros) ("Pet owners may encounter misinformation or inappropriate substitution from pharmacists who are not trained in veterinary pharmacology, who are prepared to discharge all of the responsibilities of a pharmacist when dispensing to a pet."); Greeley Comment (providing examples of pharmacists who have offered inappropriate counseling to pet owners); Workshop Tr. at 56-57 (Andrew J. Bane) ("Specific training is required to properly evaluate, dispense, educate and counsel pet owners on the proper use and administration of medications to different species of pets. . . . [W]e feel that pharmacists trained only in human medicine is not interchangeable with a pharmacist specializing in veterinary medicine."); *id.* at 87-88 (veterinarians are in the best position to dispense pet medications so that they have the opportunity to administer the first dose in the veterinary hospital, allowing pet owners to understand proper dosing and reactions to watch for); SVHP Comment at 2 ("The vast spectrum of doses, contraindications, side effects, and drug interactions that occur in animal species and breeds are not included in retail pharmacy prescription software and alert systems, and a safety net for animal patients is currently lacking in the average retail pharmacy practice. The average pharmacist, at the present time, is not likely to have sufficient knowledge to confidently and appropriately prepare, dispense, or counsel pet owners with regard to handling, administration, and monitoring of prescribed therapy."); Gay (VetRxDirect) Comment (#576) ("There are hundreds of veterinary prescription medications as well as hundreds more human medications that are prescribed for companion animal use. The average pharmacist in the United States does not have adequate knowledge to dispense all of these medications safely, nor do they possess the ability to give advice about their use to pet owners. . . . And without basic knowledge of veterinary pharmacology by the average pharmacist in the United States, it would be unwise, dangerous and unethical to dispense medicines they are not familiar with."); Pedersen Comment (claiming that human pharmacists are untrained in veterinary pharmacology, which potentially increases medication errors).

[230] According to AVMA recommendations, "[p]rescribing veterinarians should ensure that information regarding the proper use of the prescribed drug and the risks associated with its use are communicated to the client, regardless of the drug source." *See AVMA Client Requests for Prescriptions*, *supra* note 52 (Recommendation 7). Some veterinarians have argued that because pharmacists are more likely to make dispensing errors or provide incorrect information to pet owners, prescription release may result in a higher volume of adverse events for pets. The AVMA argues that these situations could require additional treatment for pets, at additional cost to pet owners, in comparison to the veterinarian dispensing the medication properly in the first instance. *See* AVMA Comment at 3. However, no data have been presented to support these assertions. In addition, it is theoretically possible that post-dispensing costs might be higher for veterinarians when a prescription is filled by an alternative retailer, even when it is filled correctly. For example, clients may require more follow-up counseling when they purchase pet medications from a

retail pharmacist rather than the veterinarian, and the veterinarian may not always be able to charge the client for this follow-up care. However, FTC staff is unaware of data to support this theory.

[231] AVMA Comment at 1. *See also id.* at 4 ("The AVMA is currently reaching out to pharmacy stakeholders to help ensure optimal communications and interactions between individual prescribing veterinarians and pharmacists for the well-being of our patients."); SVHP Comment at 1 (referencing "the emerging collaborative process that the professions of pharmacy and veterinary medicine have been undertaking over the last decade.").

[232] *See* Workshop Tr. at 127 (Mark Cushing) (stating his belief that most pharmacists already coordinate with veterinarians if they have questions); OR. VET SURVEY, *supra* note 143, at 1 ("When a retail pharmacist has a concern about a prescription issued by a veterinarian, a majority will contact the veterinarian to discuss the issue. In some instances, veterinarians have established a good business relationship with a local pharmacist, and together they work hand-in-hand to meet the needs of the client and the best interests of the patient."). The Oregon Board of Pharmacy acknowledged that the information exchange with the Oregon VMA prompted continued dialogue between the Board and veterinarians, and has resulted in more educational outreach by the Board regarding pharmacist dispensation of pet medications, as well as recommendations that Oregon pharmacy schools offer more courses in veterinary pharmacology. Also, Oregon pharmacies that dispense pet medications are now required to keep veterinary drug reference materials on hand, "such as Plumb's Veterinary Drug Handbook or the Merck Veterinary Manual." Cima, *supra* note 218.

[233] *See infra* Section IV.A.5, Product Pedigree and Safety Issues Associated with Secondary Distribution, at 81.

[234] *Purchasing Pet Drugs Online: Buyer Beware*, U.S. FOOD & DRUG ADMIN., http:// www. fda.gov/forconsumers/consumerupdates/ucm048164.htm (last updated Mar. 11, 2010).

[235] *Id.*

[236] *See, e.g.*, B. Taylor Comment (arguing that veterinarians need the ability to monitor the sources from which their clients purchase pet medications; mandatory written prescriptions take away this ability, thereby compromising follow-up care for pets).

[237] AVMA Comment at 2 ("Assuming that pharmacies acquire FDA-approved products through legal channels and store and ship them in the appropriate manner per manufacturer guidelines and state pharmacy rules, there should not be a concern with product safety or quality. We are unaware of any legal restrictions preventing pet prescription products from being dispensed by nonveterinary retail pharmacies. The key requirements are that the pharmacy is compliant with pharmacy laws and regulations and the prescriber must be authorized to provide the prescription.").

[238] *See, e.g.*, K&L Gates Comment at 6 ("The market for these counterfeit and low quality products is only encouraged by the lack of availability of low price alternatives in readily available retail outlets (i.e., pharmacies). There is no better way to protect against these low quality alternatives than by making affordable, high quality products readily available in retail pharmacies that are equipped to identify and eliminate counterfeits and evaluate substitutions within established guidelines.").

[239] *See, e.g.*, AVMA Comment at 7; Oregon VMA Comment (#422) at 2; AHI Comment at 5; Workshop Tr. At 204-05 (Douglas G. Aspros); Arp, *supra* note 35; S. Anderson (Ass'n for Veterinary Clinic Success) Comment ("Some veterinary practices will have difficulty in conforming with proposed legislation, and I believe that it will force several of these small businesses out of business."); A. Anderson Comment. *See also* Maine Hearing on L.D. 676, *supra* note 156 (separate statements from 15 veterinarians) (expressing concerns that mandating automatic prescription release would be burdensome and time-consuming to veterinary practices, and that this would likely increase the costs of veterinary care).

[240] AVMA Comment at 7. *See also id.* at 3 ("Faxed prescription requests from pharmacies also create inefficiencies. These requests are generated by the client or pharmacies, and veterinary clinics can receive numerous faxes a day. These faxes require the review of

patient medical histories before authorization can be granted or denied. Additional inefficiencies associated with faxed requests include when the dispensing pharmacist has follow- up questions for the veterinarian.").

[241] *Id.* at 7.

[242] *Id.*

[243] *See* ASPCA Comment at 5; K&L Gates Comment at 12; N. Smith Comment at 5.

[244] *See* Wilson & Rossi, *supra* note 124 (arguing that information technology presents opportunities to reduce medication errors in both the human medical and veterinary professions: "Electronic prescribing has helped reduce prescription, dispensing and administrative errors."); *id.* ("Computerized physician order entry (CPOE) is a system for physicians to prescribe pharmaceuticals online, and has probably had the biggest impact of any automated intervention in reducing medication errors."). CPOE systems could also reduce the time normally associated with providing portable prescriptions.

[245] *See* AMVA Comment at 8; SVHP Comment at 1 ("It is burdensome and unnecessary to require a written prescription as well as a written notification that the prescription may be filled elsewhere, regardless of whether the client is having the prescription filled by the veterinarian."); Foster (F&S) Comment at 7 ("If the consumer decides to have the veterinarian dispense the medication, the veterinarian need not write a prescription.").

[246] *See* AVMA Comment at 2 (portable prescriptions may be provided by handing "a written prescription to the client, by prescribing via telephone or electronically to a pharmacy, or by signing a faxed prescription from a pharmacy upon request, as allowable under individual state veterinary medical and pharmacy rules."). *See also AVMA Client Requests for Prescriptions*, *supra* note 52 (Recommendation 1) ("The veterinarian may choose to either issue the prescription in writing for the client, or contact the pharmacy electronically or by phone.").

[247] Proposed legislation has varied on this requirement. H.R. 1406, H.R. 4023 and S. 2756 would have required that a copy of each prescription, whether in written, oral or electronic format, be provided to consumers. Conversely, Maine Senate Bill S. 207 and New Jersey Senate Bill S. 2915 would have required that written copies of each prescription be provided to consumers.

[248] *See* Neely Comment (the human medical community is moving away from written prescriptions in favor of other methods, such as fax or phone, to avoid errors that arise when written prescriptions are misread).

[249] *See* AVMA Comment at 6 ("The AVMA contends that it is not appropriate for federal law to deny veterinarians the ability to charge a fee . . . for providing a written prescription to clients . . . . Writing prescriptions and subsequent follow-up work, including phone calls with pharmacists, takes time and it is not unreasonable to charge a fee for that time."); Malon Comment ("At the very least, veterinarians should be able to be compensated for creating the appropriate prescription for an animal (this should not necessarily be a free service)."). *See also* AM. ANIMAL HOSP. ASS'N, *supra* note 104, at 245 ("In 2012, the average prescription fee charged by a veterinary practice for medications dispensed from its own hospital was $10.04, and the fee charged for a prescription to be filled elsewhere was similar ($10.68).").

[250] *See* K&L Gates Comment at 11 ("Restrictions on fees and waivers are necessary to prevent their use as means to indirectly prevent competition. Veterinarians are free to charge whatever they wish for their services, but charging a client an additional fee for writing a prescription serves only an anti-competitive purpose. Presumably, no such fee would be charged if the client opted to purchase its drugs directly from the veterinarian. Yet, the administrative costs associated with dispensing (e.g. labeling, recordkeeping, etc.) are surely as high, if not higher, than the costs resulting from writing and recording a prescription. The sole purpose for charging such a fee would be to discourage clients from requesting a prescription and thereby preserving the veterinarian's monopoly."). *See also*

IOWA VET SURVEY, *supra* note 143 ("We charge $8/script to [provide prescriptions for clients to fill at an online outlet or retail pharmacy], so we don't get too many [requests]").

[251] *See, e.g.*, *Principles of Veterinary Medical Ethics of the AVMA*, *supra* note 38 (Principle VII.f.ii.) ("A veterinarian may charge a fee for the services the veterinarian provides in conjunction with the use of third-party providers such as laboratories, pharmacies, and consulting veterinarians.").

[252] *See* Foster (F&S) Comment at 7 ("Certainly veterinarians, just as physicians, have a right to be paid for their services, including the processing of faxes, record-keeping, correspondence and other tasks associated with prescriptions. I feel this is best accomplished with a simple office call or professional services fee, which are common practices in the human medicine. To do otherwise pressures clients and reduces prescription portability.").

[253] *See, e.g.*, Workshop Tr. at 186 (Wendy Hauser) ("You bet I have my clients sign a waiver if they want to order online, and the reason that I do is because I can't guarantee the safety of those drugs. . . . I look at that waiver as informed client consent, period. I do like the fact that I feel it releases me from some liability."); A. Anderson Comment; Greeley Comment. Several examples of liability waivers used by veterinarians are on file with the authors.

[254] Legislation proposed at the federal and state level would prohibit veterinarians from requiring waivers of liability from clients who obtain portable prescriptions. *See supra* description of H.R. 1406, at note 67; H.R. 4023 and S. 2756, at note 72; and Maine S. 207 and New Jersey S. 2915, at note 171.

[255] *See* MYERS, *supra* note 104, at 2 ("Increased legal risk. If a pet experiences a complication from a human drug and the client files a complaint with the state board or court, how will you defend yourself when a FDA veterinary approved drug was available?"). In written testimony to the Maine Legislature, one veterinarian contended that veterinarians are required by the FDA to dispense and prescribe veterinary approved drugs when available, and are only allowed to prescribe a human drug if there is no animal drug that can successfully treat the condition when used in accordance with the approved label. Furthermore, this veterinarian stated that veterinarians who deviate from these guidelines face the risk of unfavorable actions by the FDA and are not protected by liability insurance. *See* Maine Hearing on L.D. 676, *supra* note 156 (statement of Derralyn Rennix, DVM, Poland Animal Hosp.). *See also id.* (statement of Renee L. Bourgeois, DVM) ("The FDA recommends dispensing the veterinary version of a given medication even if a less expensive generic version exists."). However, a thorough reading of the FDA's guidance on extra-label drug use in veterinary medicine reveals that this restriction applies only to food animals, not household pets. *See The Ins and Outs of Extra-Label Drug Use in Animals*, *supra* note 58 ("In companion (non- food-producing) animals, you can prescribe an approved human drug for an extra-label use even if an approved animal drug is available.").

[256] *See, e.g.*, Letter from Hawaii Board of Pharmacy to Hawaii Pharmacists Concerning Veterinary Prescriptions (Jan. 2014), http://hawaii.gov/dcca/pvl/news-releases/ pharmacy_ announcements/veterinary- prescriptions/PharmacistVetPrescription.pdf ("If a pharmacy changes or alters the veterinary prescription, who is liable or responsible for any ill consequences to the veterinary patient that may result? Response: *A pharmacist is not allowed to change or alter a prescription without first consulting with the prescriber.*").

[257] *See* K&L Gates Comment at 11 ("Pharmacies are liable for any medication errors that they make when dispensing a drug product. Veterinarians do not need any special liability protection."); AVMA FAQS, *supra* note 52, at 4 ("In general, veterinary liability is based on the standard of care in your jurisdiction. Standards may vary among jurisdictions, but in general, if you 1) prescribe an appropriate medication at the correct dose for the patient; 2) talk with the client about the various alternatives to the medication (if any); and 3) share risks with the client and get client consent on the medication to be used, then it is less likely that you will be held responsible, even if your patient has an adverse reaction or the pharmacy filled the prescription incorrectly.").

Some stakeholders argue, however, that even if veterinarians would not ultimately be found liable, without a liability waiver they may find it more difficult to get lawsuits filed against them dismissed. *See* Wilson (Priority Veterinary Mgmt. Consultants) Comment (#475).

[258] *See* K&L Gates Comment at 11 ("[R]equiring a waiver of liability would only serve an anti-competitive purpose . . . [T]he true purpose of such a waiver would be to scare pet owners into believing that filling their prescription at a pharmacy is going to put their pet at risk. The waiver, like the fee, would simply be a tool to indirectly stifle competition from retail pharmacies."). *But see* AVMA Comment at 6 ("The AVMA contends that it is not appropriate for federal law to deny veterinarians the ability . . . to require a waiver of liability for providing a written prescription to clients, although we have not seen evidence of widespread use of such waiver forms. . . . The decision to require a waiver should be left to the business judgment of the clinic owner, subject to state liability laws, rather than be dictated by federal law.").

[259] *See* AM. ANIMAL HOSP. ASS'N, *supra* note 104, at 246 ("Focus on educating clients about the realities of purchasing elsewhere, but don't exaggerate those realities. For example, not all online pharmacies are buying product that can't be legally sold in the United States, but do talk to your clients about the ramifications of their purchase choices. Make sure they understand product guarantees and the true price difference between your practice and other outlets; it's often not as large as they think. Emphasize your availability if something goes wrong – for example, if the pet has an adverse reaction.").

[260] *See* AVMA Comment at 7-8 ("One unintended consequence we can foresee is the increased chance of prescription abuse and fraud. . . . [V]eterinarians will have to take measures to mitigate circumstances where clients use the requirement as an opportunity to acquire inappropriate numbers of prescriptions. Although prescriptions are written now for clients, the sheer number of prescriptions being written would be expected to increase because unlike the current situation . . . a prescription would be required in each and every instance the decision is made for a prescription drug. Increased numbers of prescriptions given to clients, recycled, or discarded if not needed by the client could yield increased opportunities for fraud by use of written prescriptions."); A. Anderson Comment; Maine Hearing on L.D. 676, *supra* note 156 (statement of Sharon Waugh, DVM, Alfred-Waterboro Veterinary Hosp.) ("Finally Act LD 676 is ambiguous as it could be interrupted [sic] that it requires the veterinarian to provide clients with written prescriptions even if the medication is dispensed though [sic] the veterinary hospital. This would allow drug abusing and drug seeking pet owners to fill the same prescription multiple times. Thus, the act *unintentionally encourages drug abuse*.").

[261] *See* Workshop Tr. at 187 (Wendy Hauser) ("I think inappropriate drug requests are another reason that we have concerns. If the blood work isn't accurate, if the drug isn't safe and appropriate for the patient.").

[262] *See* Workshop Tr. at 36 (Paul D. Pion); Coffin Comment ("Rightly or wrongly, pharmacy sales have always been a significant portion of veterinary hospital revenue."). *See also* Lee Comment (claiming that many U.S. veterinarians mark up pet medications three to ten times their cost in order to profit from these sales); K&L Gates Comment at 4 ("Historically, veterinarians have dispensed most of the drugs that they prescribe. This allows the veterinarian to make product margin (additional profit) when selling the drugs. The current distribution process also permits veterinarians and their office staff to benefit from various incentive programs sponsored by the manufacturers of the animal drugs that the office dispenses."); S. Anderson (Ass'n for Veterinary Clinic Success) Comment ("[T]he sale of medications is an important element in the care of veterinary patients. The sale of these products cannot be isolated from other elements in patient care . . . .").

[263] *See* AM. ANIMAL HOSP. ASS'N, FINANCIAL & PRODUCTIVITY PULSEPOINTS 86, 94 (7th ed. 2013) (in 2011, prescription drugs comprised 18.8 percent of the total income for the average veterinary practice and OTC products, including non-prescription flea/tick products, comprised 5.5 percent); AM. VETERINARY MED. ASS'N, 2010 AVMA BIENNIAL

ECONOMIC SURVEY 15 fig.12, 51 tbl.21 (2010) (in 2009, prescription drug sales accounted for 16 percent of mixed animal practices, 17.1 percent of companion animal predominant practices, and 17.6 percent of companion animal exclusive practices, while nonprescription drug and product sales accounted for 9.1 percent, 7.9 percent and 5.5 percent, respectively); Ackerman, *supra* note 104 (pet medication sales are a significant source of revenues and an important profit center in the current veterinary practice model). During the course of FTC staff's research and interviews with industry participants, individual veterinarians claimed that pet medication sales comprised anywhere from 15-30% of their practice revenues, with the majority hovering around 20%.

264 *See* Paul, *supra* note 36 ("Dispensing and prescribing is already a dwindling part of our practices. When clients ask for written prescriptions, most states now require us to provide them . . . . If passed, new congressional legislation will mandate that veterinarians provide a written prescription even if we fill the prescription in house. . . . The result of such legislation: Pet owners who didn't know they could go to their neighborhood pharmacy for prescriptions will now know – and will go."); *Pets Feel the Bite of Recession*, THE PERT GRP. (Feb. 22, 2012), http://www.thepertgroup.com/news-items/detail/92 ("Pending legislation could erode even more of what pet owners spend at the vet. Under the Fairness to Pet Owners Act, veterinarians would be required to write prescriptions whether or not they actually dispensed the medication. Traditional pharmacies would be able to fill scripts, creating additional competition. A majority of respondents [to a survey of 1,200 dog and cat owners] indicated that they would fill those prescriptions outside the veterinary channel, at least some of the time. The Internet and pet super stores continue to gain share in several product categories due to lower costs, variety and convenience.").

265 *See* K&L Gates Comment at 5 ("Some veterinarians have sought to protect the income stream derived from dispensing by refusing to issue prescriptions for drugs that are stocked by the veterinarian. . . . In some instances, veterinarians have refused to provide a prescription to a mail-order Internet pharmacy in order to protect the veterinarian's dispensing income even at the risk of losing the client."); Arp, *supra* note 35 (some veterinarians are not interested in working cooperatively with online or brick-and-mortar pharmacies because they do not want to give up the income from pet medication sales); Bowsher, *supra* note 100 ("Of course, getting your pet's generics for $4 may not be as easy as that 1-2-3. Your vet may be reluctant to write the prescription that you'll need – because PetRx programs save *you* money but take income away from vets. . . . If your vet hands you a prescription, they know you're going to take it elsewhere, which means they won't be able to sell it to you at a higher price."). Patty Khuly, *On the 'Fairness to Pet Owners Act' And Other Prickly Access-to-Pet-Med Issues*, VETERINARY PRACTICE NEWS (June 29, 2012), http:// www.veterinarypracticenews.com/June-2012/On-The-Fairness-To-Pet-Owners-Act-And-Other-Prickly-Access-to-Pet-Med-Issues/ (stating that although the AVMA considers it unethical for veterinarians to refuse to provide prescriptions to clients, it "has never come anywhere close to condemning it," and "state and local VMAs have also been loath to cry foul when practitioners routinely engage in this brand of personal income stream protectionism . . . Given our obvious degree of reluctance to self-police on this issue, is it any wonder the federal government is now advancing legislation to drag us kicking and screaming into the modern drug retail industry?").

266 Veterinarian prescription revenue has already been declining, so the relevant question becomes whether automatic prescription release would simply reinforce this pre-existing trend.

267 *See supra* notes 129-132 and accompanying text. *See also* AM. ANIMAL HOSP. ASS'N, *supra* note 263, at 86 ("As clients find more sources of less expensive medication, pharmacy income as a percentage of the practice's total income may decrease. We have not seen a statistically significant decrease in the past few years, however, which may mean that many clients are willing to pay for the convenience of not having to shop for the best deal or make a second stop to purchase medications for their pets.").

[268] *See, e.g.*, AVMA Comment at 6 ("We are not certain how HR 1406 would affect veterinary sales of pet medications. Small animal veterinary practices have varied business models, ranging from large hospitals with substantial in-patient tertiary care to house-call businesses with minimal dispensing of drugs. To that end, veterinarians' sale of pet medications differs just as broadly, making speculation difficult.").

[269] *See, e.g.*, Workshop Tr. at 38-39 (Paul D. Pion) ("The veterinary profession has a need to supplement the inability to charge adequately for services. . . . [T]hey have sustained the ability to charge affordable pricing for services by supplementing with product fees.").

[270] *See, e.g.*, Workshop Tr. at 207 (Wendy Hauser) (stating that if small animal practices were to lose their pharmacy revenues, they would have to increase revenues somewhere else to make up for this loss and the most likely place for this to happen is with the fees charged for services); *id.* at 39 (Paul D. Pion) ("I think that there's a danger here if you stress the veterinary profession too much further here that with the increased competition you'll damage quality of service available to the public.").

[271] Workshop Tr. at 38-39 (Paul D. Pion) ("For the veterinary profession, I see it as a big detriment, overall, this evolution, because I think it's damaged the public's trust in the veterinary profession. . . . I think when you have a situation where you're advertising to the public that veterinarians are overcharging you for these products, the public is going to start to ask what else are they overcharging me for.").

[272] SVHP Comment at 1 (H.R. 1406 "would further increase resentment of pharmacists by veterinarians over perceived lost revenue and would derail the emerging collaborative process that the professions of pharmacy and veterinary medicine have been undertaking over the last decade.").

[273] *See* PACKAGED FACTS REPORT 3D, *supra* note 12, at 34; NCVEI/BAYER USAGE STUDY, *supra* note 24, at 18-28, 59-60, 63, 78-83 (suggesting that veterinary visits declined in 2009-10 due to the recession and veterinary fee increases).

[274] *See* PACKAGED FACTS REPORT 3D, *supra* note 12, at 33-37. *See also* Press Release, Animal Health Inst., *supra* note 17 (indicating that sales of animal health products including biologics, pharmaceuticals, and feed additives for companion animals and food production animals, also have steadily increased from 2010 to 2013, despite recession- generated sales declines in 2008 and 2009).

[275] For example, veterinarians have lost a significant portion of OTC product sales, which would not be impacted by prescription release requirements. *See* PACKAGED FACTS REPORT 3D, *supra* note 12, at 153 ("The potential loss of flea/tick product revenue is an important concern in the veterinary channel. However, the veterinary channel will have to adapt to a changing marketplace and determine new ways to add value to the process of protecting pets from parasites."); AM. ANIMAL HOSP. ASS'N, *supra* note 104, at 245 ("Drugs and medical supply purchases constitute the second largest expense in veterinary hospitals and, historically, one of the more profitable centers of the practice. The pricing of medications, heartworm preventative, and over-the-counter items such as flea and tick products has become more difficult, however, as the availability of these items elsewhere has increased. This is not a new problem; these products have been available over the counter for years, and continue to cause worries for veterinary practice owners.").

[276] *See, e.g.*, Neely Comment; Pedersen Comment; Coffin Comment; Greeley Comment; IOWA VET SURVEY, *supra* note 143 ("I have tried to avoid the use of writing prescriptions. As prescription writing becomes mandated, I will adjust other charges to defray the loss of income from dispensed medications."); Maine Hearing on L.D. 676, *supra* note 156 (separate statements from 15 veterinarians) (e.g., testimony of James E. Hotham, DVM, Hotham's Veterinary Services, Inc.: "The sales of prescription drugs helps us to keep our service fees down and provide affordable prescriptions to our clients. If this income is lost to my business, it will ultimately mean a decrease in jobs and an increase in fees to make up for the decreased revenue."). *See also* Smith, *supra* note 56 ("The proposed Fairness to Pet Owners Act . . . would require vets to write out prescriptions when customers ask for them.

This would make it easier for pet owners to shop around and find the best price, but could cut into veterinary office profits. Veterinarians, who depend on prescriptions for as much as one-fourth of their income, say that as drug sales decline, their fees will go up, which may make their services too expensive for some people.").

Some veterinarians practicing in rural areas point out that consumer access to legitimate sources for pet medications may be limited in these areas, where veterinarians are currently the main source of these products. *See, e.g.*, Washenfelder Comment. If these veterinarians are forced to increase the prices of their services due to losses in pharmacy revenues, they fear that veterinary care will become even less affordable for their clientele, which could have a negative impact on pet health and pet ownership, in general. *See, e.g.*, Webb (Lindquist Veterinary Care Ctr.) Comment; Maine Hearing on L.D. 676, *supra* note 156 (statement of Derralyn Rennix, DVM, Poland Animal Hosp.) ("We are not the veterinary clinics of larger metropolitan areas. We must rely on income generated from our prescription medications in order to provide this type of affordable [rural] community care for our patients. Income generated from our prescription medications help us to be able to offset the actual costs of bringing a pet in for an exam or procedure. Without income from the prescription medications, the cost to bring a pet to the veterinarian for services would have to increase in order for Maine veterinary hospitals to continue to operate.").

277 *See, e.g.*, Workshop Tr. at 81 (Paul D. Pion) ("In the end, pet owners will end up paying more for their pet care, or fewer pets will be seen, which will deteriorate the health care of our pets and our population."); Maine Hearing on L.D. 676, *supra* note 156 (separate statements from 15 veterinarians) (e.g., testimony of James E. Hotham, DVM, Hotham's Veterinary Services, Inc.: "At the end of the day if this bill is passed, the client and patient will end up paying more for veterinary services and really see little or no savings on prescription drugs.").

278 Ackerman, *supra* note 109; NCVEI/BAYER USAGE STUDY, *supra* note 24, at 66-67; Workshop Tr. at 38 (Paul D. Pion) (stating that veterinarians have become too dependent on product sales and should focus more on providing professional services); Lee Comment ("Veterinarians should not be pharmacies. We are medical professionals. We should be charging to write a script to an outside pharmacy. If as a profession we would just charge more appropriately for examinations and services, we would not need to rely on marking up medications to turn a profit."); AM. ANIMAL HOSP. ASS'N, *supra* note 104, at 245-46 (stating that veterinary practices "need to focus on a combination of strategies: generating a greater percentage of their income from nonproduct sources, competitive pricing, and creating value to encourage clients to purchase products from the practice."). *See also* Coffin Comment (stating that he believes most veterinary practices would become healthier fiscally if automatic prescription release were mandated, and veterinarians could no longer rely as heavily on pharmacy revenues).

279 Some veterinarians seem less concerned about a loss of revenue due to a shift toward increased retail sales of pet medications, and view that change as simply part of the evolution of the industry. These veterinarians appear to be making necessary adjustments to remain competitive in the changing marketplace. *See* Katie Burns, *Bayer Selling Flea and Tick Products Directly to Retailers*, J. AM. VETERINARY MED. ASS'N (Mar. 1, 2010), https:// www. avma.org/News/JAVMANews/Pages/100315g.aspx (Dr. Karen E. Felsted, CEO of National Commission on Veterinary Economics Issues, stating that veterinary prescription drugs and other veterinary products have been readily available outside of veterinary clinics for several years and that many veterinarians have already adapted to this changing distribution model, sometimes by shifting the emphasis from product revenues to services revenues and running their practices more productively and efficiently); Coffin Comment.

280 Workshop Tr. at 22-23 (Douglas G. Aspros). There are a variety of possible explanations for this shift in veterinary practice revenues. For instance, losing pharmacy sales to alternative

retailers will cause the ratios to change, but the change could also occur if new services, such as diagnostic tests, become available to sell.

[281] Arp, *supra* note 35 (quoting Karen Felsted, chief executive of Felsted Veterinary Consultants). *See also* N. Smith Comment at 7; Zeidner (1-800 CONTACTS) Comment at 16 (stating that the ophthalmic sector as a whole has experienced significant growth since the passage of the FCLCA).

[282] *See* NCVEI/BAYER USAGE STUDY, *supra* note 24, at 20-27 (suggesting that veterinary fee increases contributed to a decline in visits to veterinary practices); *id.* at 59 ("Contrary to common belief, demand for veterinary services is not inelastic; Frequency and size of fee increases are factors" in the decline in visits to veterinary practices); Ackerman, *supra* note 109 (suggesting that there is a ceiling for the prices veterinarians can charge for services and a limit to the veterinarian's ability to raise fees without commensurate value); Zeidner (1-800 CONTACTS) Comment at 13-16 (claiming that despite concerns of opponents of automatic prescription release for contact lenses, eye examination prices have not increased substantially to compensate for lost product sales).

[283] *See* NCVEI/BAYER USAGE STUDY, *supra* note 24, at 42 (suggesting that veterinarians consider both competition for services and competition for medications when making business decisions).

[284] Although the majority of veterinarians interviewed by FTC staff did not believe that they would go out of business due to a decline in pet medications revenues, some stakeholders suggested otherwise. *See* Maddigan (Willamette Valley Animal Hosp.) Comment ("Veterinary economics are currently under great pressure and the loss of revenue from pharmacy sales will either result in the closure of many vet hospitals around the country or result in higher prices for all services to compensate for the loss of pharmacy revenue."); S. Anderson (Ass'n for Veterinary Clinic Success) Comment ("Diluting veterinary practice income in any way would have a very detrimental impact on practices throughout the country, and especially for smaller practices. . . . Some veterinary practices will have difficulty in conforming with proposed legislation and I believe that it will force several of these small businesses out of business.").

[285] This type of effect is common in markets where consumers bear significant switching costs from changing the product that they use, or where suppliers of a durable good anticipate earning significant profits from aftermarket sales of complementary products or services. For example, sellers of photocopiers might anticipate future sales of consumables or services when setting the prices of photocopiers. *See, e.g.*, Joseph Farrell & Paul Klemperer, *Coordination and Lock-In: Competition with Switching Costs and Network Effects*, *in* 3 HANDBOOK OF INDUS. ORG. 1967-2072 (Mark Armstrong & Robert H. Porter eds., 2007); Dennis Carlton & Michael Waldman, *Competition, Monopoly, and Aftermarkets*, 26 J.L. ECON. & ORG. 54 (2010), *available at* http://jleo.oxfordjournals.org/content/26/1/54.full.

[286] During the FTC workshop, one panelist described the possibility of a similar pricing equilibrium in the markets for eye examinations and contact lenses, for which prescriptions have been subject to mandatory release since 2004. Dr. James Cooper points out the possible allocative inefficiency that could result from cross- subsidization between products and services. Cooper argues that it is inefficient when the prices for examinations and contact lenses are, respectively, below and above the competitive level. Workshop Tr. at 275 (James C. Cooper). A comparable inefficiency could occur with respect to veterinary examinations and pet medications.

[287] ASPCA Comment at 5 ("The affordability of veterinary care should not be tied to where the client decides to purchase medications. Pet owners should have the freedom to shop around for both affordable veterinary care and affordable veterinary drugs. Consumers denied information about the cost of medications and services could be paying unnecessarily high prices.").

[288] *See, e.g.*, Maddigan (Willamette Valley Animal Hosp.) Comment; Fankhauser Comment; S. CAL. VET SURVEY, *supra* note 143 ("[I]f I know ahead [that a client may request a portable prescription], I might give another injection or add a couple of minutes to surgery").

[289] *Principles of Veterinary Medical Ethics of the AVMA*, *supra* note 38 (Principle I.c.) ("The choice of treatments or animal care shall not be influenced by considerations other than the welfare of the patient, the needs of the client, and the safety of the public.").

[290] Lau, *Parasiticide Diversion*, *supra* note 56 (stating that there is an "inherent conflict of interest in a veterinarian's time-honored practice of writing prescriptions for or recommending medications that they also sell" and that this aspect of the larger debate surrounding the sale of pet medications often receives little attention).

[291] *See* N. Smith Comment at 5 (comparing veterinarians selling pet medications to a proverbial fox guarding a hen house and questioning veterinarians' "claim of objectivity and aggressively seeking the best customer value. . . .").

[292] *See* Workshop Tr. at 185 (Race Foster); Foster (F&S) Comment at 11 ("Consumers need to know that there is no conflict of interest involved when their veterinarian prescribes a particular medication. The present practice by at least one large drug manufacturer to financially incentivize clinics to prescribe its medications raises serious conflict of interest questions."); John Russell, *Drug Companies' Loose Purse Strings Court Vets*, INDIANAPOLIS STAR (Dec. 18, 2014), http:// www.indystar.com/ story/ news/ investigations/ 2014/12/18/drug-companies-loosen-purse-strings-to- woo-vets/20492301/ (describing how "the pet medicine industry is allowed to target veterinarians with marketing practices banned from the realm of human medicine" and suggesting that this could threaten the objectivity of veterinarians who prescribe drugs for pets). *See also* PACKAGED FACTS REPORT 3D, *supra* note 12, at 89 (describing the Elanco Earnings program that rewards veterinary practices for purchasing Elanco's parasiticide products); *id.* At 94 (describing the Merial 12.12.12. program directed to veterinarians, which may have contributed to 400,000 additional doses of Heartguard Plus sold in 2012).

[293] For example, consultants have suggested that veterinarians charge premium pricing for products that are not readily available at alternative retail outlets, and avoid stocking commodity products (e.g. human generics and OTC products) that are available for lower prices elsewhere. Furthermore, veterinary consultants have advised veterinarians to resist the urge to save clients money by prescribing human generics, in favor of prescribing veterinary-label products, reasoning that these products not only have been approved for safe use in animals, but also typically can be priced higher than products available at retail outlets. *See* Ackerman, *supra* note 104 (arguing, among other things, for the use of injectables that must be administered by veterinarians whenever possible, to guarantee compliance and health benefits, and also because these products may be priced higher due to their limited availability at retail outlets); MYERS, *supra* note 104, at 1 ("Prescribe veterinary drugs instead of human generics. Pharmacies, grocery stores, and warehouse clubs are promoting deeply discounted generics. Writing scripts for human generic drugs and sending clients to local pharmacies will encourage them to request scripts for future medications. Your goodwill gesture to save clients money may backfire."); Arp, *supra* note 35 (referencing veterinary consultant, Ernie Ward, DVM, who advises that one tactical and proactive reaction to pharmacy competition is switching to medications and products that are exclusive to the veterinary channel).

[294] *See, e.g.*, Workshop Tr. at 186 (Wendy Hauser) ("[D]rugs are selected not based on buyback programs or buy- in programs, and percentage discounts. They're selected because they're the best medications that I can offer my patients, period.");Workshop Tr. at 118 (Mark Cushing) (insisting that veterinarians do not attempt to maximize revenues by prescribing high-priced branded veterinary label products, and instead are willing to provide prescriptions, often for human generics, that may be filled through retail pharmacies).

[295] *Principles of Veterinary Medical Ethics of the AVMA*, *supra* note 38 (Principle VI.f.iv.) ("A veterinarian may not accept payment of any kind, in any form, from any source, such as a

pharmaceutical company or pharmacist, manufacturer of medical appliances and devices, for prescribing or referring a patient to said source. In each case, the payment violates the requirement to deal honestly with clients and colleagues. The client relies upon the advice of the veterinarian on matters of referral and prescribing. All referrals and prescriptions must be based on the skill and quality of the veterinarian to whom the patient has been referred or the quality and efficacy of the drug or product prescribed.").

[296] *See* discussion of regulatory mechanism, *supra* notes 219-224 and accompanying text.

[297] *See, e.g.*, Letter from Thomas Zerzan, President, Merial US Operations, to Veterinary Clients (Feb. 11, 2010), http://www.aldievet.com/docs/merial_20100219142042.pdf ("Merial's policy has always been to sell FRONTLINE® products only to licensed practicing veterinarians."); *Frontline Plus* Canine, MAIN ST. ANIMAL HOSP. OF BRADFORD, INC., http://www.mainstanimalhospital.com/index.php?option=com_opencart&Itemid=37&route =product/product&produ ct_id=50 (product webpage stating Merial's Frontline sales policy as follows: "Why are FRONTLINE Brand Products only available through my veterinarian? It is Merial's sales policy to sell our small animal products only where a veterinarian/client/patient relationship exists. Merial believes that the veterinarian is the only professional qualified to serve the health care needs of pets, the concerns of their owners and the appropriate use of our small animal products such as FRONTLINE Brand Products."); Letter from Stephen A. Connell, Dir. of Technical, Academic and Consumer Servs., Elanco, to Veterinary Clients (2012) [hereinafter Elanco Letter], *attached to* Shaprut Comment ("Elanco has maintained a strict policy that limits the distribution of our products to licensed veterinarians. Unauthorized sources of Elanco products, including Internet, big box retail and warehouse club pharmacies do not purchase Elanco products from Elanco or any of our authorized veterinary distributors."); Letter from Jim Heinle, Exec. Dir., U.S. Companion Animal, Merck Animal Health, to Pet Owners (June 14, 2013), http://www.merck-animal-health-usa.com/binaries/Activyl_Letter_tcm96-112654.pdf (stating that Merck Animal Health limits the distribution of companion animal medications to licensed veterinarians, and recommends that pet owners not purchase products from unauthorized sources, including Internet retailers); Pfizer Comment (#329) at 1; Novartis Comment at 3. *But see* Foster (F&S) Comment at 9 ("For the record, there are drug manufacturers and distributors who do not practice restricted distribution. These include Virbac, Farnam, Bayer, FidoPharm, Boehringer-Ingelheim, Cardinal Health and Anda.").

[298] *See, e.g.*, Novartis Comment at 3 ("The expertise, training and compassion possessed by veterinarians has been essential to helping NAH [Novartis Animal Health] achieve its objective of preserving and enhancing the quality of life of companion animals and ensuring the optimal application of innovative treatments. Accordingly, NAH brings its products to consumers and their pets exclusively through practicing veterinarians. NAH considers these highly skilled professionals to be our partners in addressing unmet medical needs. We have found no better, more effective way to ensure that innovative science is best directed to the benefit of pets. By distributing these treatments through veterinarians, pet owners receive the information necessary to use our products in the most safe and effective manner for the benefit of their companion animal."); *See also* Elanco Letter, *supra* note 297 ("We are committed to bringing high-quality, innovative products to pets. We believe your veterinarian is your best resource in recommending these products to you – and in keeping your best interests at heart. We encourage you to purchase veterinary products through your veterinarian, who is trained to make the best recommendations for you and those you love.").

[299] Workshop Tr. at 250-51 (Kent D. McClure). *See also* Elanco Letter, *supra* note 297 ("To ensure product efficacy and quality, we strongly recommend you purchase Elanco products only through your veterinarian. If a product is purchased outside of the veterinary-client-patient relationship, the following may occur: [t]he product may have been outside a documented chain of custody and we cannot ensure it has been handled according to label requirements; [a] product acquired through unauthorized sources, with or without a

prescription, will not qualify for any product guarantee reimbursements or be eligible for any consumer promotional offers; [w]e cannot guarantee the product hasn't been tampered with in some way; [t]he product may have been defaced and important information may be missing; [t]he product may be counterfeit.").

[300] Pfizer Comment (#329) at 3.

[301] *Id. See also* Workshop Tr. at 76 (Mark Cushing), 87 (Andrew J. Bane) (arguing that it is a rational decision for manufacturers to exclusively distribute their products through licensed medical professionals who are trained to understand the physiology and pharmacology of a host of animal species, and that likewise, it is a rational decision for distributors to honor these contractual requirements and sell only to veterinarians).

[302] *See, e.g.*, Novartis Comment at 4 ("Veterinarians understand patient history and drug interactions and serve as a control point for dispensing medications, which is key to supporting proper drug usage. Contact points such as treatment, prescription, dispensing and follow up appointments with pets and pet owners create a base of experience and opportunities for feedback that are unmatched. These contacts, and the continuity of care fostered by a strong VCPR, are critical to the effective administration of animal health care. When this continuity is broken the health and safety of companion animals are threatened. It is our position that nothing should interfere with this relationship or these contact points."); Workshop Tr. at 85, 87 (Clinton Vranian); Pfizer Comment (#329) at 1 ("From our experience, we feel strongly that veterinarians are the most effective educators of pet owners when it comes to ensuring animal health. Therefore, we believe that preserving the direct relationship between the veterinarian, the client and the patient – in all facets of animal healthcare, including the dispensing of medications – is critically important to ensuring pet health . . . .").

[303] *See* Workshop Tr. at 36-37, 94 (Paul D. Pion); *id.* at 86 (Clinton Vranian); Novartis Comment at 2-3 ("NAH continues to believe that distribution through the professional channel continues to present the best path to enhance animal well-being through innovation. . . . Like human pharmaceuticals, prescription pet medications are cost- intensive to develop and bring to market. . . . However, the market for these products is orders of magnitude smaller than in the human marketplace. Thus, there is a business challenge in getting the word out about new and innovative treatments in a cost effective manner. As a result, NAH relies heavily on education of the veterinarian through personal visits to detail all relevant aspects of the product and accessible technical product support, as pet owners generally turn to their veterinarian when their pet has a problem. NAH relies very little on advertising to the general public, or even through professional media. . . . The vast majority, if not all, of our marketing practices are designed to educate the veterinarian and defer to his or her professional judgment when it comes to patients. . . . [F]or a medication to earn a place in a clinic, a veterinarian must believe in the science, integrity and quality of the product and the company behind it. He or she will then overlay that information with their experience and the needs of their patients. . . . The impression that this business model somehow restricts access to medicine is false. In fact, this business model enhances access to a wide range of medicines that could not be developed without it. Much of the discussion at the Pet Medications Workshop centered around 'blockbuster' drugs. But many of the life-saving medicines most important to the health of companion animals have extremely small markets. It is only by maintaining the VCPR that these medicines can be made available.").

[304] Novartis Comment at 4 ("For one thing, by educating and distributing our products to practicing veterinarians, NAH has built relationships and developed a knowledge base with these veterinary professionals, which has helped sharpen our focus on the safety and health of companion animals. Working directly with the veterinarians who administer our products has driven innovation that has resulted in products that deliver therapies for previously unmet medical needs in pets.").

[305] N. Smith Comment at 1 (arguing that "coordinated restricted distribution practices undertaken by pet product manufacturers and veterinarians" have contributed to a fundamentally flawed

marketplace); Valley Vet Supply Comment at 3 ("A few of the major veterinary pharmaceutical companies have joined with the veterinary practitioners in collusion to keep their prescription pharmaceutical dispensing within the veterinary clinics, to the exclusion of licensed pharmacies. Their unwritten message to the practicing veterinarians is, "You choose our brand in your practice and we will limit your clients' consumer choice and competitive pricing options." This sales policy is implemented under the pretense it is necessary to ensure a VCPR. That is a fallacy, as a valid VCPR must exist at the time a prescription is written."); Kroger Comment at 1(suggesting that the limited distribution systems for pet medications and "anti-competitive behavior among veterinarians, and the product manufacturers that support them" have led to "inflated prices for consumers."). *See also* Matter Comment (arguing that drug manufacturers have colluded among themselves to maintain an oligopolistic pricing structure for pet medications, and that veterinarians are unfairly blamed for the high prices of these products).

[306] *See* In re: Disposable Contact Lens Antitrust Litigation, No. MDL 1030 (complaints filed M.D. Fla. 1994). For further discussion of this case, *see supra* note 226 and accompanying text; Zeidner (1-800 CONTACTS) Comment at 3.

[307] *See supra* note 305.

[308] *See* Edie Lau, *Bayer Opens Flea Product Sales to Retail Outlets*, VIN NEWS SERV. (Feb. 10, 2010), http://news.vin.com/VINNews.aspx?articleId=14996 [hereinafter Lau, *Bayer Opens Product Sales*] ("Bayer's new sales policy elicited a flurry of opinions . . . . Many comments posted on VIN were angry. Some practitioners said they would immediately stop carrying Bayer products. Others brainstormed on how they could register collective displeasure with the company's new stance."); Edie Lau, *PetSmart First Retailer to Carry Advantage under New Bayer Policy*, VIN NEWS SERV. (Mar. 17, 2010), http:// news.vin.com/ VINNews. aspx?articleId=15360 [hereinafter Lau, *PetSmart to Carry Advantage*] ("Bayer's move has been both praised and denounced by practitioners. Some credit the company with recognizing the realities of diversion and being honest about the benefits of retail trade to their business. Others see Bayer as having used veterinarians to cultivate consumer loyalty to their products, then cutting them out of the sales loop now that the products are well-recognized. So displeased are some about the change that they are turning away from Bayer.").

In 2008-2009, the Florida Office of the Attorney General investigated a complaint that veterinarians were threatening a group boycott of certain manufacturers who they believed were not taking sufficient measures to honor exclusive distribution policies and prevent product diversion. Ultimately, a settlement was reached with a veterinary trade organization and an individual veterinarian after the Florida Office of the Attorney General alleged that they had encouraged a veterinarian letter-writing campaign intended to threaten a group boycott. However, no evidence of collusion between veterinarians and manufacturers was reported. *See* Edie Lau, *Merial Details Company Stance on Product Diversion*, VIN NEWS SERV. (Feb. 26, 2010), http://news.vin.com/VINNews.aspx?articleId=15110 [hereinafter Lau, *Merial Stance on Diversion*].

[309] *See, e.g.*, AHI Comment at 2 ("Manufacturers utilize a variety of distribution channels to sell animal health products. Each manufacturer independently determines the channels most effective for the distribution of its products. In the companion animal market, manufacturers currently sell their products through distributors or directly to veterinarians, veterinary hospitals, retailers, and pharmacies (both on-line and bricks & mortar). Some companies limit the channels utilized for the sale of some of their products and some utilize different outlets for different categories of products. These types of practices are among those that the FTC has publically acknowledged as appropriate and common across industries.").

[310] *See* Foster (F&S) Comment at 9 ("For the record, there are drug manufacturers and distributors who do not practice restricted distribution. These include Virbac, Farnam, Bayer, FidoPharm, Boehringer-Ingelheim, Cardinal Health and Anda. This is a big plus for consumers in terms of price and choice and the number of animal patients having access to

proper treatment."). However, it appears that the vast majority of animal pharmaceutical sales are subject to exclusive distribution. Of the ten largest animal pharmaceutical manufacturers in 2012, at least five of them were known to have exclusive distribution policies, representing nearly 75 percent of industry sales in 2012. *See* PACKAGED FACTS REPORT 3D, *supra* note 12 at 6-7; *supra* note 297 (describing the exclusive distribution sales policies of five of the largest animal pharmaceutical manufacturers in 2012, including Merial, Elanco, Merck, Pfizer, and Novartis).

311 *See* Complaint at ¶¶ 16-18, Bayer Healthcare LLC v. Eli Lilly and Company, No. 1:11cv3047 (S.D.N.Y. May 4, 2011). For explanation of product diversion, *see infra* Section IV.A.3, The Secondary Market for Pet Medications, at 74.

312 *See* PACKAGED FACTS REPORT 3D, *supra* note 12, at 61. *See also id.* at 62 (reporting that Bayer's Animal Health Division has increased its pet medication revenues and consolidated its position in the market since its channel cross-over).

313 *See* Lau, *Bayer Opens Product Sales*, *supra* note 308; Lau, *PetSmart to Carry Advantage*, *supra* note 308; Edie Lau, *Bayer Wins Some, Loses Some*, VIN NEWS SERV. (Apr. 28, 2010), http://news.vin.com/VINNews.aspx?articleId=15609 [hereinafter Lau, *Bayer Wins Some*].

314 *See* PACKAGED FACTS REPORT 2D, *supra* note 14, at 78-80; PACKAGED FACTS REPORT 3D, *supra* note 12 at 63, 65.

315 Economic theory suggests that unless the manufacturer creates a financial incentive for dealers to promote the manufacturer's product, dealers will fail to devote any resources to promoting the manufacturer's product. *See* Benjamin Klein & Kevin M. Murphy, *Vertical Restraints as Contract Enforcement Mechanisms*, 31 J.L. & ECON. 265 (1988). Furthermore, a dealer that devotes resources to promoting a manufacturer's product may have higher costs than a dealer that fails to devote such resources, which could enable the non-promoting dealer to undercut the promoting dealer's price. In these situations, the manufacturer may protect the dealer by limiting "intrabrand" competition through some mechanism, so as to prevent non-promoting dealers from "free riding" on promoting dealers' efforts to increase consumer demand. *See* Lester G. Telser, *Why Should Manufacturers Want Fair Trade*, 3 J.L. & ECON. 86 (1960).

316 *See* Foster (F&S) Comment at 9 (suggesting that price support is the only reason drug manufacturers refuse to sell pet medications to fully licensed pharmacies, particularly those with Vet-VIPPS certification); *id.* at 4 ("As far as we can tell, restricting distribution has only one purpose: to maintain prices at higher levels than they would be with open competition. Who pays? Consumers."); Kroger Comment at 1 (stating that exclusive distribution builds loyalty from the veterinarians by allowing them to benefit financially, but that consumers will pay inflated prices as a result).

317 *See Principles of Veterinary Medical Ethics of the AVMA*, *supra* note 38 (Principle VI.) ("A veterinarian shall continue to study, apply, and advance scientific knowledge; maintain a commitment to veterinary medical education; make relevant information available to clients, colleagues, and the public; and obtain consultation or referral when indicated."); *id.* at sec. VI.b. ("Veterinarians should strive to improve their veterinary knowledge and skills, and they are encouraged to collaborate with other professionals in the quest for knowledge and professional development.").

318 Workshop Tr. at 113-14 (Nate Smith) ("The brand value associated with that vet recommendation is I can charge higher prices, I can have higher margins, because it's what the veterinarian has established from a brand perspective as the most efficacious, the most optimal medical treatment.").

319 *See, e.g.*, Jim Downing, *Gilded Lilly? Bayer Challenges Elanco Claims*, VIN NEWS SERV. (June 24, 2011), http://news.vin.com/VINNews.aspx?articleId=18945 ("Restricting retail sales of pet medications to licensed veterinarians with valid veterinarian-client-patient relationships is meant to be mutually beneficial: Veterinarians market drugs for the

pharmaceutical companies in exchange for the assurance that clients won't be able to purchase those products outside of a veterinary clinic.").

[320] *See* PACKAGED FACTS REPORT 2D, *supra* note 14, at 59 ("A key premise of pet medications marketing is that veterinarians will, whether directly or indirectly, help to sell the products, driven by their own desire to provide clients with the best healthcare options available and to realize higher practice revenues and profits. Accordingly, all of the large pharmaceutical marketers of pet medications court veterinarians, with sales representatives routinely calling on animal hospitals and private practices to promote their products and distribute free samples and gifts.").

[321] *See supra* note 292 and accompanying text.

[322] Telephone Interview with Kim-Jung et al., *supra* note 126 (By definition, an approved OTC drug is one for which adequate directions can be provided for a layperson to use safely and effectively. This would not apply to unapproved products available through certain retailers). Furthermore, FDA-approved nonprescription drug products intended for use in humans may be administered to animals under the direction of a veterinarian, in the presence of a valid veterinarian-client-patient relationship, and as according to the Federal Food, Drug, & Cosmetic Act and implementing regulations regarding extra-label drug use in animals (Title 21, Code of Federal Regulations, Part 530- Extralabel Drug Use in Animals).

[323] *See* Foster (F&S) Comment at 2 ("The entire point of being labeled an OTC product is to assure the public that the product has been judged safe for consumer use without a prescription and that consumers can shop online or walk into a store and buy the product, no doctor visit needed."); Magee (F&S) Comment at 11 ("In my opinion there is no medical justification for drug manufacturers restricting distribution of over-the-counter pet medications . . . .[I]t is hypocrisy of the highest order for a drug manufacturer to go to the trouble and expense of licensing a medication as over-the-counter and then claim, for so-called safety reasons, it should only be dispensed through veterinarians.").

The AVMA seems to offer somewhat conflicting statements regarding OTC products. On the one hand, the AVMA acknowledges that prescriptions are not required for OTC products and that the FDA has determined that directions for their use should be adequate for the public to follow. AVMA FAQs, *supra* note 52, at 1. On the other hand, the AVMA appears to agree with manufacturer justifications for selling OTC products only through veterinarians, claiming that "it seems more likely that the product will be used properly . . . if the veterinarian is supplying the medication and is counseling the pet owner on the proper use of the medication." *Id.* at 2.

[324] Magee (F&S) Comment at 12-13 (claiming that "the recommendation by the AVMA that a veterinarian should honor a client's request for a written prescription is moot if the client cannot fill the prescription anywhere except a veterinarian's office" and that, in its opinion, exclusive distribution "restricts competition and the consumer winds up paying higher prices."); *id.* at 15.

[325] Foster (F&S) Comment at 8 ("There is no reason to deny products to licensed pharmacies which are compliant with pharmacy laws and regulations."). *See also supra* notes 220 and 237 and accompanying text.

[326] Foster (F&S) Comment at 4 (describing safety concerns as a "false issue"); PetCareRx at 2-3; Valley Vet Supply Comment at 4 ("And the claim that pharmacists may not be equipped to fill a veterinarian's prescription as written because the pharmacist has not trained in veterinary pharmacology or physiology is overstated. Pharmacists complete rigorous training and continuing education, and are will equipped to fill any health provider's valid prescription. In addition, the veterinarian with a VCPR has the knowledge and ultimate responsibility for prescribing the proper medication and dosage."). *See also supra* note 225.

[327] PetCareRx Comment at 3 ("Some [manufacturers] also actively discourage purchase of their products from third-party pharmacies. These tactics include exaggerating safety concerns about pharmacy-purchased products, refusing to honor guarantees or warranties for, or

accept returns of, products purchased from sources other than veterinary offices, and refusing to provide even informational support to purchasers of such products."); Workshop Tr. at 147 (Race Foster); Foster (F&S) Comment at 7-8 (". . . there is a cohort of some manufacturers and a few veterinarians who paint every online pharmacy with the same brush, claiming directly or implying to consumers that no online pharmacy is truly qualified to fill pet prescriptions. . . . However, not every online pharmacy falls into that category.").

[328] *See* discussion of regulatory mechanism, *supra* notes 219-224 and accompanying text.

[329] *See* Foster (F&S) Comment at 4 ("As a requirement for a pharmacy to purchase medications from a manufacturer, maintenance of the direct veterinary-client-patient-relationship is a false issue. F&S only dispenses products when it receives a veterinarian's prescription from a veterinarian or pet owner who has obtained a prescription from a licensed veterinarian through a valid client-patient-relationship.").

[330] *See* discussion of Vet-VIPPS program, *supra* notes 49-52 and accompanying text.

[331] In addition to online pharmacy solutions, central fill pharmacies may also offer detailed reporting services and other medication management services to veterinary practices.

[332] Workshop Tr. at 54-55 (Andrew J. Bane). *See also id.* at 32-33 (Paul D. Pion).

[333] *See, e.g., We're VetSource*, VETSOURCE, http://www.vetsource.com/#About: (describing VetSource as employing pharmacists and pharmacy technicians, but not veterinarians). *See also* Magee (F&S) Comment at 14.

[334] Magee (F&S) Comment at 13-14. "Hypocritically, drug manufacturers sell to pharmacies, but only to those who have a financial arrangement in place with veterinarians. This directly contradicts the drug manufacturer assertion that prescription pet medication should only be sold by those with a valid [veterinary]-patient-client- relationship." *Id.* at 15. *See also* PACKAGED FACTS REPORT 3D, *supra* note 12, at 158-59 (describing how Vets First Choice, a leading central fill pharmacy, offers a solution that helps protect veterinary practice revenues in an increasingly competitive environment).

[335] *See generally* PACKAGED FACTS REPORT 3D, *supra* note 12, at 153 ("Although much is made of the gray market in this category, it appears to be a natural outcome when manufacturers elect to restrict supply to more expensive channels."); Workshop Tr. at 103-04 (Clinton Vranian) ("It's clear that this is an economic force and where there's sufficient demand for a product, the consumer or the market is going to find a way.").

[336] *See* PetMed Express, Inc., *supra* note 21, at 6 ("Historically, substantially all the major pharmaceutical manufacturers have declined to sell prescription and non-prescription pet medications directly to us. In order to assure a supply of these products, we purchase medications from various secondary sources, including a variety of domestic distributors."); PetCareRx Comment at 2 ("PetCareRx must purchase its pet medication supplies from different categories of suppliers for one main reason: historically, manufacturers have restricted their sale of prescription pet medications only to veterinarians and, in some purchase agreements, have prohibited veterinarians from re-selling such medications to distributors or third-party pharmacies. While some manufacturers have abandoned this anticompetitive practice, others continue to proffer the antiquated and flawed view that safety concerns warrant restricting distribution of prescription pet medications to veterinarians.").

[337] *See* Edie Lau, *The Flea Market*, VIN NEWS SERV. (Apr. 6, 2009), http:// news.vin.com/ VINNews.aspx?articleId=12576 [hereinafter Lau, *Flea Market*].

[338] According to SymphonyIRI sales data, "vet-only" brands have significant sales in the mass-market retail channels, which is noteworthy given that these brands do not appear to be authorized for distribution in the supermarkets and mass merchandisers that represent the large majority of SymphonyIRI-tracked sales. PACKAGED FACTS REPORT 2D, *supra* note 14, at 68-69 (noting that Merial's Frontline brand has been a leader in the non- veterinary retail channel for the dog and cat categories for several years, despite Merial's exclusive distribution policy).

[339] For extensive discussion of the secondary distribution system for OTC pet medications, see a series of articles written by Edie Lau, Jim Downing, and Peggy Guy (pseudonym) for the VIN News Service, from 2009 through 2012. Lau, *Flea Market*, *supra* note 337, https://web.archive.org/web/20120618130806/http://news.vin.com/VINNews.aspx?articleId =12576 (archived version) (the table at the top of this archived version of Edie Lau's article provides links to each article in the 13-part series on product diversion that ran from 2009 until 2011); Edie Lau, *Veterinarian Investigates Illicit Diversion of Flea Products*, VIN NEWS SERVICE (May 8, 2012), http://news.vin.com/VINNews.aspx?articleId=22512 (the first article in a 3-part series from 2012).

[340] The use of the term "unauthorized distributor" is not intended to imply that something illegal is necessarily occurring, as many of these distributors appear to be fully licensed within the states in which they operate. These distributors also may be referred to as "aggregators."

[341] *See generally* Workshop Tr. at 31 (Paul D. Pion).

Stakeholders have described other variations on this general approach. One retail pharmacy described a scenario in which "a single entity, often a veterinarian, becomes an unauthorized distributor and creates a network of other veterinarians who purchase an oversupply of product from manufacturers. The oversupply from this network of veterinarians is then aggregated into a central supply source that is sold – i.e. diverted – directly to retailers." Powers (F&S) Comment at 2.

In another scenario, an employee of a drug manufacturer (e.g. sales representative) and a veterinarian solicit a retailer to purchase a large volume of prescription or OTC pet medications. By involving a veterinarian, the manufacturer can still claim that it sells only through veterinarians. The veterinarian is generally paid for this effort through rebates and quantity discounts, and the retailer typically pays 15 to 20 percent more than the veterinarian pays. *Id.* at 1-2.

In addition, the NABP has identified the following practices: (1) veterinarians who serve as consultants to pharmacies or wholesalers, purchase drugs under their license, and then transfer the products to the pharmacy or wholesaler; (2) veterinarians who own pharmacies, purchase drugs under their veterinary license, and then transfer the products to the pharmacy; (3) wholesalers who purchase pet medications directly from manufacturers, despite claims by manufacturers that these products are restricted to the veterinary channel; and (4) wholesaler distributor license obtained under the name of a veterinary hospital that later goes out of business, only to have a distributor continue to purchase products under the veterinary hospital's license. Workshop Tr. at 63-66 (Gregg Jones).

[342] For purposes of this report, the term "veterinary diversion" generally refers to veterinarians who sell pet medications to unauthorized wholesale distributors or non-veterinary retailers (e.g., retail pharmacies), thus creating the secondary market for pet medications. This report does not analyze situations where veterinarians sell prescription drugs to consumers without first establishing a VCPR or where non-practicing veterinarians operate retail establishments that sell prescription drugs to consumers without requiring a valid prescription.

In the human medications industry, the term "diversion" always implies something illegal is occurring, such as the diversion of controlled substances to unlicensed sellers and, ultimately, consumers who lack a proper prescription. With respect to the animal market, there are some widely varying regulations that deal with veterinary drug distribution, and the term "diversion" may not always imply something illegal and therefore may not have the same negative connotations. Workshop Tr. at 107-08 (Gregg Jones).

[343] Until recently, the AVMA Principles of Veterinary Medical Ethics described veterinarian merchandising of prescription drugs outside the context of a VCPR and the resale of medications outside the manufacturer sales policies as unethical. *See Principles of Veterinary Medical Ethics of the AVMA,* http:// web.archive.org/ web/ 20120729082115/ http://www.avma.org/issues/policy/ethics.asp_(approved Nov. 2010) (Principles III.C.2. & VI.D.). However, the newly revised AVMA Principles of Veterinary Medical Ethics no

longer include this language. *See Principles of Veterinary Medical Ethics of the AVMA*, *supra* note 38.

[344] The NABP stated that there are pharmacies that remove secondary bar coding on certain types of pet medications intended to identify the veterinarian that purchased the product. The pharmacies may also remove these medications from the original packaging, place them into proprietary vials, and dispense the product in a similar manner to human drugs. *See* Workshop Tr. at 63-66 (Gregg Jones).

[345] *See* Workshop Tr. at 31 (Paul D. Pion) ("Manufacturer and distributor reps, it turns out, are a big part of this. How high it goes up that they're encouraged to do this, to make their numbers, and to increase their income, we don't know. But we know that they're a big part of this. And there's a lot of indications that manufacturers, despite saying that they don't want to sell into these channels, and distributors, are doing so directly as well."); *id.* at 103-05 (Clinton Vranian) (suggesting that some manufacturers use the secondary market to obtain sales they might not have obtained through the veterinary channel). One retail pharmacy stated that diversion is sanctioned by manufacturers who publicly claim to sell products exclusively through the veterinary channel, while privately allowing their sales representatives to engage in product diversion to retailers. According to this stakeholder, manufacturers use this practice to increase their sales volumes through retailers, but at inflated prices to the consumer. Powers (F&S) Comment at 1-3. *See also* Foster (F&S) Comment at 5-6 ("We have first-hand knowledge of drug manufacturer reps trying to set up product diversion.").

[346] At the workshop, Novartis explained that it had a history of trying to stop diversion, but found that it was impossible. "[A] secondary supply can be done legally and it's not our place to prevent a legal business from operating in any way." Novartis also stresses that it aggressively pursues counterfeit or unapproved product reaching the secondary market, but otherwise does not implement measures to control diversion. "Our best estimate is between two and five percent maybe on an annual basis winds up in the secondary market. The cost of trying to stop that, setting aside competitive issues, is just cost prohibitive. We focus on bringing clients back to the veterinarian and controlling what we can control. In the end, our objective through these measures is to protect the quality and health and life of animals. It's not to protect the channel, control distribution, limit competition or support inefficient businesses." Workshop Tr. at 103-05 (Clinton Vranian).

[347] *See* Lau, *Merial Stance on Diversion*, *supra* note 308 (referencing conversations with executives at Merial, Lau states "the company is limited in its ability to aggressively pursue diverters [of OTC Frontline] because diversion [of this product] is not illegal and because Frontline is the market leader, putting Merial under particular scrutiny to avoid breaking laws against restraint of trade, anti-competitive behavior and collusion.").

Elanco also has a stated policy of trying to stop diversion. "Since 2010, Elanco has identified close to 400 veterinarians/diverters who failed to meet our corporate sales policy and their ability to purchase Elanco Companion Animal products has been revoked. Elanco is constantly evaluating new ways to identify and stop those who choose to participate in this deceptive action." Yet, Elanco acknowledges that, despite these efforts, it is aware that some of its products are being sold by online and retail pharmacies. Elanco Letter, *supra* note 297.

[348] *See* Lau, *Flea Market*, *supra* note 337 ("Judging from fiery discussions that crop up repeatedly on Veterinary Information Network (VIN) online discussion boards, a prevailing sentiment is that manufacturers have used and betrayed veterinarians: used, by enlisting veterinarians to promote their products, promising them exclusive claim to the retail profits; and betrayed by not enforcing the policies once pet owners came to trust the brands."); Lau, *Parasiticide Diversion*, *supra* note 56 ("Many clinicians are passionately upset that drug companies as a whole are failing to control distribution of product that the companies themselves say should be sold only by veterinarians. Rumor says that some of the companies are complicit in making their product available to general retailers and online pharmacies. Companies say

they fully support veterinarians and don't tolerate diversion, but most refuse to detail how they combat over-the-counter sales or explain how so large a volume of product escapes their control.").

[349] *See, e.g.*, Elanco Letter, *supra* note 297. There appear to be multiple levels of manufacturer product support, the most basic being purchase price reimbursement or product replacement in the event of a defective product. There is also diagnostic reimbursement, the highest level of technical support in which the manufacturer pays for diagnostic analysis to determine the reason for a pet's adverse reaction to a medication. Workshop Tr. at 129-31(Clinton Vranian).

[350] *See e.g.*, Shaprut Comment; *The Danger of Veterinary Internet Pharmacies*, ANIMAL MED. CTR. OF S. CAL., http://www.animalmedcenter.com/news-and-press/article/the-danger-of-veterinary-internet-pharmacies ("You should also know that neither the drug maker nor your veterinarian will stand behind a product's guarantee if you purchase the product online."); *Frequently Asked Questions*, CLANTON ANIMAL HOSP., http://www.cahvet.us/faq.html; *Pharmacy*, SUNNYCREST ANIMAL CARE CTR., http:// www.sunnycrestanimalcare.com/ services/veterinary-care/pharmacy/.

[351] For example, Novartis provides technical support for its products irrespective of point of sale. To receive diagnostic reimbursement from Novartis, a veterinarian must initiate the complaint, but this does not depend on the product being purchased at the veterinary clinic. Workshop Tr. at 130-31 (Clinton Vranian). According to an article published by VIN News Service, spokesmen for Merial and Pfizer stated that they guarantee their products regardless of where they were purchased. Lau, *Parasiticide Diversion*, *supra* note 56 (suggesting that drug companies must not be overly concerned about counterfeit pet parasiticide products because they are willing to guarantee these products regardless of whether they are purchased through a retail channel). Elanco, on the other hand, has a stated policy of refusing product guarantee reimbursements for prescription and OTC products acquired through unauthorized sources. Elanco Letter, *supra* note 297.

[352] A few states appear to have statutes that explicitly prohibit veterinary diversion of prescription drugs, or have issued legal advisory opinions or official written guidance indicating that veterinary diversion is illegal. Most states, however, do not have veterinary or pharmacy practice statutes that expressly address veterinary diversion of prescription or OTC pet medications. At most, some states require that veterinarians must establish a VCPR before dispensing, distributing or selling pet medications, and these requirements might be construed to prohibit veterinary diversion to wholesale distributors and non-veterinary retailers. Some state veterinary board officials informed FTC staff that they interpret these statutes to prohibit veterinary diversion, while other state veterinary board officials informed FTC staff that they are uncertain whether existing statutes prohibit veterinary diversion or they believe it is allowed. Also, it appears that in many states where veterinary diversion of prescription pet medications may arguably violate some state laws, the sale of OTC pet medications is largely unregulated and veterinary diversion of these products may not be prohibited, particularly where veterinarians are allowed to obtain wholesale distributor licenses.

[353] *See, e.g.*, Workshop Tr. at 58 (Andrew J. Bane) (arguing that diversion of prescription pet medications occurs in violation of veterinary practice and state pharmacy board statutes in nearly every state and claiming that "[g]enerally, veterinarians are authorized to dispense prescription products via the respective veterinary practice acts of the states within which they practice. These acts require that the prescription dispensing by the veterinarian is to occur within the context of the valid Veterinarian-Client-Patient-Relationship. This requirement is violated when veterinarians wholesale products outside of the context of this relationship to other businesses. Additionally, anyone reselling prescription products needs to be properly licensed according to the state boards of pharmacy, just as is required of legitimate wholesale veterinary distributors.").

[354] According to the NABP, under the Food, Drug and Cosmetic Act, human drug distributors must be licensed by their resident state and human drug sales must be tracked back to a manufacturer or authorized distributor, in accordance with rules established by the FDA. These requirements do not exist for veterinary drug distribution, however, and the licensing of wholesale distributors of veterinary drugs varies widely by state. Workshop Tr. at 65 (Gregg Jones). Furthermore, there are no audit trail requirements for veterinarians to demonstrate whether they purchase products under their veterinary license and resell under their wholesale license. *Id.* at 107. *See also id.* At 129 (Paul D. Pion) (claiming that state pharmacy veterinary boards have often been unable to clarify for him whether veterinary diversion is legal in their state); Lau, *Flea Market*, *supra* note 337 ("Diversion [of OTC pet medications] may violate company sales policies, but it is not illegal per se.").

[355] *But see* Kan. Bd. of Veterinary Exam'rs v. Maloley (KBVE 2006) (Case No. 3052.11) (board disciplinary action against a veterinarian who purchased prescription and OTC veterinary products from manufacturers and distributors and resold them to other establishments, including Internet retailers, in violation of established marketing polices and without having a VCPR with the ultimate consumers who received the products from the retailers); Kan. Bd. of Veterinary Exam'rs v. Otto (KBVE 2006) (Case No. 04047) (board disciplinary action against a veterinarian who solicited and arranged for the purchase by himself and other Kansas veterinarians of large quantities of OTC pet medications for resale to persons other than the end user, including other retailers); Tex. Bd. of Veterinary Medical Exam'rs v. Box, Agreed Order 2009-24 (Oct. 26, 2009) (board disciplinary action against a veterinarian who allowed a retailer seller of veterinary drugs and supplies to use his license to purchase bulk veterinary pharmaceutical drugs and supplies; it appears that the Respondent rectified the situation by becoming licensed as a wholesale distributor of prescription drugs with the Texas Department of State Health Services); Tex. Bd. of Veterinary Medical Exam'rs v. Wilkinson, Negotiated Settlement, Docket Number 1991-16 (Feb. 1991) (board disciplinary action against a veterinarian who allowed his license to be used for the unauthorized delivery of prescription drugs to a retailer; failure to register as a wholesale drug distributor; and not establishing a VCPR with the end-user of the prescription drugs). *See also* Jessica Tremayne, *Kansas veterinary board takes actions against DVM licenses*, DVM360.Com (May 1, 2006), http://veterinarynews.dvm360.com/kansas-veterinary-board-takes-actions-against-dvm-licenses (stating that the Kansas Board of Veterinary Examiners sent a letter to about 2,400 licensed Kansas veterinarians stating that legal action will be taken against them if caught reselling products in a manner that violates manufacturer directions).

[356] *See* PetCareRx Comment at 1; Kroger Comment at 1-2; PACKAGED FACTS REPORT 3D, *supra* note 12, at 37 ("For many years, flea/tick spot-ons have been subject to massive gray market (unauthorized) distribution of products that are supposed to be restricted to the veterinary channel . . . . While this perhaps boosts flea/tick care sales by making the products more affordable and more widely available in non-veterinary channels, it is putting even more price pressure in the market, as Frontline has experienced.").

Some stakeholders acknowledge that the secondary market may have expanded consumer access to pet medications, but continue to debate the extent to which the secondary market may have led to lower prices. *See* Workshop Tr. at 38 (Paul D. Pion) ("the gray market starts to appear, and what this did was expand the market. It reached consumers who didn't go to veterinary clinics. It didn't really lower prices much, because it was still all mostly coming through veterinary chains, and so there wasn't much of a margin, because veterinarians weren't marking them up as much as people believe, in general.").

[357] Foster (F&S) Comment at 5-6 ("[B]y refusing to sell direct to retailers but selling to them under the table, manufacturers are forcing extra layers of cost into the system. . . . In addition, pet owners cannot always be assured that their preferred pharmacy will have the products they need when they need them, because the diversion process removes a regular supply of products to retailers."); Powers (F&S) Comment at 2 ("Consumers suffer because

the multiple steps involved in diversion artificially inflate prices and create an inconsistent supply for retailers and pet owners."). *See also* Workshop Tr. at 70-71, 73 (Nate Smith).

358 An exception would be if a manufacturer knowingly entered into some type of diversion scheme, in which it sold product directly to a veterinarian, who then sent the product directly to a retailer. Some stakeholders have reported that in these situations, product may be officially sold to the veterinarian, but actually sent directly to a warehouse owned by the retailer. Retailers may still pay significant mark-ups for these products, but the product flows through fewer entities.

359 Workshop Tr. at 100 (John Powers) ("Any product, whether it's hardware or housewares, where you include another step in the distribution channel, is going to raise prices for the consumer ultimately. Most companies have a minimum mark-up they can work on and still be profitable. Cost enters into that equation. So, every incremental cost you add, from the time the product is manufactured until it gets to the ultimate retailer, will definitely affect the price of that product to the consumer."). *See also id.* at 98-99 (Nate Smith) ("[Y]ou're always going to look at how many players are there in a supply chain, how many times is a product received, touched, reaped, distributed, shipped somewhere else.").

360 *See* PetCareRx Comment at 3-4 ("Consumers who do purchase prescription pet medications from third-party pharmacies may pay higher prices than they would have if pharmacies could obtain all drugs directly from manufacturers or from distributors that purchase directly from manufacturers. This is because purchasing veterinarians' surplus directly or indirectly through distributors creates unnecessary inefficiencies and can result in supply shortages, both of which increases costs for pharmacies, which are then passed on to consumers."); Foster (F&S) Comment at 5 (stating that with diversion, retailers pay prices that are "15% higher or more, with no payment terms, and no volume price breaks," resulting in higher prices to consumers); Powers (F&S) Comment at 1 ("[T]hrough product diversion consumers, pharmacies and retailers become victims of elevated prices, inconsistent supply and restricted consumer choice."); N. Smith Comment at 5 ("Of course, the prices pet owners are charged for filling prescriptions from alternative channels are inflated because of the inability of those channels to obtain product directly from manufacturers.").

361 *See, e.g.*, Lau, *Bayer Wins Some*, *supra* note 313 (PetMed Express CFO, Bruce Rosenbloom, stating that the company hopes to purchase the Bayer products "at a better price than we got it previously" now that it can buy direct); Interview with representatives from PetCareRx, Inc. (Jan. 22, 2015) (to understand whether PetCareRx paid lower prices for Bayer Animal Health products as a result of the manufacturer's direct distribution of products to PetCareRx).

362 *See* Workshop Tr. at 60-61 (Brad Dayton); *id.* at 146 (Race Foster) ("Today, in our pharmacy, we have more prescriptions on file than we are allowed drug to fill."). *But see* Jim Downing, *PetMed Express Stumbles*, VIN NEWS SERV. (Dec. 8, 2011), http:// news.vin.com/ VINNews.aspx?articleId=20606 (citing Foster as stating that since 2009, obtaining OTC pet medications through secondary distribution channels has become much easier for retailers).

363 The International Association of Compounding Pharmacists ("IACP") expressed concerns about its members being able to meet the needs of patients due to their inability to procure finished drug products directly from manufacturers or authorized distributors. Workshop Tr. at 69-70 (David G. Miller). The FDA requires that compounding of medications for veterinary use must be done with commercially-available finished drug products. *See id.* Compounded products are very important to veterinary practice, as various animals may require that certain medications be prepared in a specific way that is amenable to their consumption or other application. *See generally* Indep. Pharmacy Alliance Comment at 1 ("Many owners seek compounded pet medications that can be ingested in liquid form or blended with pet foods to ensure better medication treatment and pet cooperation to ensure pet medication utilization."). IACP states that, because of manufacturer sales policies,

compounding pharmacies cannot buy drugs directly and, instead, must obtain products from veterinarians, which leads to potential disruptions in the supply chain. *See* Workshop Tr. at 68-69 (David G. Miller).

364 *See* Foster (F&S) Comment at 6 ("Consumers . . . pay in aggregate millions of dollars a year more than they would have if normal market forces were allowed to come into play. In addition, pet owners cannot always be assured that their preferred pharmacy will have the products they need when they need them, because the diversion process removes a regular supply of products to retailers."); PetMed Express, Inc., *supra* note 21, at 6 ("We cannot guarantee that if we continue to purchase prescription and non-prescription pet medications from secondary sources that we will be able to purchase an adequate supply to meet our customers' demands, or that we will be able to purchase these products at competitive prices."); *id.* at 7 ("We need to properly manage our inventory to provide an adequate supply of these products and avoid excessive inventory . . . . In the event that subsequent orders fall short of original estimates, we may be left with excess inventory. Significant excess inventory could result in price discounts and increased inventory carrying costs. Similarly, if we fail to have an adequate supply of some SKUs, we may lose sales opportunities. We cannot guarantee that we will maintain appropriate inventory levels. Any failure on our part to maintain appropriate inventory levels may have a material adverse effect on our financial condition and results of operations.").

365 Workshop Tr. at 98 (Brad Dayton) (stating that time delays are the biggest inefficiency).

366 PetCareRx Comment at 3-4.

367 *See* Workshop Tr. at 101-02 (Clinton Vranian).

368 *Id.* at 102 (John Powers) (stating that some manufacturers that used to encourage retailers to carry their prescription products have recently made the decision to cut off their supply).

369 *See, e.g., id.*

370 *See* Workshop Tr. at 57 (Andrew J. Bane) ("[T]his gray market distribution channel creates substantial risk of adulterated or counterfeit compounds being introduced."); *id.* at 122-23 (David G. Miller); GADA Comment at 5 ("Once product is diverted from the manufacturer's authorized distribution channel, product quality and integrity cannot be ensured."); SVHP Comment at 2 ("The SVHP also believes that the existing gray market utilized by non- veterinarians to obtain prescription veterinary medicines invites fraud, deception and safety issues for pets and their owners."); Brown Comment (#521); J. Forbes Comment; *Cf.* Kroger Comment at 2 ("There will be operators of high quality documentation and handling. We are participating in this distribution method, and are highly confident in our business partner, and the standard operating procedures that have been built to ensure a safe supply channel. Unfortunately there will be operators of poor quality storage and distribution, which could be a threat to safety.").

371 *See* Workshop Tr. at 57 (Andrew J. Bane) ("The lack of regulatory oversight means that the appropriate mechanisms are not in place to ensure that prescription products are stored and shipped under their required conditions."); *id.* at 122-23 (David G. Miller).

372 *See id.* at 57 (Andrew J. Bane) ("On the matter of gray market distribution of veterinary prescription products, we feel that this unregulated product trafficking has the potential to endanger pet health. . . . This also means that there's a lack of transparency in the chain of custody of the products for the dispensing pharmacists as well as for the pet owner."); *id.* at 108-09 (Nate Smith) (stating that diversion can be problematic for retailers if it compromises their ability to establish a proper chain of custody); Gay (VetRxDirect) Comment (#576) ("Without pedigrees in the distribution of prescription veterinary medicines, there is a significant risk of fraud, substitution, and mishandling.").

373 Workshop Tr. at 122-23 (David G. Miller).

374 *Id.* at 122 (David G. Miller) ("Our preference is to always purchase either directly from the manufacturer, or through a wholesaler who has a direct relationship that is licensed and regulated.");Workshop Tr. at 108 (N. Smith) ("We would prefer sourcing the product from the manufacturer to know that that supply chain has had all the integrity, all the controls.").

See also Edie Lau, *Are Pet Drugs Like Contact Lenses?*, VIN NEWS SERV. (Sept. 19, 2012), http://news.vin.com/VINNews.aspx?articleId=24419 ("PetMed Express would like very much to purchase pet medications directly from manufacturers. ").

[375] Workshop Tr. at 65-66 (Gregg Jones).

[376] Telephone Interview with Gregg Jones, Compliance Manager, et. al., Nat'l Ass'n of Bds. of Pharmacy (Sept. 11, 2012).

[377] Conversations with the NABP confirm that evaluation of supply sources has been included in the Vet-VIPPS accreditation process since early 2012, to mitigate any risk that products may be counterfeit or adulterated. Pharmacies that rely on secondary distribution sources must demonstrate that the drugs they acquire are authentic and originated with the manufacturer. Telephone Interview with Carmen Catizone, Exec. Dir., Nat'l Ass'n of Bds. of Pharmacy (July 12, 2012); Telephone Interview with Gregg Jones, Compliance Manager, et. al., Nat'l Ass'n of Bds. of Pharmacy (Sept. 11, 2012). *See* Edie Lau, *Accreditation Body Questions Pharmacists on Veterinary Drug Suppliers*, VIN NEWS SERV. (June 28, 2012), http://news.vin.com/VINNews.aspx?articleId=23189 (stating that supply sources are now being evaluated as part of the Vet-VIPPS accreditation process).

[378] *See* PetCareRx Comment at 2; Kroger Comment at 2; Workshop Tr. at 131-32 (John Powers) (noting that Vet- VIPPS certified online pharmacies are required to have a policy for handling and storing product).

[379] Workshop Tr. at 131-32 (John Powers) (stating that both the veterinary and retail channels have problems with misused, expired, or poorly handled products).

[380] *See* Workshop Tr. at 122-23 (David G. Miller) ("We need to open the marketplace up so that legitimate, licensed pharmacies can purchase the same way that a veterinarian can purchase [directly] from . . . a manufacturer or wholesaler. Then there will be no need for a secondary market."); Foster (F&S) Comment at 6 ("By eliminating manufacturer driven diversion practices, prices will remain affordable and proof of distribution becomes transparent, traceable, and trusted. Veterinarians and consumers deserve transparency from drug manufacturers."); Valley Vet Supply Comment at 3 ("The proper licensing of veterinary pharmacies provides safety and efficacy for the consumer purchasing animal medications (pet, equine, and food animal). Full cooperation and validation in product distribution from veterinary drug manufacturers would further ensure product validity, safety and efficacy. Mandatory EDI sales reporting (a common practice) from licensed pharmacies back to pharmaceutical manufacturers could provide tracking of product sales to the end user for added distribution security and assurance."); Workshop Tr. at 53, 131 (John Powers).

[381] Workshop Tr. at 82 (Paul D. Pion). Similarly, the Society of Veterinary Hospital Pharmacists argues that "the integrity of these products must be ensured by requiring distributive pedigrees and legitimate distribution channels that would minimize the risks and dangers demonstrated by the current gray market." SVHP Comment at 2.

[382] Pfizer Comment (#329) at 2 ("We train veterinary distributors and veterinarians on proper transportation, handling and storage, and we track those metrics to ensure the quality and integrity of our products – which helps to ensure their ultimate safety to pets. Despite our efforts, the same cannot always be said in situations where our products are diverted away from the veterinary market and sold outside of our tracked and verified distribution channel (e.g. gray market distribution)."). *See also* AHI Comment at 3 ("[M]any manufacturers have invested tremendous resources to educate veterinarians about their products."); Workshop Tr. at 126 (David G. Miller) (explaining that manufacturers teach veterinarians about the products that they develop and bring to market); *id.* At 86-87 (Clinton Vranian) (stressing the importance of manufacturer education of veterinarians).

[383] *See* PetMed Express, Inc., *supra* note 21, at 4 ("We believe having strong relationships with product manufacturers will ensure the availability of an adequate volume of products ordered by our customers, and will enable us to provide more and better product information."). *See also* SVHP Comment at 2 ("The SVHP also recommends consideration and collaboration on the part of the Board of Pharmaceutical Specialties, boards of

pharmacy, pharmaceutical companies, and veterinary drug distributors to develop a system to qualify pharmacists and pharmacies that have the expertise to dispense companion animal prescription medications."); Brown Comment (#521) (stating that a direct distribution system would eliminate concerns about product pedigree in the secondary distribution system, but that pharmacists still would not be able to safely dispense pet medications without comprehensive training in veterinary pharmacology).

384 In an interview discussing Bayer's decision to end its exclusive distribution policies, Dan Peizer, marketing manager for Bayer Animal Health, described how Internet and brick-and-mortar retailers would now be able to receive direct product support from Bayer. "This is important because it assures retailers that they are providing pet owners with product direct from the manufacturer backed by our full technical support." *An Advantage for Pet Stores*, PET BUS. (Dec. 1, 2010), www.petbusiness.com/articles/2010-12-01/An-Advantage-for--Pet-Stores. *See also Distributor Locator*, BAYER ANIMAL HEALTH, https:// web.archive.org/ web/20120111135750/http://www.bayer- ah.com/petSpecialty/index.cfm (archived version) (instructing pet specialty retailers that they can purchase Bayer's animal products directly from an authorized distributor, which assures them that they are receiving quality product backed by the support of Bayer Animal Health; reliable supply and availability; and merchandising and marketing support from the distributor and Bayer Animal Health).

385 *See* Workshop Tr. at 124 (Clinton Vranian) (suggesting that product training for pharmacists regarding veterinary products "may wind up increasing the price of certain products."). *See also supra* note 303 and accompanying text.

386 *See, e.g.*, PACKAGED FACTS REPORT 3D, *supra* note 12 at 61 (describing how in certain circumstances, the sales opportunities outside the veterinary channel far outweigh the concerns regarding negative pushback from veterinarians and distributors); Lindsey Wojcik, *Another One Bites the Dust*, Pet Bus. (Jan. 31, 2012), www.petbusiness.com/articles/2012-01-31/Another-One-Bites-the-Dust- (describing Bayer's expansion into the non-veterinary retail channel and suggesting that other manufacturers could follow suit).

387 FED. TRADE COMM'N, *supra* note 88, at 9; GADA Comment at 3-4 ("The extensive availability and use of human generic drugs over brand name alternatives results in enormous cost savings."); *See* Reiffen & Ward, *supra* note 88; GENERIC PHARM. ASS'N, GENERIC DRUG SAVINGS IN THE U.S. 1 (6th annual ed. 2014), http:// www.gphaonline.org/ media/cms/GPhA_Savings_Report.9.10.14_FINAL.pdf (indicating that human generic medicines saved the U.S. healthcare system "nearly $1.5 trillion over the past 10 years (2004-2013)").

388 GADA Comment at 1; K&L Gates Comment at 1 ("[G]eneric animal drugs dispensed by retail pharmacies provide an alternative to inject price competition into the animal drug distribution/dispensing system while maintaining the high standards of safety and quality that pet owners rightly demand.").

389 *See supra* note 89; K&L Gates Comment at 5-6; Workshop Tr. at 47-48 (Michael H. Hinckle).

390 21 U.S.C. § 360b(n). Generic animal drugs are subject to an FDA approval process that is similar to human generic drugs, in which applicants "must demonstrate that the drugs are safe and effective for their intended use and are manufactured under the same quality standards that apply" to the branded drugs. GADA Comment at 1.

391 PACKAGED FACTS REPORT 3D, *supra* note 12, at 54.

392 *Id.* at 55 ("That approximately 90% of the drugs used for animals have no generic equivalent also signals strong market potential. Many of the patents on relevant drugs have expired, and the time needed to gain additional FDA review of a generic pet drug is relatively short: less than five years, compared with the decade or more it takes to develop a human drug from scratch. Accordingly, some analysts predict that generics will account for half of all pet medications within a decade."); *id.* at 57 ("With several patents on branded pet drugs having already expired and many more scheduled to expire in the next few years, competition in pet generics can only be expected to intensify. . . .").

[393] PACKAGED FACTS REPORT 2D, *supra* note 14, at 64 (referencing survey conducted by Advanstar Veterinary Healthcare Communications). *See also* PACKAGED FACTS REPORT 3D, *supra* note 12, at 58 ("As the market develops, generic pet medications will likely also become more attractive to pet owners from a price perspective. . . . Moreover, as veterinary costs continue to go up, those savings may be even more important on the pet side, where the vast majority of pet health costs are paid out of pocket as opposed to through insurance programs.").

[394] PACKAGED FACTS REPORT 2D, *supra* note 14, at 63. *See also Frequently Asked Questions*, PUTNEY, http://putneyvet.com/education/faqs (describing benefits of generic animal drugs to veterinary practices); *Veterinary Viewpoints*, PUTNEY, http:// putneyvet.com/ education/viewpoints (veterinarians describing patient compliance and financial benefits of stocking and prescribing generic animal drugs).

[395] *See* PACKAGED FACTS REPORT 3D, *supra* note 12, at 38 (". . . the race to market of generics may boost sales in the short term by increasing volume sales, but the longer term may be a dampening effect on dollar sales due to generics' lower prices. Any 'new' sales via retail channels will also involve market cannibalization, since they will come primarily at the expense of veterinary channel sales.").

[396] *See supra* notes 31 and 37 and accompanying text; GADA Comment at 2.

[397] AVDA Comment at 1 ("The primary market for veterinary supplies consists of some 55,000 veterinarians practicing in more than 25,000 veterinary practices throughout the United States."); GADA Comment at 3.

[398] GADA Comment at 3.

[399] *See, e.g.*, Workshop Tr. at 109-10 (Clinton Vranian); GADA Comment at 3.

[400] GADA Comment at 3.

[401] *Id.* at 5 ("The traditional model under which pet owners obtain pet medications has some inherent efficiencies. Distributors offer a wide array of products from numerous manufacturers and in essence, serve as a one-stop-shop for veterinarians. In turn, when pet owners have their pets treated by veterinarians, they can often get the medical advice and services and the medications they need all at the veterinary practice as part of the same transaction. As discussed above, blocking generic drugs from this model means generic drug manufacturers cannot take advantage of these efficiencies and cost-effective generic drug options become less available to pet owners.").

[402] In general, exclusive dealing agreements may have procompetitive justifications or may result in anticompetitive harms, depending on the particular circumstances surrounding the agreements. Potential benefits of exclusive dealing agreements may include enhanced marketing support or other services for the manufacturer's brand that are useful to consumers. Potential harms of such agreements may include dominant manufacturers blocking rivals from accessing a necessary sales channel, thereby marginalizing them, forcing them out of the market, or deterring their entry into the market in the first place.

[403] Workshop Tr. at 115-16 (Paul D. Pion) (explaining why these types of agreements are no longer common, that they are in no one's interest except the manufacturer, and that neither consumers nor veterinarians benefit from these agreements in terms of price or convenience.); *id.* at 36-38 (explaining how, in the past, these types of agreements artificially inhibited competition, and kept prices to consumers higher than they would have been otherwise); *id.* At 112-13 (Andrew J. Bane) (stating that there are fewer instances of manufacturer-distributor exclusive agreements in recent years and that pharmacists are not likely to enter into any exclusive arrangements with manufacturers); Lau, *Bayer Wins Some*, *supra* note 313 (describing exclusive dealing agreements that Merial had with certain distributors until 2009, in which "Merial prohibited distributors who carried their flea, tick and heartworm products for dogs and cats from selling competitors' flea, tick and heartworm products." The article states that these agreements with the largest distributors eventually ended due to distributor consolidation.).

[404] *See* GADA Comment at 3-5 (claiming to be aware of at least two large pioneer companies that entered into these types of exclusive dealing agreements with large, national distributors); Workshop Tr. at 116-17 (Michael H. Hinckle); *Frequently Asked Questions*, *supra* note 394 ("Some large pharmaceutical companies require distributors to sign agreements stating they will not distribute a generic product that competes with one of their name-brand products. This limits where veterinarians can access FDA-approved generics.").

[405] GADA Comment at 3.

[406] Workshop Tr. at 112, 118 (Mark Cushing).

[407] *Id.* at 111 (Clinton Vranian).

[408] GADA Comment at 4-5. *See also* Workshop Tr. at 116-17 (Michael H. Hinckle). However, some generic animal pharmaceutical companies continue to develop products. *See, e.g.*, *Veterinary-Approved Products*, PUTNEY, http://putneyvet.com/products; *Frequently Asked Questions*, *supra* note 394.

[409] K&L Gates Comment at 5. One workshop participant opined that without direct access to branded products, retail pharmacies will be less likely to carry generic products because the sales opportunities will be too limited and thus there is no incentive for mainstream wholesalers to carry generic pet medications. Workshop Tr. at 48-49, 97 (Michael H. Hinckle). This argument may be inconsistent, however, with evidence presented that retailers have been increasing their presence in the branded pet medications market through secondary distribution. *See supra* Section II.B, Retail Options Available to Consumers of Pet Medications, at 9; Section IV.A.3, The Secondary Market for Pet Medications, at 74.

[410] *See* K&L Gates Comment at 2 ("[T]he current distribution and dispensing practices are the result of a combination of veterinarians' desire to dispense directly to their clients and animal drug companies' marketing efforts that cater to that desire. . . . Veterinarians benefit from the profit margin on the drugs they dispense, and drug manufacturers benefit from veterinarian support of the branded drugs without the need to compete with generic products dispensed by pharmacies or retail outlets. The real loser, however, is the consumer who pays a higher price to receive the brand pet medication from his or her veterinarian when an equivalent generic drug could have been purchased from a pharmacy at a much lower price absent this arrangement."); Kroger Comment at 1 (stating that branded manufacturers use exclusive distribution to limit the threat of generic competition, and thereby maintain a higher pricing structure for their products).

[411] K&L Gates Comment at 5-6. As discussed in greater detail *infra*, notes 417-422 and accompanying text, some stakeholders have indicated that the lack of automatic generic substitution for pet medications may constrain market opportunities for generic alternatives, even when pet owners do fill veterinary prescriptions through retail channels.

[412] GADA Comment at 5. *See also* K&L Gates Comment at 7; Workshop Tr. at 202 (Michael H. Hinckle) ("Prices would be lower if we had a robust, generic industry, and it would also be helpful for everyone in the sense that a robust generic industry drives the innovator companies to develop the new generation of products instead of using marketing techniques to continue to evergreen their existing products.").

[413] *See supra* notes 15-16 and accompanying text.

[414] Workshop Tr. at 167-70 (Michael H. Hinckle) (arguing that potential cost savings might be available to consumers "if they had a prescription and if there was a distribution process that would allow the substitutable generics to get into the retail pharmacies."). *See also* K&L Gates Comment at 6 ("The current practices, and specifically veterinarian reluctance to provide portable prescriptions, deny consumer access to affordable generic drugs that are dispensed at the retail pharmacy. While it is true that many state-level veterinary practice ethical rules call for veterinarians to provide a prescription upon customer request, these rules fail to take into account the natural trepidation that pet owners feel in requesting a prescription. In actual practice, if the prescribed drug is stocked by the veterinarians, the office staff typically provides the drug at check-out without any mention of the customer's other options. Only when the veterinarian elects not to stock the prescribed drug is the

customer typically provided with a prescription."); Workshop Tr. at 202 (Michael H. Hinckle) ("There is definitely a problem that needs a solution . . . when Congress passed the Generic Drug Act for animal drugs, it had reason to believe that eventually [consumers] were going to get affordable drugs. That's not happening, and I think it's in large part because there's not enough demand because people just don't ask for the prescriptions many times. For whatever their reason may be. That lack of demand means that there's not a market for the generic drugs.").

[415] *See* Workshop Tr. at 168-69 (Michael H. Hinckle).

[416] K&L Gates Comment at 11.

[417] Workshop Tr. at 49, 117 (Michael H. Hinckle).

[418] *See* FED. TRADE COMM'N, DRUG PRODUCT SELECTION 273 (1979), *available at* http://www.bookprep.com/read/mdp.39015008517792; Alison MASSON & ROBERT L. STEINER, BUREAU OF ECON., FED. TRADE COMM'N, GENERIC SUBSTITUTION AND PRESCRIPTION DRUG PRICES: ECONOMIC EFFECTS OF STATE DRUG PRODUCT SELECTION LAWS (1985), http:// www.ftc.gov/ sites/ default/ files/ documents/ reports/ generic-substitution-prescription-drug-prices-economic-effects-state-drug-product-selection-laws/massonsteiner.pdf.

[419] *Approved Animal Drug Products (Green Book)*, U.S. FOOD & DRUG ADMIN. (Jan. 2015), http://www.fda.gov/animalveterinary/products/approvedanimaldrugproducts/default.htm.

[420] K&L Gates Comment at 3-4.

[421] *See id.* at 13 ("The pro-competitive effect of H.R. 1406 could be greatly enhanced by a provision requiring FDA to publish therapeutic equivalence codes for animal drugs in the same manner as the agency does for human drugs. . . . [B]y publishing its bioequivalence determinations in a form that is familiar to pharmacists (i.e., the therapeutic equivalence codes published in the human drug *Orange Book*), FDA could facilitate consumer access to generic animal drugs that the agency has determined are fully interchangeable with their pioneer counterparts."). Although arguably the FDA provides enough information on its website for pharmacists to determine whether a generic animal drug is interchangeable with a pioneer drug, the substitution process would be much easier for animal drugs if the Green Book contained these codes. *See id.* at 3.

[422] *See Approved Animal Drug Products (Green Book)*, *supra* note 419.

[423] Workshop Tr. at 189-90 (Michael H. Hinckle). This may already be happening, at least to a certain extent. *See, e.g., Education Center*, PUTNEY, http:// putneyvet.com/ education (focusing on initiatives to educate veterinarians about the value and efficacy of generic animal drugs).

[424] *See, e.g.*, B. Taylor Comment ("Generic products lack consistency and veterinarians should have the right not to prescribe them for the pet's best interest."); S. CAL. VET SURVEY, *supra* note 143 ("Many clients get generic Rimadyl from online pharmacies; about half seem to switch back to brand name Rimadyl because they say the generic doesn't seem to be effective."). Indeed, even the AVMA appears to question the differences between the brand name version and the generic version of a pet medication. *See* AVMA FAQS, *supra* note 52, at 2 ("[W]e have heard some anecdotal and unconfirmed reports of pets that had been receiving a brand name medication, but did not do as well when given a generic version of the same medication. Although all USP versions of a drug meet the purity standards for that drug, all of the ingredients and the processes involved in making the trade name versions are often protected by patent or other intellectual property laws, and there may be differences in the minor ingredients that could produce slightly different results between the versions, while still providing the main drug that meets USP standards. Think of it as following a recipe – even if you have the same ingredients and follow the instructions, the end result might vary a little bit. This is not a common problem with medications, and is often resolved by switching back to the effective [i.e., branded] version of the medication.").

[425] This may be accomplished by identifying changes in relevant factors that occur in the states that adopt prescription release policies from the time before the policy is adopted to the time after the policy is adopted, and then evaluating these same factors in the states that do not adopt such policies. Thus, the states that do not adopt prescription release policies would serve as the control group by which to compare any changes that occur in the states that do adopt such policies. In economic terms, this is known as a difference-in-differences approach.

[426] *FTC Announces Pet Medications Workshop; Will Explore Competition and Consumer Protection Issues Related to the Pet Medications Industry*, FED. TRADE COMM'N, http://www.ftc.gov/policy/public- comments/initiative-433.

[427] Comments are numbered when there was more than one comment received that listed the same commenter name and/or organization name. The numbering refers to the order that they are listed on the public comments webpage. *Id.*

In: The Pet Medication Industry
Editor: Anita R. Alvarez
ISBN: 978-1-63485-316-3

Chapter 2

COMMENTS OF W. RON DEHAVEN, EXECUTIVE VICE PRESIDENT AND CEO, AMERICAN VETERINARY MEDICAL ASSOCIATION. WORKSHOP ON "PET MEDICATION ISSUES"*

Dear Sir or Madam:

I am writing on behalf of the American Veterinary Medical Association, established in 1863 and the largest veterinary medical association in the world. As a not-for-profit association established to advance the science and art of veterinary medicine, the AVMA is the recognized national voice for the veterinary profession. The AVMA's more than 82,500 members, representing over 83% of all veterinarians in the United States, are involved in a myna' d of areas of veterinary medical practice, including private, corporate, academic, industrial, governmental, military, and public health services.

The Federal Trade Commission is seeking public comments in connection with a workshop to examine competition and consumer protection issues in the pet medications industry. The workshop will consider how current industry distribution and other business practices affect consumer choice and price competition for pet medications, the ability of consumers to obtain written prescriptions that they can fill wherever they

* This is an edited, reformatted and augmented version of comments offered September 10, 2012 in response to a request from the Federal Trade Commission in preparation of a public workshop on October 2, 2012.

choose, and the ability of consumers to verify the safety and efficacy of pet medications that they purchase. The workshop will also examine the extent to which recent changes to restricted distribution and prescription practices in the contact lens industry might yield lessons applicable to the pet medications industry.

The AVMA has concerns with mandatory prescription writing for veterinarians. Veterinarians are already writing prescriptions for clients, which is supported by state laws and the Principles of Veterinary Medical Ethics of the AVMA.[1] The AVMA asserts that veterinarians should honor client requests for written prescriptions when the decision ion is made to treat a patient with a particular prescription drug. However, mandated prescription writing is unwarranted.

Our utmost concern is the well-being of our patients. Therefore, the AVMA is taking several steps to promote optimal outcomes for consumers obtaining prescription drugs for their pets from independent pharmacies:

- We are interacting with pharmacy stakeholders to help ensure that licensed pharmacists understand their roles and responsibilities for counseling and educating clients when filling a veterinary prescription, including verification with the prescribing veterinarian should the pharmacist have any questions about the medication or dosage.
- We educate veterinarians through various communication channels about prescription drug rules and the importance of following the Principles of Veterinary Medical Ethics of the AVMA and state rules.
- We are interacting with pharmacy stakeholders to determine how best to train licensed pharmacists on basic veterinary pharmacology issues.

We offer our current thinking on some of the questions the FTC has posed concerning the distribution of pet medications.

How are pet medications distributed to consumers?

For the purposes of this letter, we define the term pet *ardication* as being synonymous with the term *animal drug,* which is defined in the Fairness to Pet Owners Act of 2011 (HR 1406),[2] in part, as being "a drug intended to be administered to an animal...." Drugs are under the jurisdiction of the US Food and Drug Administration and are defined under the Federal Food, Drug, and Cosmetic Act as being substances "intended for use in the diagnosis, cure, mitigation, treatment, or prevention of disease in man or other animals.[3]" We would refer you to individual drug manufacturers, the Animal Health Institute, individual distributors, or the American Veterinary Distributors Association as better sources of specific information on the distribution of pet medications.

Veterinary drug dispensing— When a veterinarian has determined that a patient needs a prescription drug, the drug can be distributed by dispensing directly from the clinic inventory, by dispensing from the clinic's online store (inventory supplied by a third-party distributor), by providing a written prescription to the client, by prescribing via telephone or electronically to a pharmacy, or by signing a faxed prescription from a pharmacy upon request, as allowable under individual state veterinary medical and pharmacy rules. In the case of controlled substance prescriptions, US Drug Enforcement Administration and state rules apply. Direct dispensing as well as written, faxed, and oral prescriptions, is allowable for Schedule III, IV, and V controlled substances. Schedule II controlled substances may only be dispensed directly by the veterinarian or prescribed in writing before being dispensed by a pharmacy.

How has competition to sell medications to pet owners evolved in light of these distribution practices?

We do not have specific data regarding changes in competition of drug product sales; however, it appears that more options for pet medication sales are available to consumers.

How do these practices affect product supply and quality?

Assuming that pharmacies acquire FDA-approved products through legal channels and store and ship them in the appropriate manner per manufacturer guidelines and state pharmacy rules, there should not be a concern with product safety or quality. We are unaware of any legal restrictions preventing pet prescription products from being dispensed by nonveterinary retail pharmacies. The key requirements are that the pharmacy is compliant with pharmacy laws and regulations and the prescriber must be authorized to provide the prescription.

That said, wide availability of drugs through various retailers appears to be associated with quality concerns in some situations. In the online article *Purchasing pet drugs online• buyr becgare,* the FDA reports, "Some of the Internet sites that sell pet drugs represent legitimate, reputable pharmacies..., but others are fronts for unscrupulous businesses operating again' st the law. The FDA has found companies that sell unapproved pet drugs and counterfeit pet products, make fraudulent claims, dispense prescription drugs without requiring a prescription, and sell expired drugs."[4]

How do these practices affect consumer choice?

The consumer would be anticipated to have more purchasing options.

What efficiencies or inefficiencies are associated with these practices?

The availability of animal drug products from various retailers likely creates both efficiencies and inefficiencies for veterinarians. Given that not all veterinarians, particularly mobile practitioners, are able to stock every prescription product they might prescribe for their patients, there is an efficiency associated with pharmacies carrying certain prescription products.

Inefficiencies associated with distribution practices are largely geared toward animal health concerns. Specifically, treatment with medications dispensed directly from a veterinary clinic can be started promptly and there are no anticipated concerns associated with the quality of the drug product. On the other hand, if a prescription drug is not obtained from a pharmacy immediately or at all, or if it is later realized that the pharmacy does not stock the needed medication, then treatment may be delayed to the detriment of the animal's health.

In addition, we understand that pharmacists are not required to have training in animal pharmacology. Whereas veterinarians have been educated to be cognizant of unique pharmacological needs across species, including the idiosyncrasies of different animal species (eg, feline sensitivity to acetaminophen and lagomorph sensitivity to certain antimicrobials), pharmacists might not have this awareness. We have learned that this has resulted in incorrect counseling, wrong dosages, or unauthorized drug substitutions, which could harm animal patients and create the need for additional treatment that would have been unnecessary had the correct medication or information been dispensed initially.

Faxed prescription requests from pharmacies also create inefficiencies. These requests are generated by the client or pharmacies, and veterinary clinics can receive numerous faxes a day. These faxes require the review of patient medical histories before authorization can be granted or denied. Additional inefficiencies associated with faxed requests include when the dispensing pharmacist has follow-up questions for the veterinarian.

What, if any, product safety or counterfeiting issues exist with respect to these practices? Have there been instances in which false or misleading information about product safety risks was disseminated to consumers?

The FDA has expressed concern about counterfeit drugs and product safety issues associated with unscrupulous Internet businesses acting unlawfully *(Sre* How do these practices affect product supply and quality?). The AVMA has observed foreign prescription drugs available on nonpharmacy retail websites. In 2009, the AVMA submitted a letter[5] to eBay in response to our observation of foreign-source heart-worm preventive drugs made available for purchase by the public without a prescription. This would create an animal health concern if, for example, the drug were stored inappropriately or used in a heartworm-positive dog.

Are there other factors that should be considered when analyzing the competition and consumer protection issues related to the distribution of pet medications?

Other factors should be considered when analyzing the competition and consumer protection issues related to the distribution of pet medications. Specifically, although veterinary students receive substantial education in veterinary medical pharmacology, pharmacy students do not necessarily receive such formal education. The AVMA is currently reaching out to pharmacy stakeholders to help ensure optimal communications and interactions between individual prescribing veterinarians and pharmacists for the well-being of our patients.

In addition, state authorities need to enforce rules with regard to prescription drug sales. Almost all states require a valid veterinarian-client-patient relationship (VCPR) for a veterinarian to prescribe or dispense medications for their patients.[6] This ensures that the veterinarian is familiar with the patient's condition and history to make the proper diagnosis and decide on treatment, including prescribing the veterinary drugs in appropriate circumstances. However, based on information AVMA and state veterinary medical associations have received from members over the years, pharmacists have allegedly dispensed prescription products without the veterinarian of record's knowledge. The AVMA asserts that the decision for use of a prescription drug in an animal should be made by the veterinarian— not a pharmacist— within the confines of a VCPR.

How varied are current veterinarian practices with respect to providing written, portable prescriptions to clients?

Twenty-six states[7] have specific laws, agency regulations, or policy statements that require veterinarians to provide their clients with a written prescription upon request. In addition, veterinarians in other states are at risk of state board discipline for unprofessional conduct in general for failure to honor a client's request for a prescription.

Within the confines of state laws, veterinary practices vary with respect to providing written prescriptions to clients. Some veterinarians do not stock prescription products, so all of their prescriptions are written and must be filled at a pharmacy, whereas others offer written prescriptions before dispensing; others fall on a spectrum in between.

Veterinarians who are AVMA members are expected to follow the AVMA Principles of Veterinary Medical Ethics,[1] which state that veterinarians should honor a client's request for a prescription in lieu of dispensing (Section III-C). In addition to the threat of discipline against their licenses, veterinarians have other incentives to honor clients' requests for prescriptions. A veterinarian who denies such a request risks alienating clients and harming his or her practice. In cases where the patient's condition may worsen quickly without medication and the client wishes to purchase the medication at a pharmacy, denial of a written prescription may place the veterinarian at legal risk.

To what extent are consumers aware that they can request a portable prescription from their veterinarian and have the prescription dispensed elsewhere?

Aside from anecdotal estimates or conducting a voluntary survey, there is no way to quantitatively determine the extent to which pet owners realize they can go elsewhere to fill prescriptions. Advertisements for public consumption have been observed in various communication vehicles for several years.

Which states require prescription portability for pet medications? Which do not? Are there states in which a proposal for prescription portability for pet medications was rejected by the legislature and, if so, why?

The AVMA is aware of 26 states with statutes, rules, or agency policy statements that require veterinarians to provide their clients with a written prescription upon request.[7] California and Arizona laws additionally require a prescriber to provide a client with written disclosure that the client has a choice between obtaining the prescription from the dispensing prescriber or obtaining the prescription at a pharmacy.

Even in states that have not adopted formal laws or regulations in this area, state boards of veterinary medicine could find in acting on a complaint that failure to honor a client's request for a prescription constitutes unprofessional conduct, leading to discipline against a veterinarian. Unprofessional conduct refers to a departure from or failure to conform to the standards of acceptable and prevailing practice of veterinary medicine.

In 2011, a bill in the Maine Senate, An Act To Enact Requirements Concerning Veterinary Prescriptions (S 207; legislative document 676),[8] which proposed mandatory prescription writing for veterinarians, much like HR 1406, was defeated. A similar bill, An Act Concerning Veterinarians and Supplementing Chapter 16 of Title 45 of the Revised Statutes (A 2995),[9] was introduced in the New Jersey Assembly on May 24, 2012, and has not advanced in that state's legislature.

In states that do require prescription portability, what recourse do consumers have if a veterinarian refuses to provide a written, portable prescription?

Consumers may file a complaint for unprofessional conduct with the state's veterinary licensing and disciplinary board. In some states, state veterinary medical associations offer consumers the opportunity to file complaints with ethics or grievance committees. In addition, some states provide consumers a private cause of action for violation of a statutory right. Consumers also may attempt to get assistance from their state's attorney general in enforcing the state's laws.

What evidence exists to support a need for federal legislation requiring veterinarians to provide written prescriptions to their clients?

We believe that state regulatory mechanisms pertaining to veterinary prescription writing are adequate and that there is no need for a federal mandate. Both veterinary medicine and pharmacy practices have traditionally been regulated by the states. A federal mandate would be a dramatic and unwarranted departure from state professional regulation and should be done only if there is a particular problem that needs to be addressed. We are not aware of consumers widely being denied their requests for prescriptions and see no need for a federal mandate that would undercut existing state regulation of veterinary medicine and pharmacy practices.

What risks or inefficiencies may be posed by prescription portability for pet medications? Potential risks associated with prescription filling at pharmacies include those pertaining to lack of formalized veterinary medical pharmacology educational requirements for pharmacists. Untrained pharmacists can unknowingly provide incorrect counseling or substitute inappropriate medications to the detriment of the patient. Another risk is the potential for delay in treatment should the preferred pharmacy not carry the needed medication or should the client be delayed in picking up the drug from the preferred pharmacy. Additionally, we have concerns that written prescriptions can result in increased instances of prescription drug abuse or fraud when filled outside of the veterinary clinic.

Is there a need for federal legislation requiring veterinarians to notify clients that they have the right to fill their prescriptions at the pharmacy of their choice?

At this time, the AVMA does not believe there is the need for federal legislation requiring veterinarians to notify clients that they have the right to fill their prescriptions at the pharmacy of their choice. State pharmacy and veterinary practice laws already govern veterinary prescription writing.

Is it appropriate to deny veterinarians the ability to charge a fee or require a waiver of liability for providing a written prescription to clients?

The AVMA contends that it is not appropriate for federal law to deny veterinarians the ability to charge a fee or to require a waiver of liability for providing a written prescription to clients, although we have not seen evidence of widespread use of such waiver forms. Writing prescriptions and subsequent follow-up work, including phone calls with pharmacists, takes time and it is not unreasonable to charge a fee for that time. The decision to require a waiver should be left to the business judgment of the clinic owner, subject to state liability laws, rather than be dictated by federal law.

How might the passage of HR 1406 affect price, consumer choice, and other forms of competition in the pet medications market?

We are unable to determine how passage of HR 1406 would be expected to affect price, consumer choice, and other forms of competition.

How can the prices charged to consumers for pet medications by veterinary clinics and retailers best be quantified and compared?

We do not have data regarding prices charged to consumers by veterinary clinics for comparison to those charged by retailers and are not certain whether quantifying and comparing such data would be feasible. Veterinary business models range from small, single doctor practices to large, multidoctor, multifacility practices as well as from practices that treat only one species to practices that treat multiple species.

To what extent do retailer prices for pet medications affect the prices of medications sold at veterinary practices or other aspects of veterinary clinic operations?

Given the variety of veterinary business models, we are unable to comment on how retailer prices for pet medications affect prices of medications or other aspects of individual veterinary clinic operations.

To what extent would HR 1406 affect veterinarians' sales of pet medications?

We are not certain how HR 1406 would affect veterinary sales of pet medications. Small animal veterinary practices have varied business models, ranging from large hospitals with substantial inpatient tertiary care to house-call businesses with minimal dispensing of drugs. To that end, veterinarians' sale of pet medications differs just as broadly, making speculation difficult.

What compliance costs would veterinarians face if HR 1406 were enacted?

Compliance costs are anticipated to be substantial. An administrative burden is associated with writing the prescription every time the veterinarian determines a prescription drug is needed, regardless of whether the client has even decided whether he or she wants to, or can, go elsewhere.

The amount of time taken to write, call in, or fax a prescription currently adds a few minutes to every appointment when it occurs. The time is multiplied when patients require multiple medications. Should HR 1406 pass, there would be a substantial impact on the scheduling of appointments to make allowances for the cumulative time taken for prescription writing for each patient. Dedicating either professional or support staff time or both to prescription writing activity changes staffing duties and responsibilities. Alterations in appointment flow to account for the time required to comply with prescription writing would need to be made. Extending office hours to offset the resultant time lost to prescription writing would result in business costs associated with such a decision. The verification requirement, including follow-up phone calls from the pharmacies, for every prescription will also create an administrative burden and further impact appointment scheduling.

The requirement that veterinarians provide a written prescription to clients who choose to have their prescription filled at the veterinarian's clinic adds another cost of compliance. Veterinarians would have to take measures to store or properly dispose of these written prescriptions in accordance with state laws, taking into account efforts to prevent misuse and to document that a prescription was properly dispensed to the client.

One unintended consequence we can foresee is the increased chance of prescription abuse and fraud. In complying with the provisions of HR 1406, veterinarians will have to take measures to mitigate circumstances where clients use the requirement as an opportunity to acquire inappropriate numbers of prescriptions. Although prescriptions are written now for clients, the sheer number of prescriptions being written would be expected to increase because unlike the current situation, under HR 1406, a prescription would be required in each and every instance the decision is made for a prescription drug. Increased numbers of prescriptions given to clients, recycled, or discarded if not needed by the client could yield increased opportunities for fraud by use of written prescriptions.

Should possible amendments to HR 1406 be considered?

The AVMA is strongly opposed to HR 1406 and does not believe any amendments should be considered. The AVMA wishes to engage in dialog with relevant stakeholders should any amendments to HR 1406 be offered.

Are there other factors that should be considered when analyzing the competition and consumer protection issues related to the portability of pet medication prescriptions? We would again like to underscore the applicable education and knowledge that the veterinarian of record has with regard to veterinary medical pharmacology and, in particular, the medical history of his or her individual patients. Veterinary medications dispensed in the veterinary clinic come from a qualified veterinary team who can answer the client's questions and assure clients they have the proper drug for the patient. Our primary goal is to ensure that our clients receive the best quality information about their pet's medications.

Aside from pharmacists' lack of formal education in veterinary pharmacology, not all pharmacies have state licensure in good standing. Prescription products obtained from unlicensed pharmacy retailers pose a risk to the animal's e being and create an ethical, and potentially legal, conundrum for the prescribing veterinarian.

Part of the AVMA's mission is to improve both animal and human health, and we are concerned with possible human health ramifications that could result from mandated prescription writing. We are concerned about scenarios wherein the client leaves the clinic with prescription in hand, only to call the clinic back and claim that the prescription has been lost; rewriting the prescription for the benefit of the animal is acceptable but could unknowingly lead to drug diversion. The sudden increase in volume of written prescriptions could increase the chance that individuals will be able to fraudulently and illegally procure prescription drugs.

In closing, the AVMA appreciates the FTC's careful analysis of how the Fairness to Pet Owners Act of 2011 (HR 1406) would affect veterinary practitioners and the availability and access to drugs for treating household pets, including dogs, cats, birds, and certain exotic species. Although the AVMA is supportive of a client's right to fill a prescription at their pharmacy of choice, we are strongly opposed to any federal mandate that requires a written prescription be provided, regardless of whether the client chooses to, or can, go elsewhere. The AVMA believes HR 1406 is redundant and will cause undue regulatory and administrative burdens on veterinary practices. It is burdensome and unnecessary to require a written prescription as well as a written notification that the prescription may be filled elsewhere, regardless of whether the client is having the prescription filled by the veterinarian.

- The provision requiring verification of prescriptions, regardless of whether the pharmacy is accredited or licensed, places the veterinarian in both a legal and ethical dilemma. At the same time, it puts consumers at risk.

- FIR 1406 encroaches on state jurisdiction; state pharmacy and veterinary practice laws already govern compliance by veterinarians.
- Clients already have the flexibility to fill a prescription at their veterinary clinic or at a pharmacy of their choice. The AVMA is supportive of a client's right to choose where to have a prescription filled.
- The AVMA believes that veterinarians are uniquely educated to provide the best professional guidance and education to pet owners when dispensing prescription products.

Thank you for your time and consideration. The AVMA appreciates the opportunity to comment and would like to continue the dialog on this and other important matters. For further clarification on the AVMA's comments, please contact either Dr. Ashley Morgan (202-289-3210; amorgan@avma.org) or Dr. Lynne White-Shim (800-248-2862 ext. 6784; 1white@avma.org).

Respectfully,
W. Ron DeHaven,
DVM, MBA Executive Vice President and CEO

End Notes

[1] AVMA. Principles of Veterinary Medical Ethic, ()I the AVMA. Available at: www.avma.org/ KB/Policies/Pages/Principles-of-VeJerinary-Medical-Ethics-of-the-AVMA.aspx. Accessed Jul 26, 2012.

[2] Fairness to Pet Owners Act of 2011, HR 1406, 112th Gang, 1st Sess (2011-2012).

[3] US FDA. Animal drugs: a brief overview of CVM's drug approval process. Available at: www.fda.gov/AnimalVeterinary/ResourcesforYou/ucm268128.htm. Accessed Jul 26, 2012.

[4] US FDA. Consumer updates. Purchasing pet drugs online: buyer beware. Available at: www.fda.goviforconsumers/consumerupdates/ucm048164.htm. Accessed Jul 26, 2012.

[5] AVMA. Veterinary prescription drugs sold on eBay. Available at: www.avma.org/Advocacy/ National/Other/Pages/Veterinary-prescription-drugs-sold-on-eBay.aspx. Accessed Jul 26, 2012.

[6] AVMA. VC PR requirement for prescriptions. Available at: www.avma.org/ Advocacy/ State AndLocaVPages/vcpr-and-prescriptions.aspx. Accessed Jul 26, 2012.

[7] AVMA. Client request for prescriptions. Available at: www.avma.org/Advocacy/ StateAndLocal/Pages/veterinary-prescription-orders.aspx. Accessed Sep 9, 2012.

[8] S 207, 125th Leg, 1st Sess (Me 2011).

[9] A 2995, 215th Leg, 1st Reg Sess (NJ 2012-2013).

In: The Pet Medication Industry
Editor: Anita R. Alvarez
ISBN: 978-1-63485-316-3

Chapter 3

ONLINE PET PHARMACIES: PROTECT YOURSELF AND YOUR PET: BE A.W.A.R.E.*

U.S. Food and Drug Administration

- "Affordable pet prescriptions!" "Pet meds at discount prices!"
- "No prescription required!"
- "Your best source for pet meds!"

If you've ever searched online for prescription pet medicines, you've likely seen similar eye-catching, attention-grabbing claims. They sound convincing, promising convenience and lower prices, but are these claims always true?

Many online pet pharmacies are reputable. Some, however, may be businesses breaking Federal, State, and sometimes, International laws. These illegal online pharmacies may sell medicines that are counterfeit, outdated, mislabeled, or incorrectly formulated. The medicines may not contain the actual drug or may contain incorrect amounts of drug. Some may not work as well if the product is old (expired) or has been stored in conditions that were too hot, cold, or humid. Others may not have the proper directions

* This is an edited, reformatted and augmented version of an online document issued by the U.S. Food and Drug Administration at the following website: http://www.fda.gov/AnimalVeterinary/ResourcesforYou/AnimalHealthLiteracy/ucm203000.htm (updated 12/2/15 and viewed 3/14/16).

for use. If you are unhappy with the products you ordered, you may not be able to get your money back from an illegal online pharmacy.

If you want to purchase your pet's prescription medicines online, you can protect yourself by doing your homework and being online pharmacy *A.W.A.R.E.*

A— Ask Your Veterinarian

Before you purchase online, talk with your veterinarian! Is an online pharmacy appropriate for your pet and for your situation? Does the medicine require additional monitoring and/or adjustments to the dose or the timing of doses that would best be handled by your veterinarian?

W—Watch for Red Flags

When buying from online pharmacies, keep an eye out for red flags. Be careful if …

- the pharmacy doesn't require a veterinarian's prescription for a prescription medicine.

Online pharmacies that sell prescription veterinary medicines without requiring a veterinarian's prescription are breaking the law. Under the Federal Food Drug and Cosmetic Act, a pharmacy can't sell you a veterinary prescription medicine without a valid prescription or order from a licensed veterinarian. Online questionnaires or consults don't take the place of a veterinarian's prescription. Online pharmacies that sell drugs without requiring valid veterinary prescriptions rob both you and your pet of the protection provided by a veterinary physical exam.

- the pharmacy has no licensed pharmacist available to answer questions.

Can someone answer your questions about your pet's medicines? Some pharmacies may not be prepared to respond your questions or they may have limited knowledge about medications for animals.

- the pharmacy's website does not list its physical business address, phone number, or other contact information.

If something goes wrong with your order, can contact them?

- the pharmacy is not based in the United States.

If you use a foreign online pet pharmacy, there's not much the U.S. government can do to help you get your money back if you have a problem with your order.

- the pharmacy is not licensed by the State Board of Pharmacy where the business is based.

If the pharmacy operates in the U.S., you can check the National Association of Boards of Pharmacy (NABP) website to see if the pharmacy is properly licensed: http://www.nabp.net/consumers/board-of-pharmacy-contacts/

- the pharmacy's website does not protect your personal information.

Keep yourself safe from identity theft! Make sure the site you use is secure before you give the pharmacy your credit card number and other personal information. Look for easy-to-understand privacy and security policies.

- the pharmacy's prices are dramatically lower than your veterinarian's or other online pharmacies' prices.

If it seems too good to be true, then it probably is.

- the pharmacy ships you medicines that you didn't order or medicines that look very different from what your pet normally takes.

Don't give these medicines to your pet! Contact your veterinarian and the online pharmacy immediately!

A—Always Check for Pharmacy Accreditation

Beside following federal and state licensing and inspection requirements, many good online pharmacies are also accredited. In 2009, the National Association of Boards of Pharmacy (NABP) created a voluntary accreditation program called Vet-VIPPS (Veterinary-Verified Internet Pharmacy Practice Sites). Vet-VIPPS-accredited online pharmacies:

- are appropriately licensed in the states from which they ship drugs
- have successfully completed a review and online survey
- undergo yearly Vet-VIPPS review and re-accreditation, and
- undergo NABP on-site surveys every three years.

Vet-VIPPS-accredited pharmacies must also meet other criteria including protecting client confidentiality, ensuring strict quality assurance, and validating prescription orders.

R—Report Problems and Suspicious Online Pet Pharmacies

If your pet has a problem with a medicine you bought online (for example, a reaction to the medicine or the medicine isn't working), contact the company that makes the medicine. You can also report problems directly to the Food and Drug Administration (FDA) Center for Veterinary Medicine (CVM) by calling 1-888-FDA-VETS or emailing AskCVM@fda.hhs.gov. For a copy of FDA's reporting form (FDA Form 1932a) and for more information on how to report problems, visit the following web page: http://www.fda.gov/AnimalVeterinary/SafetyHealth/ReportaProblem/ucm055305.htm.

Protect yourself, your pets, and others! Don't fall victim to illegal online pet pharmacies. Report suspicious online pet pharmacies to the FDA and the NABP:

FDA: http://www.fda.gov/Safety/ReportaProblem/ucm059315.htm

NABP: http://www.nabp.net/

E—Educate Yourself about Online Pet Pharmacies

The best defense you have against illegal online pet pharmacies is education. Do your homework and be online pet pharmacy A.W.A.R.E. before you buy your pet's medicines online. *An informed consumer is an empowered consumer.*

For more information about buying pet medicines from online pharmacies, visit FDA's website at:

http://www.fda.gov/AnimalVeterinary, or call FDA at 1-240-402-7002.

A-Ask your veterinarian

W-Watch for red flags

A-Always check for pharmacy accreditation

R-Report problems and suspicious online pet pharmacies

E-Educate yourself about online pet pharmacies

Whenever your pet needs prescription medicines, your veterinarian is a good, reliable resource.

Your veterinarian:

- physically examines your pet and knows your pet's medical and treatment history
- knows which medicines are safe for your pet
- educates you about potential side effects associated with your pet's medicines
- shows you how to properly use the medicines prescribed for your pet.

INDEX

D

E

F

G

H

I

J

L

Q

R

S

T

U

W